*InDesign for
QuarkXPress Users*

InDesign for QuarkXPress Users

David Blatner
Christopher Smith
Steve Werner

PEACHPIT PRESS

✻

David: To Richard

Steve: To Amma and Harry

Christopher: To Grant and Elizabeth

✿

INDESIGN FOR QUARKXPRESS USERS
David Blatner, Christopher Smith, and Steve Werner

Copyright © 2003 by David Blatner, Christopher Smith, and Steve Werner

PEACHPIT PRESS
1249 Eighth Street
Berkeley, California 94710
(800) 283-9444
(510) 524-2178
(510) 524-2221(fax)

Find us on the World Wide Web at: http://www.peachpit.com
Peachpit Press is a division of Pearson Education

Editor: Serena Herr
Production coordinator: Lisa Brazieal
Indexer: Caroline Parks
Cover illustration: Ron Chan, www.ronchan.com
Cover design: Mimi Heft and Ron Chan
Interior design and production: David Blatner (moo.com) and Jeff Tolbert

ISBN 0-321-15948-9
9 8 7 6 5 4 3 2 1

Printed and bound in the United States of America

overview

contents

Part 3: Building Documents

Part 4: Typography

Part 7: Where Text Meets Graphics

Part 8: Color and Transparency

Part 9: Long Documents

Part 10: Printing

Part 11: Exporting

Appendix A

introduction

Have you ever bought a new cell phone—or a washing machine, or a power tool—and muddled through the instruction manual? The people who write the manual assume that we've never had a cell phone before—or a washing machine or a power tool—so they start from the beginning. Don't forget to plug it in, they remind us, as though we thought electricity comes from the air.

Granted, there is a place for instruction manuals that start from the very beginning (a very good place to start, as Julie Andrews would tell us), but what we often need is a manual that knows what we already understand and just tells us what's different and what's the same. That's what this book is all about. We know you already know how to use QuarkXPress. We know many of you recently added a new tool—Adobe InDesign—to your existing toolbox of desktop publishing applications. We know you want to get up and running as fast as possible. Others of you may be reading this book because you're considering whether you should even start using InDesign.

We've been there; we feel your pain.

Learning a new program is no fun, especially when you're facing a publication deadline. We want to help you learn InDesign faster and easier by leveraging your knowledge, using what you know about QuarkXPress as a springboard to greater efficiency with this new program.

How to Read This Book

Because each chapter of this book covers a basic task or concept—text wrap, for instance, or exporting PDF files—we don't expect many of you will read the whole thing cover to cover. Rather, we think it makes sense to read the first few chapters, just to get up and running, and then skip around the book, gathering what you need when you need it. We also suggest searching out the chapters that give background information (labelled "Think Outside the Box"), such as Chapter 43 (about fonts) and 62 (about graphics). These chapters focus particularly on areas where InDesign's technology has leaped ahead of of XPress's.

Note that we have no intention of having this book cover everything you ever wanted to know about InDesign. Sure, we cover a lot of ground, and we take an in-depth look at many of the features (especially those that have no equivalent in XPress). But we expect that you'll use this book in conjunction with other resources on InDesign (see "For More Information," below).

Why Use InDesign

Before we go any further, we should probably ask an important question: If you already know how to use QuarkXPress, why bother with Adobe InDesign? If you're sitting on the fence between the two programs, you've probably spent a lot of time asking yourself this recently. If you've already fallen head over heels for InDesign, then your boss, your printer, and your clients are likely asking you. So, let's look at some of the reasons we find InDesign so compelling.

Features

While InDesign and XPress both have a core set of features which are similar (and sometimes identical), they each have some features that the other does not. For example, QuarkXPress has custom lines (dashes and stripes), drag-and-drop text, and the ability to mix together spot colors into custom swatches—InDesign does none of these things. Nevertheless, if you analyze the two programs's feature lists, InDesign is ultimately the overwhelming winner. Here are a few reasons why.

- **User Interface.** InDesign has been life-changing for us because we can start trusting what we see on screen so much more than with XPress. InDesign incorporates a type of "Display PostScript," so you can see what text, bitmapped images, and vector graphics really look like before you print a proof. Plus, there's a Preview mode that hides all guides and non-printing items, an Overprint Preview mode that simulates over-printing inks on screen, and the ability to zoom in to 4,000 percent.

Unlike XPress, you can place guides precisely, lock them, color them, copy-and-paste them, and even put them on a layer. You can turn on a graph-paper document grid for quick alignment. You can truly lock an object (XPress's Lock feature is lame, letting you move and even delete locked objects). You can display your document in more than one win-dow (for multiple views). The list goes on and on.

- **Typographic Features.** If you care about type, InDesign is the program for you. InDesign makes hyphenation and justification decisions based on the look of a whole paragraph rather than one line at a time. Plus, support for hanging punctuation, automatic kerning based on the shape of the characters, and all the OpenType features (like automatic frac-tions and swashes) means you can get high-quality typography without having to painstakingly do it manually.

- **Graphics and Transparency.** Most folks do their really cool layout work in Photoshop. InDesign's transparency features mean that you can spend more time doing *layout* in your page-layout application. For example, because InDesign understands native Photoshop (.PSD) files and retains their transparency, you may never have to make a clipping path in Photoshop again; just erase the background to the checkerboard transparency and import into InDesign. Similarly, you don't have to use an XTension or switch to Photoshop just to make a drop shadow or to feather the edges of an object because InDesign has these features built in. To all you cynics out there: Yes, this stuff really does print beautifully; it doesn't crash RIPs or cause service bureaus to spontaneously combust (we show you how in the Printing section of the book).

- **Tables.** InDesign's table features far outshine XPress's, letting you set automatic alternating fills or strokes, link tables across pages, and even convert Microsoft Word and Excel tables into editable InDesign tables.

- **Printing and Exporting.** Everyone knows that the printing architecture in InDesign 1.0 and 1.5 was terrible (just like it was in QuarkXPress 1.10 and 2.12, for those of you with a long memory). But InDesign 2 changed all of that, and now many service providers prefer it over XPress! It now features built-in preflighting, the ability to export high-quality PDF files directly to disk (without Distiller), embedding fonts in EPS files, and generating DSC-compliant device-independent PostScript (something we techno-geeks have been asking from Quark for 12 years).

- **Other Stuff.** The list of features InDesign has and XPress does not goes on and on: It's scriptable on Windows as well as the Macintosh. You can edit all the keyboard shortcuts. If you crash (all software crashes sooner or later), InDesign recovers your document so you don't lose much (if any) work. You can base master pages on other master pages or turn a document page into a master page. It is Unicode compliant, so you can set multiple languages (even those with non-Roman character sets) in the same document. And more!

Granted, features aren't everything. But features are like tools on a Swiss Army knife—the right feature at the right time can be a major lifesaver! Of course, there was no one feature that convinced us that InDesign is a great tool; rather it is the broad assortment of InDesign's features that make our work easier.

On the other hand, if you absolutely cannot live without one of the features that is only found in XPress, then you're stuck (until Adobe adds that feature). Just for the record, here's a list of some other features XPress 5 has that InDesign 2 does not (in our experience, few XPress users ever use these features anyway):

- Custom kerning and tracking tables
- Merge and Split ("pathfinder") features
- Rotated text within frame
- Forms objects (like popup menus), image maps, and rollovers in HTML Web documents
- Customizable text underscores
- Hexachrome color support
- Image contrast and halftone settings

Performance
Here's one more feature that XPress 5 has that InDesign does not: It runs better on older, slower computers. InDesign's feature set comes at a cost: It's RAM and processor hungry—anything less than a Pentium 4 or G4 processor with 256 MB of RAM will make your InDesign experience

frustrating, especially with longer documents. Generally, any machine on which you'd be happy running Photoshop will also support InDesign.

But computing power is only half the equation when it comes to being productive in a program. In 2002, Pfeiffer Consulting conducted extensive tests exploring what happened to business productivity when companies began to use InDesign. The results were fascinating (you can read them yourself at *www.pfeifferreport.com*). In short, they found that what saved the most time was not the raw speed of the computer or the software, but was reducing the number of steps required to build a document.

At first, it made us crazy that InDesign imports Microsoft Word documents significantly slower than XPress (particularly long documents). Then we found that while we lose a little time at import, we gain a lot more time because InDesign does so much automatically (or with a single step) that we had to do manually in XPress (with many steps). For example, anyone who has spent the afternoon trying to get text to look just right by adding manual line breaks, discretionary hyphens, and other typographic tweaks will be astonished at how little of that is necessary because of InDesign's paragraph composer. (That said, Adobe engineers have assured us that they're working on making the import feature faster in future versions of InDesign.)

Similarly, InDesign saves steps by letting you make drop shadows in the page-layout program, drawing a frame for you when you import text or graphics (if you don't already have one), converting Word and Excel tables to editable tables upon import, and even maintaining the editability of vector artwork (from Illustrator or FreeHand) that you paste onto your pages.

The Pfeiffer Report found astonishing efficiency increases in some areas of work (like making PDF files) and found that InDesign equalled XPress in other areas. In their benchmark testing, it took designers two to three times longer to create a document in XPress than in InDesign.

What's Your ROI?

For many people, especially at larger companies, the biggest hurdle to using InDesign is not learning the features (you've already got that handled by buying this book) but convincing "the suits." After all, arguments like "It's got more features!" and "I can go home early if I use it" don't go over well with those folks we affectionately call the bean counters.

When approaching your boss, you need to use phrases like "return on investment" (ROI) and "increasing workflow integration for gigahertz productivity enhancements." (The latter expression doesn't actually mean anything, but it's very impressive.)

Of course, measuring ROI in the publishing industry is difficult. For a small design firm, the investment is simply the cost of the new software and a couple of books or training classes to help you learn it. The return can be anything from cooler designs that help you get more clients to saving time on producing a big job.

Larger companies tend to think about the cost of retraining (both in money and hours lost from the production cycle), and the returns come in reducing headcount and expenses. Fortunately, the Pfeiffer Report also looked at ROI issues, briefly mentioning how Australia's largest magazine publisher, ACP, cut their prepress costs in *half* while moving 40 magazines (including *Cosmopolitan* and 7 weeklies) to InDesign. Designers and the production team put one issue of a magazine to bed with XPress and the next issue was created—cover to cover—with InDesign. It was a highly successful operation, and the company reportedly saved so much money (in the relative cost of the software plus in reducing prepress expenses) that they could afford to buy new computers for everyone (we're still waiting for ours).

Add a Tool, Don't Replace It

Our publisher keeps calling this a "switcher book," for people who want to switch to InDesign. Our response is: No, it's for people who want to *add* InDesign to their repertoire. We expect that there are very few people who will be in the position to completely drop QuarkXPress, just like we all have copies of PageMaker on our machines, even though we have no intention of creating any new documents with that program. Therefore, for the foreseeable future, it's likely that you'll need to know how to use both programs (or at least keep someone on staff who does).

But doesn't InDesign open XPress documents? Sure it does, but not necessarily perfectly. In Appendix A, we explain what does and doesn't translate and how you should best use this feature.

Our colleague Sandee Cohen notes that people who start using InDesign often try to fit it into the same workflow they're accustomed to. Sure, you can replace XPress with InDesign and keep doing everything else the same, but you're going to miss out on a lot InDesign has to offer. Using InDesign is all about finding new and better ways of working—integrating all your tools together for maximum efficiency.

For More Information

As we said earlier, as deep as we can go in the next 400 pages, we don't expect to answer every question you ever have about InDesign. For example, we don't cover how to script InDesign or import/export XML. Fortunately, there are other resources out there. Here's a few places you can go for more information.

- *Real World Adobe InDesign 2.* While we are a bit biased (this book was written by David Blatner and long-time industry expert Olav Martin Kvern), this is also the book recommended by members of the InDesign development team at Adobe.

- *Adobe InDesign 2 Visual Quickstart Guide.* Sandee Cohen offers a wonderful step-by-step introduction to InDesign. We like this better than the *Adobe InDesign Classroom in a Book*, though that one is good, too.

- **Adobe InDesign Web Site.** Most corporate Web sites are filled with marketing materials. You'll find plenty of that at Adobe, but it's alongside excellent useful information, too. It's definitely worth a trip to *www.adobe.com/products/indesign*. Also, the answers to many of your most puzzling InDesign questions can be answered by the knowledgeable and helpful volunteers in the InDesign User to User Forums at *www.adobe.com/support/forums/main.html*

- **InDesign Users Groups.** At the time of this writing, there are InDesign Users Groups in San Francisco, Seattle, Chicago, Atlanta, and New York City; we expect more to appear soon (see *www.indesignusergroup.com*). If you've got one near you, check it out.

Acknowledgements

We'd like to give special thanks to a few of the people who helped us turn a crazy idea into the book you're now holding. First, many thanks to the folks at Adobe who gave us a great product and have helped support this book, including Will Eisley, Tim Cole, Mark Neimann-Ross, Eliot Harper, Thomas Phinney, Lonn Lorenz, Matt Phillips, Michael Wallen, Jim Ringham, David Cohen, Mike Silverman, Susan Prescott, Carrie Cooper, Tim Plumer, Joe Smith, Ron Ditorro, and Olav Martin "Ole" Kvern.

Thanks to our Peachpit editor, Serena Herr, for her extraordinary patience and (usually) gentle nudges to get it done. To Jeff Tolbert for his great (and fast) production. To Lisa Brazieal for her help in riding this wild Harley all the way to the printer. To Conrad Chavez, for his excellent technical editing. And to Caroline Parks, whose eagle eye produced a terrific index.

Our sincere appreciation for a wealth of good information goes to Sandee "Vector Babe" Cohen, Deke "The Man" McClelland, Cyndie Shaffstall at The PowerXChange, the InDesign beta testers, and participants in the BlueWorld InDesign list and the InDesign User to User Forums.

Steve: "Thanks to Bent Kjolby and the staff at Rapid Lasergraphics for giving me the freedom to develop and teach my classes. Thanks to my students, who have taught me so much. Thanks to Astrid Wasserman of Key3Media and Thad McIlroy for encouraging me to teach at Seybold Seminars. And finally thanks to Harry and all our friends who have provided me with the support I needed during the months it took to write this book."

Christopher: "Thanks to the instructors at AGI Training, especially Brian Reese, Larry Happy and Jennifer Smith for their input as we have made our own transition from QuarkXPress to InDesign. A special thanks to Grant for encouraging me (frequently) to take a break from writing and read Dr. Seuss books with him. "

David: "My deepest appreciation goes to my beloved wife, Debbie, and our delightful son, Gabriel, who are such blessings in my life. Thanks, too, to a host of generous friends and family who remind me that as much as I like digital, analog is even better."

PART 1

The User Interface

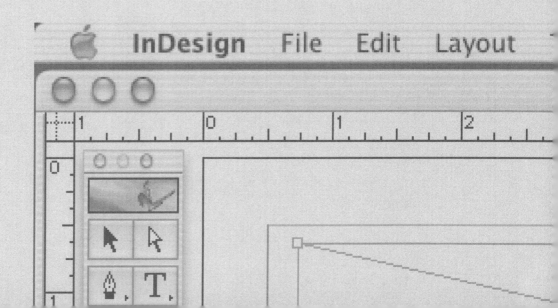

1

The Tools Palette

Many QuarkXPress users are also Adobe Illustrator users, which makes the job of learning the InDesign tools much more simple. InDesign borrows heavily from the Illustrator tool box, so you will see a great many familar tools if you are an Illustrator user. But don't skip over this chapter just because you know the Illustrator tools. There are some subtle but important differences between the two software programs.

You can position InDesign's Tools palette in the traditional two columns, a single vertical column or horizontally as a single row (see Figure 1-1). Laptop users or those working on smaller screens will appreciate the single row or column that is a more efficient use of space. To change the palette layout, click the maximize window button at the top of the palette. This rotates you through the various view options. You can also set the layout of the tools in the General section of InDesign's preferences. If you accidentally close the tools palette, you can easily re-open the palette by selecting Tools from the Window menu.

Unlike XPress, each tool has a key command associated with it (see Figure 1-2). As long as you are not entering or editing text, you can use the key commands to move from one tool to another. Plus, you can press the Tab key to show or hide all palettes. Use Shift-Tab to show or hide all palettes except the Tools palette.

Tools for Selecting

The Selection tool and Direct Selection tool are both used for selecting objects on your page. The Selection tool (press V) is most like the Item

Figure 1-1
Tools palette layouts

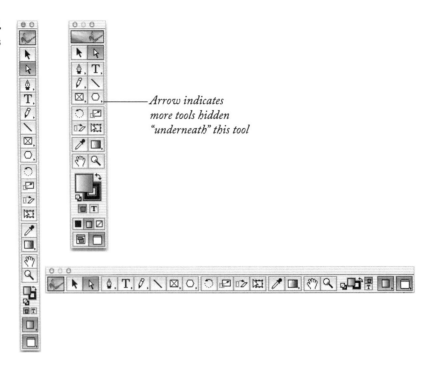

*Arrow indicates
more tools hidden
"underneath" this tool*

tool in QuarkXPress, as you use it to select objects and their contents at the same time. For example, you can use the Selection tool to move a frame and its contents to a new location on a page.

The Direct Selection tool (press A) is somewhat like the QuarkXPress content tool. You can use this tool to move the content of a picture frame, but you can also use it to select and modify individual frame points or portions of a frame. When using this tool notice that its appearance will change subtly based upon what is being selected.

While these two tools may appear to be interchangable because of their similar names, using the incorrect selection tool can make your life miserable. For example, selecting a picture frame with the Direct Selection tool and then making a change in the Transform palette affects the content, but not the frame itself—which may or may not be what you wanted. We cover these tools in greater detail in Chapter 11 and 20.

Type Tools

The Type tool (press T) and Path Type tool (press Shift-T) are similar to QuarkXPress's Content tool (though they only work in text frames). Of course you can use the Type tool for adding or editing text within frames

Figure 1.2
Keyboard shortcuts
for selecting tools

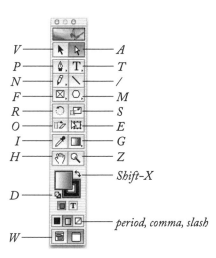

and on paths. However, you can also use the Type Tool for creating frames that will contain text or graphics. Learn more about this in Chapter 10.

Drawing Tools

You can use the drawing tools to build lines or frames. We cover these in more detail when we discuss creating and editing shapes in Chapter 12.

Pen
Like both QuarkXPress and Illustrator, you use the Pen tools to create Bézier lines and frames. The basic Pen tool (press P) draws shapes, adds points on a path, or deletes points on a path (depending on what's beneath the cursor). While InDesign offers several other tools "under" the Pen tool in the Tools palette, we never actually select them, because you can get them on the fly using keyboard shortcuts.

Pencil
You can use the Pencil tool (press N) for creating free-form paths, or for building frames—but only if you have a steady hand. Select the Smooth and Erase tools, hidden underneath the Pencil tool, to help create a perfect path. (We think that this tool is completely out of place in a page-layout application, but we suppose it's nice to have the option.)

Line
When you simply need a straight line, the Line tool (press the backslash key) makes this easy. Although the Pencil or Pen tools will also work, they

require a very steady hand or the use of modifier keys (like the Shift key) to keep your lines straight. InDesign doesn't have a line tool that only draws horizontal and vertical lines, like XPress does, but you can just hold down Shift while dragging with this tool to constrain the line.

Frame

The three Frame tools (press F) allow you to draw rectangular, oval or polygon frames to contain text or graphics. You can draw a perfectly square or circular frame by holding down the Shift key when using the oval and rectangle tools. You can also draw a frame from the center of where you have clicked by holding down the Option/Alt key while drawing the frame.

You can set the number of sides in the polygon by double-clicking on the Polygon tool prior to drawing with it. You can also draw a specific size rectangle or oval frame by clicking once on the page after selecting either of these tools.

Shape

The Shape tools work identically to the Frame tools, however the frames created by the Shape tools have a default stroke (border) around them, and you can only select these shapes by clicking on the perimeter of the frame or their non-printing center point. While they are intended to serve as graphical elements and not frames, shapes and frames are really interchangeable— you can place text or graphics inside of objects created with either the Shape or Frame tools. We find the overlap of these tools to be confusing for first time InDesign users, and maybe the folks at Adobe will find something better to take the place of the drawing tools.

Editing Tools

As we mentioned earlier, it is important to note whether you have selected the frame or the contents of the frame, because these editing tools change whatever is selected (see Chapter 18).

Rotate

InDesign's Rotate tool (press R) works very similarly to QuarkXPress's: select the object you wish to rotate then drag with this tool to determine the axis of rotation. You can click on the object even if it was not previously selected and InDesign will select the object along with its axis of rotation (but this only works if nothing on the page was previously selected).

Scale

Use the Scale tool (press S) to increase or decrease the size of a selected object on the page, including text and picture frames. We tend to shun this tool in favor of using the Transform palette or Command/Ctrl-Shift dragging the corner or side handles of an object with the Selection tool (which allows you to scale an object and its contents without switching to a special tool).

Shear

If you have ever wanted your text to resemble the the Leaning Tower of Pisa, or look like movie credits moving off into the distance, then this is the tool for you. With the Shear tool (press O) you can take an object on your page and apply a skew that'll make your eyes twitch. You can easily over-manipulate objects with this tool, so take advantage of InDesign's multiple undo feature if you find your objects in an awkward position.

Free Transform

You can use the Free Transform tool (press E) to rotate and scale objects. To scale, select one or more objects, choose this tool, and drag one of the corner or side handles in the direction you wish to scale. To rotate, click outside the bounding box and drag. Unlike the Shear tool, which can move in multiple directions concurrently, this tool requires separate actions to rotate or to scale.

Eyedropper

After working with the Eyedropper tool (press I) you will wonder how you ever got along in XPress without it. You can use the Eyedropper tool to copy colors or text formatting from one location to another without building a swatch, or a paragraph or character style. Double click on the Eyedropper tool to set preferences relating to what it will duplicate when copying formatting.

To copy the color from an imported image, move the Eyedropper tool over the image and click once. The color your clicked on should fill the eyedropper and should also be shown in the Color palette and either the fill or stroke color in the bottom of the Tools palette, based upon whichever is in the foreground. You can then apply the color to any InDesign object or save it as a swatch.

If you have already selected a color and would like to replace it with another color, hold down the Option/Alt key while clicking with the

Eyedropper tool and the tool becomes white and points down and to the left, indicating that it is ready to pick up another color if you click.

You can learn more about this and how the Eyedropper tool can be used for copying and pasting text formatting in Chapter 82.

Gradient

You can use the Gradient tool (press G) to modify the length and direction of existing gradients or to apply a gradient to one or more selected objects. One or more objects must first be selected on your page before you use the Gradient tool. After selecting an object, click and drag over it with the gradient tool to determine the direction of the gradient. The longer you drag, the longer the gradient. For an abrupt transition between colors in the gradient click and drag over a shorter distance. We discuss gradients in more detail in Chapter 81.

Navigation Tools

Like QuarkXPress, InDesign provides some tools for navigating through your document.

Grabber Hand

Just as in XPress, you can use the Grabber Hand tool (press H) to scroll around a page or even between pages. With the Grabber Hand tool, you may never need to use the scroll bars to move around your document again. While XPress lets you press the Option/Alt key to temporarily activate the Grabber Hand tool, InDesign reserves the Option/Alt key for duplicating objects. So, in InDesign you get the Grabber Hand temporarily by holding down the space bar while using other tools, *or* holding down the Option/Alt key if you're editing text with the Type tool.

Zoom

Just like its QuarkXPress counterpart, you can use the Zoom tool (press Z) to change the view magnification in your document window. Of course, it's a hassle to select the tool just to change the view, so there are shortcuts for temporarily activating the zoom tool. Like Photoshop and Illustrator, pressing Command/Ctrl-spacebar temporarily activates the Zoom tool. Add Option/Alt key to decrease the page magnification. Also like Illustrator and Photoshop, you can press Command/Ctrl and the plus and minus signs to increase and decrease the magnification.

Determining Color Selections

The Tools palette also lets you control how InDesign applies fills and strokes. You can reset the currently selected colors to the default colors (press D), identify whether the text or frame is being modified, and even apply the last used solid color, gradient or no color from the Tools palette.

InDesign lets you apply color or gradients to either an object's stroke or fill. You can click on the fill or stroke icons in the Tools palette or the Swatches palette to determine where color selections are applied, but it's faster to use the X key to toggle between fill and stroke. If you accidentally apply a color to a fill but intended it for the stroke (or vice versa) press Shift-X to toggle the colors between the stroke and fill.

QuarkXPress users are often surprised to find that InDesign lets you apply colors to objects by pressing keyboard shortcuts. This can get you in trouble if you're not careful about what you press! For example, you can apply "no color" to the selected object (stroke or fill) with the forward slash key. You can also apply the last-chosen solid color with the comma key and the last selected gradient with the period key

The last two buttons in the Tools palette control the Preview mode, which we discuss in Chapter 3.

2

Views and Navigation

While we could keep this chapter about navigating around your document short and simply tell you to use the scroll bars, it wouldn't be any fun and would keep you from discovering all of the efficient and innovative navigation tools that are packed into InDesign!

Let's start by looking at navigation on a single page, then we'll look at navigation between pages in a document.

Navigating on a Page

The faster and more fluidly you can navigate around your document, the more efficient you're going to be.

Document Window Navigation

InDesign displays the current page magnification in the lower-left corner of your document window—more or less the same place as XPress displays it (see Figure 2-1). You can select from any of the preset magnification levels (in the popup menu next to the magnification setting), which range from five percent to 4000 percent. You can also enter a magnification value other than the presets; just remember to hit the Enter or Return key for your value to be accepted.

Zoom Tool

The Zoom tools in XPress and InDesign are very similar, even looking the same. You can quickly select the zoom tool by clicking Z on your keyboard (when the text cursor isn't active).

Figure 2-1

The document
window navigation
panel

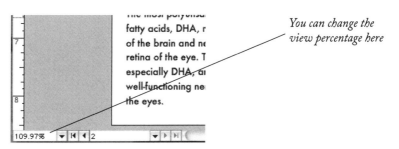

*You can change the
view percentage here*

However, just as in QuarkXPress, many people use this tool inefficiently. You can be much more productive with this tool by drawing a marquee around the objects you wish to magnify. This allows you to avoid having to click multiple times to increase the zoom level. To zoom out with this tool, hold down the Option/Alt key.

You can temporarily activate the zoom tool by selecting the Command/Ctrl key and the spacebar together. You can add the Option/Alt key to this combination to reduce the magnification.

Useful Key Commands for Navigating

InDesign provides you with several key commands to help you achieve the optimum page magnification. Use Command-0/Ctrl-0 (zero) to fit the current active page into your window. Be careful: InDesign sometimes thinks that you are working on a different page than you think! To be certain that the correct page will be magnified, check the page number listed in the lower left corner of the page window before using this key command. Note that Fit in Window mode in InDesign is different than in XPress; when you resize your document window in InDesign while in Fit in Window mode, the document resizes on screen, too (in XPress, you'd have to select this view mode again).

Also, unlike XPress, InDesign is able to fit the active spread into the window, not just the active page. Access this via Command-Option-0/Ctrl-Alt-0 (this is Fit Pasteboard in Window in XPress).

You can easily access a 100% zoom by selecting Command-1/Ctrl-1 and a 200% view by selecting Command-2/Ctrl-2. You can switch between your last two zoom levels by pressing Command-Option-2/Ctrl-Alt-2.

Page Grabber Hand

Just like QuarkXPress and Photoshop, the Hand tool (H from your keyboard) allows you to "grab" a portion of the page and move your view by dragging the page within the document window. If you don't use this tool you are missing out on one of the most efficient ways to move around a document page because it lets you move both vertically and horizontally at the same time. So say goodbye to your scroll bars and hello to the hand tool! You can temporarily activate this tool while you are using another tool by holding down the spacebar (unless you are entering type, of course). When editing type, use the Option/Alt key to temporarily access this tool.

Moving Between Pages

You are able to easily move between the pages in your document using some familiar tools and some ideas borrowed from other Adobe applications.

Pages Palette

Like the Document Layout palette in QuarkXPress, the Pages palette provides you with an icon representing each page in your document (see Figure 2-2). You may double-click on a page to move to that page. As an added bonus, you can also double-click on the page numbers below the spread and InDesign jumps to the spread and centers the pages within the window. Like XPress, master pages are shown at the top of the palette; double-click on one to view it. The page number that you are currently viewing appears bold in the Pages palette.

Document Window Navigation

The current page and zoom magnification is always listed in the navigation panel in the lower-left corner of the document window. To move to a specific page, click the down arrow at the right of the page number, and select a page from the pop-up list (see Figure 2-3). To move forward or backward by one page, click the right or left facing arrows, respectively. To move to the start or end of the document, use the arrows with the vertical line adjacent to them.

Key Commands for Navigating

Just as in QuarkXPress, you can use Command-J/Ctrl-J to quickly enter a page number and move to that page. However, unlike QuarkXPress, no dialog box appears—rather, the current page number in the navigation panel is highlighted (in the lower left corner of the document window).

Figure 2-2

The Pages palette

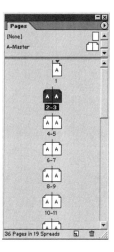

Figure 2-3

Selecting a page from the navigation panel

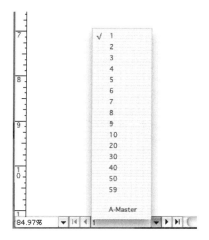

You can then enter the desired page number, followed by Enter or Return.

InDesign has the same keyboard shortcuts as XPress for navigating through your document: You can use the Page Up and Page Down keys on your keyboard to scroll up or down through your document. Plus, adding the Option/Alt key when using the Page Up and Page Down keys will take you up or down to the next full spread. Adding the Shift key takes you to the next or previous page.

The Navigator Palette

QuarkXPress users might not be familiar with the Navigator palette, which you can open from the Window menu. InDesign's Navigator palette works identically to those in Illustrator and Photoshop. The

Figure 2-4

The Navigator palette

palette shows a tiny representation of an entire page (see Figure 2-4). A red box on the page identifies the area which is currently visible on screen. At the bottom of the palette, you can use the sliding triangle to zoom in or zoom out of the page by dragging it right or left. You can see the view change in the active document window, and the red box in the palette will also update to reflect the current visible area.

The percentage value displayed in the lower left of the palette indicates the current view percentage. You can click your cursor into this area and enter a value, just as you can in the lower left of the document window.

Unlike the Navigator palette in Illustrator or Photoshop, you can also use this palette to display all pages in a document and navigate to a specific portion of a document page. You can select View All Pages from the palette's flyout menu to see all of the document pages.

In our experience, this palette is slow to redraw on all but the fastest computers. And because we often work on our notebook computers, we find that this palette takes up more space than it is worth on smaller screens, so we tend to leave this palette closed.

The Layout Menu

Of course, if you really don't like all of the other navigational options we've discussed, you can always use the Layout menu which, like XPress's Page menu, provides menu commands for moving from page to page. We find it painfully inefficient to see anyone using these commands, as they are so labor intensive. We encourage you to avoid using them.

Scrollable Mouse

We take advantage of two-button mice (though David uses a 10-button trackball on his Macintosh)—and so does InDesign. If you're using a third-party multi-button mouse on the Macintosh, make sure the second button is set to Control-click.

3

Showing and Hiding Page Elements

As QuarkXPress users, we've become familiar with hiding our page guides or showing invisible text characters. InDesign takes these basic options and expands upon them dramatically. You can show or hide all kinds of page elements separately. Even better, you can quickly preview how the page will print with the Preview feature.

Show and Hide Page Properties

Like XPress, InDesign lets you show and hide your page guides and ruler guides (see Chapters 34 and 35 for more on these sorts of guides) with a single command: Show/Hide Guides from the View menu (or press Command-;/Ctrl-;). However, while this command in XPress hides or shows all page properties, this command *only* hides or shows the ruler and page guides. InDesign lets you hide or show other page properties, too, such as frame edges, baseline grid, and even master page items.

Frame Edges

XPress users aren't used to hiding the edges of text and picture boxes as a separate step from hiding guides. But after becoming acclimated to this, you'll find that it's a very powerful tool. For instance, by using the Hide Frame Edges command from the View menu (Command-H/Ctrl-H), you can often better position an item near a guide without the frame interfering with the view. Note that this keyboard shortcut is the same as Hide Selection in Photoshop.

Baseline Grid

If you create multiple-column documents you probably use the baseline grid. You can make the grid visible from the View menu by select Show Baseline Grid (or hide it by selecting Hide Baseline Grid). The keyboard shortcut is Command-Option-'/Ctrl-Alt-' (single quote).

InDesign also gives you a second method for showing or hiding the grid, based upon the zoom level at which you are viewing the page. You can set the grid to be visible when you viewing the document at a high magnification but to hide when you are viewing the entire document at a lower magnification level. Use the Grids preferences (see Chapter 7 for more on preferences) to set the View Threshold for the baseline grid. When the document is at a magnification above the view threshold the grid is visible; when it's below the threshold, the grid is invisible. Or, if you always want the baseline grid to be visible, regardless of the magnification, set the View Threshold to 5%.

By the way, this same threshold option is available for ruler guides. Use the context menus when clicking on an existing ruler guide (Ctrl-click/ right click) to set this percentage. You can also set this percentage for all future ruler guides by entering the View Threshold in the Ruler Guides dialog accessed from the Layout menu, as seen in Figure 3-1.

Figure 3-1
View Threshold
determines the
magnification above
which ruler guides
will be visible

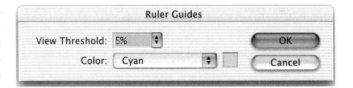

Text Threads

In XPress, it's a hassle to find out how text boxes are linked together. InDesign makes this much easier: Just turn on Show Text Threads from the View menu (Command-Option-Y/Ctrl-Alt-Y). You can hide the threads with the same command. Note that these threads are only visible when the in and out ports of the text frame are visible; that is, when you you've selected the frame with the Selection or Direct Selecction tool (see Chapter 40 for more on text threads).

Master Items

Another nice option InDesign introduces is the ability to show or hide master page items. You can use this to easily determine what items are master page items versus local, individual page items. Select Display Master Items from the View menu (or press Command-Y/Ctrl-Y) to show or hide items that are part of a master page that is applied to a document page.

Document Grid

QuarkXPress also lacks any sort of document grid–esentially a piece of graph paper that can overlay the document page. Fortunately, InDesign has this, and you can turn the grid on or off by selecting Show Document Grid from the View menu (or press Command-;/Ctrl-;). The document grid is extremely helpful when placing a number of objects on a page because you can avoid placing your own guides. You can control the document grid settings in the Preferences dialog box (see Chapter 7).

Preview Mode

One of our favorite features that InDesign has and XPress doesn't is the Preview Mode, which hides every non-printing page property (frames, guides, grids, and so on) in one quick step while placing the document on a neutral background. To do this, click the Preview Mode button at the bottom of the Tools palette (or press W—when you are not editing text, of course). Click the button or press W again to switch back to normal viewing mode.

Note that while in Preview mode, InDesign hides parts of objects that bleed onto the pasteboard, so you can see what your final printed page will look like, after trimming.

4

Palettes and Windows

InDesign displays your document in a window very similar to QuarkXPress: The scroll bars, resizing features, and closing and window-minimizing features all follow the traditional rules of the operating system you're using. Some window features are different, however. For instance, on both Mac and Windows InDesign sports a Window menu from which you can select open document windows (XPress only has one on the Windows platform).

Both InDesign and XPress also share the Tile and Cascade features, each of which take multiple documents and fit them within the available space on your monitor (though in different ways).

The Pasteboard

InDesign has a pasteboard that works very much like the one in XPress (though very differently than the pasteboard in PageMaker). The pasteboard is the area surrounding an InDesign document page where you can store items that you may not need on the page immediately. The pasteboard is equal to the width of the document page—except on the first page of a facing pages document, where it is the width of the document on the right side and twice the width of the document on the left side.

Unlike QuarkXPress there is not a preference to control the width of the pasteboard; so be careful as to not scroll too far out onto the side of the page or to position items too far out of reach!

Managing Palettes

Adobe InDesign makes liberal use of palettes, as opposed to QuarkXPress, which places most of its features in dialog boxes. This different way of presenting options creates a few challenges in keeping your workspace organized.

Palette Key Commands

Most palettes have their own key commands, which—if the palette is hidden—makes the palette appear and activates the first field within the palette. If the palette is already visible, then the keyboard shortcut hides the palette. Once the first field of the palette is active, you can use the Tab and Shift-Tab keystrokes to move between fields. For example, you can access the Character palette by using Command/Ctrl-T, then tab to the size field, type in a value, and press Enter to leave the palette. Note that you can also use the arrow keys to increase and decrease existing entries within the palettes (or Shift-arrow keys to increase and decrease in larger increments).

One of our favorite keyboard shortcuts is Command-~ (tilde), which highlights the last-used palette field. Unfortunately, Mac OS X grabbed this keyboard shortcut for "switch window" so if you want to use this feature in InDesign you have to change the keyboard shortcut (see Chapter 6).

Minimize Palettes

Adobe InDesign lets you minimize your palettes by clicking the Grow Window button at the top of the palette (see Figure 4-1). This button varies between operating systems—on the Macintosh it appears as a green button in the left corner of the palette and on Windows systems it appears as a horizontal line to the left of the Close Window button in the upper right corner of the palette.

You can also double click on the name of the palette you are viewing to have the palette expand or contract its view. Some palettes sport three views, so double-clicking on the palette name provides you with an expanded view, a reduced view, and a view where the palette is hidden except for its name.

Figure 4-1
A minimized palette

Combining and Docking Palettes

Because you are working with so many more palettes with InDesign it is important to customize your workspace to efficiently find what you need. With InDesign you can move palettes so that they are positioned together or separate palettes to view them independently. For example, the paragraph and character styles palettes are combined by default, but by dragging the title tab of one of these palettes you can separate them. Drag a palette (by it's title tab) on top of another palette to combine them (see Figure 4-2).

You can also dock palettes together by dragging the title tab of one palette over the bottom edge of another (wait until the palette's bottom edge highlights before letting go). When palettes are combined or docked, they'll always hide and show at the same time.

Figure 4-2

Combined and docked palettes

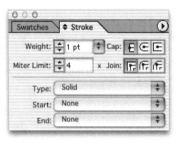
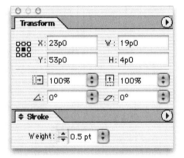

Hide Your Palettes

You can easily open palettes out and then forget to put them away, leaving your screen cluttered. We recommend closing palettes when you are done using them (a good reason to remember those keyboard shortcuts). Or, if you need to get a temporary uncluttered view of your page, press the Tab key (when not editing text) to hide all palettes—or Shift-Tab to hide all palettes except the Tools palette.

Tiny Text

If you have dozens of styles in the Paragraph Styles palette, or colors in the Swatches palette, consider selecting Small Palette Rows from the palette's flyout menu. This way, you can fit many more items in the same amount of space—though you may need to squint to read them.

5

Context Menus

Context-sensitive menus, or just "context menus" for short, can help you save a tremendous amount of time by giving you just the features you need in a menu depending on what you click on—or, more specifically, what you right-button click (Windows) or Control-click (Macintosh). While QuarkXPress 4 has only one context-sensitive menu (in the Style Sheets palette), and XPress 5 has a bunch scattered throughout the program, InDesign offers many more features within the context menus.

However, rather than listing every context menu option, we've picked out some of our favorite timesaving options that you can use.

Document Window Context Menus

When you Control-click or right-mouse button click anywhere on the page or pasteboard where there is *not* an object you can zoom in and out on the page, plus show, hide or lock page guides (see Figure 5-1). Context menus for selected page guides let you copy, paste or move the guides. Unlike QuarkXPress, you can even change the guides color under the Ruler Guides option (see Figure 5-2). Like XPress, you can also use context menus on the document ruler (the rulers at the top and left of the document window) to switch ruler measurements.

Using Context Menus With Frames

You can make almost any sort of modification to selected picture and text frames using the context menus. When working with picture frames,

Figure 5-1

Context menu on pasteboard or page

Figure 5-2

Context menu on selected guides and on rulers

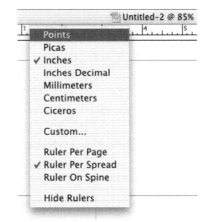

remember to take care in what is selected; if you use the Direct Select tool, you may select the image rather than the picture frame.

Here are a few common tasks available from the context menu for frames (see Figure 5-3):

- You can reduce or enlarge frame sizes with the Fit Frame to Content option. This works with both text and graphic frames.

- Use the Fit Content to Frame to proportionally or disproportionally cause graphic content inside of a frame to enlarge or reduce to fit into the frame in which it resides.

- You can set the stroke weight around a frame using context menus, including adding a stroke to an object that originally did not have one.

- You can apply a drop shadow or feather to an object.

Figure 5-3
Use the context menu to save time applying borders or fitting graphics within a frame.

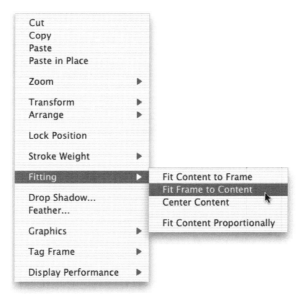

Text and Context Menus

We suggest you make your life easier by following the mantra, "When in doubt, use the context menu." Unlike QuarkXPress, InDesign provides access to most common text modification options through context menus, and offers some great time saving features too.

For instance, you can forget about Key Caps or the Character Map when looking for seldom-used characters. InDesign packs them into the Special Character submenu—one of many available from the context menus when working with text (see Figure 5-4).

Other useful context menu feature for text include:

- Spell Checking is easily accessed by using the context menus while editing text with the text tool.

- You can use the Fill with Placeholder Text option to place dummy text inside of an existing frame.

- With the Insert Special Character command you can easily add unusual characters such as a copyright or trademark symbol.

- Text Frame Options make it easy to change the number of columns applied to a text frame, remove text wrap or change the text inset.

- Use Change Case to change characters to reflect the desired capitilization—including all caps, all lower case or sentence case.

Figure 5-4

Context menu
with text

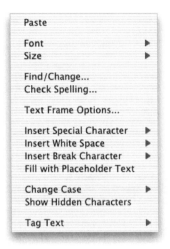

- Show Hidden Characters displays all typographic symbols, including spaces, hard returns and tabs. A great proofreading tool that you would otherwise access from the Type menu.

Keyboard Shortcuts

One of the most common arguments QuarkXPress users offer for not wanting to switch to InDesign is that they already know so many XPress keyboard shortcuts. However, the great thing about InDesign is that you can take all of your favorite shortcuts with you, get rid of the ones you don't like, change others and then add some more of your own. In short, with InDesign you can make keyboard shortcuts work for you. InDesign eliminates a common frustration for Photoshop and Illustrator users: the need to use one set of key commands in these programs but another set of commands while in QuarkXPress.

The ability to change keyboard shortcuts is great for you, but causes a problem for authors like us because we don't know if or how you changed your keyboard shortcuts. So the keyboard shortcuts we list in this book are all based on the default shortcuts that ship with InDesign. If you change them, you're on your own!

Finding Shortcuts

As with QuarkXPress, keyboard shortcuts are typically listed adjacent to the commands in the pull-down menus (see Figure 6-1). Additionally, many keyboard shortcuts from Adobe Illustrator, Photoshop and PageMaker work in InDesign, too. For example, the zoom in and zoom out shortcuts (Command-=/Ctrl-= and Command-hyphen/Ctrl-hyphen) that work in other Adobe programs also work here.

When looking for a key command, first try a Photoshop or Illustrator equivilant if you know it. If that doesn't work, look to see if the shortcut

Figure 6-1

Keyboard shortcuts are often listed next to menu commands.

is listed in a menu. Finally, you can try the Keyboard Shortcuts command from the Edit menu (see Figure 6-2). First, use the Product Area popup menu to select the type of command you are looking to find (like Text and Tables or View Menu). Then use the Commands section to identify the feature for which you want a shortcut. When you click on the name of the command InDesign lists the shortcut in the Current Shortcuts field.

As we mentioned back in Chapter 1, each tool also has a keyboard shortcut associated with it. These shortcuts are shown by hovering your mouse over any tool.

Printing Shortcuts

Perhaps the best way to learn the keyboard shortcuts is to print a complete list of all the current keyboard shortcuts. To do this, select Keyboard Shortcuts from the Edit menu and then click the Show Set button. InDesign saves a file called "Default.txt" to disk and then opens it with the system's default text editor (like TextEdit, SimpleText, or Windows Notepad). This file (which you can print) contains not only a complete list of all possible keyboard shortcuts, but also every command which *could* have a keyboard shortcut (see Figure 6-3).

User Interface

Figure 6-2
The Keyboard
Shortcuts dialog box

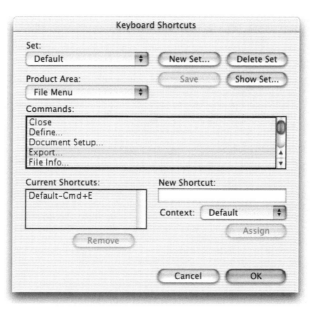

Customizing Shortcuts

While many Adobe InDesign key commands will be easy for you to use, there may be others that make your work more difficult. For example, after years of importing objects in XPress using Command-E/Ctrl-E (for Get Picture), InDesign now asks you to use Command-D/Ctrl-D (for Place). In XPress, the latter command duplicates selected objects, but if you use the former in InDesign, you open the Export dialog box. Fortunately, you can resolve this dilemma by customizing your key commands to whatever you want them to be.

The easiest way to change InDesign's keyboard shortcuts is to select a different set from the Set popup menu in the Keyboard Shortcuts dialog box. InDesign ships with one shortcut set other than its default: QuarkXPress 4.0 keyboard shortcuts. If you really like XPress's shortcuts, choose this. Suddenly, Command-E/Ctrl-E activates Place, Command-3/Ctrl-3 adds an automatic page number, and so on.

It's not hard to customize the keyboard commands further, but you do need to take some care with the Context menu. Here's what you do.

1. Select Keyboard Shortcuts from the Edit menu, then choose the Set you want to modify (or click New Set to make your own). You can alter the Default set, but we don't recommend it, as it's nice to be able to go back to the original settings.

Figure 6-3

A listing of all keyboard shortcuts which can also be printed

```
Default.txt

Product area : Object Menu
    Arrange: Bring Forward --- Default-Cmd+]
    Arrange: Bring to Front --- Default-Shift+Cmd+]
    Arrange: Send Backward --- Default-Cmd+[
    Arrange: Send to Back --- Default-Shift+Cmd+[
    Clipping Path... --- Default-Opt+Shift+Cmd+K
    Compound: Make --- Default-Cmd+8
    Compound: Release --- Default-Opt+Cmd+8
    Content: Graphic --- [none defined]
    Content: Text --- [none defined]
    Content: Unassigned --- [none defined]
    Corner Effects... --- Default-Opt+Cmd+R
    Display: Use View Setting --- [none defined]
    Drop Shadow... --- Default-Opt+Cmd+M
    Feather... --- [none defined]
    Fitting: Center Content --- Default-Shift+Cmd+E
    Fitting: Fit Content Proportionally --- Default-Opt+Shift+Cmd+E
    Fitting: Fit Content to Frame --- Default-Opt+Cmd+E
    Fitting: Fit Frame to Content --- Default-Opt+Cmd+C
    Group --- Default-Cmd+G
    Image Color Settings... --- [none defined]
    Lock Position --- Default-Cmd+L
    Reverse Path --- [none defined]
    Text Frame Options... --- Default-Cmd+B
```

2. Choose a subject from the Product Area popup menu, and then choose the command you want to change from the Commands portion of the window.

3. After selecting a command to be modified, InDesign displays the current keyboard shortcut in the Current Shortcuts field. You can eliminate a current shortcut (there may be more than one, each with a different context) by clicking the Remove shortcut without assigning a new shortcut.

4. If you want to add a new shortcut, first choose from the four choices in the Context popup menu: Alerts/Dialogs, Text, Default, and Tables (plus XML Selection if you have the XML plug-ins installed). This controls when the shortcut will be active. For instance, if you choose Tables, then the keyboard shortcut will only function when your text cursor is in a table.

5. Finally, click in the New Shortcut portion of the window, enter the keystroke you want, and click the Assign button. Your new shortcut should then be listed in the Current Shortcuts portion of the window. When done assigning keyboard shortcuts, click the OK button.

7

Defaults & Preferences

Like QuarkXPress, with InDesign you can customize your work environment to reflect your needs. From the way you measure to how your type is set and what size documents you typically produce. InDesign lets you choose how documents should typically be created, displayed and printed.

Page Settings

InDesign has two groups of defaults, we'll start with page settings that change how a page is created and displayed then we will look at the actual preferences.

Default Page Size

You can define the default page size by closing all documents, and keeping InDesign open and then selecting Document Setup from the File menu. Like with QuarkXPress, most settings made with no documents open will be reflected in all future documents. If you make preference or default changes while a document is open the changes are limited to that document. Enter the page size, orientation and whether or not you want facing pages in the Document Setup dialog box (see Figure 7-1). Once you set these, InDesign uses the values for all your future documents (until you change the defaults, of course). While this sets your default page size, you can always override these defaults in the New Document dialog box when creating new files.

Figure 7-1
The Document Setup
dialog lets you set the
document size and
margins.

Default Margins and Columns

As with the default page size, you can define default margin and column settings with no documents open by selecting the Margins and Columns command from the Layout menu and entering the distance for margins on each side of the page and the number of columns for the document (see Figure 7-2). InDesign uses these values as the default for all new documents, but you can always override them in the New document dialog box, or revisit the Margins and Columns dialog box in an open document. QuarkXPress simply handles this by remembering the last values input into the New Document dialog box, so it may take some time for you to become accustomed to InDesign's handling of these defaults.

Figure 7-2
The Margins and
Columns dialog lets
you establish default
settings when no
documents are open.

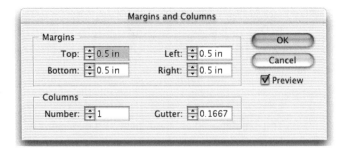

Default Preferences

Like QuarkXPress, InDesign lets you set preferences that control your working environment. Just like in XPress, if you set preferences with no documents open, they apply to all new documents, or you can set them while a document is open for them to apply to only that document. You can access preferences from the Edit menu in or the Application menu (depending on your operating system). You can jump directly to one of the nine preference sections by selecting it from the Preferences submenu, or by choosing General Preferences and then clicking the preference type along the left side of the Preferences dialog box.

General Preferences

The general preferences provide a host of options that are not found in QuarkXPress (see Figure 7-3). For example, because InDesign uses an automatic crash recovery, which is not optional like that found in XPress, you can use this dialog to set the location of the temporary file.

- **Page Numbering.** This controls the way pages appear in the Pages palette.

- **General Options.** You can also use this section to configure the Tools palette, and to disable or enable tool tips–those small pop-up windows which describe the tool name and appear when your mouse rolls over a tool or a palette icon.

- **Print Options.** This preference lets you set whether black overprints or knocks out colors beneath a black object.

- **Temporary Folder.** You can also set the folder for the location of your temporary files–Macintosh OS X users may wish to move this location to something easier to find than the Users folder. Because this controls where your preferences and saved data are stored, you can use this to help find these files if the preferences become corrupt or InDesign is trying to open an auto-saved version of a file that you don't want.

Figure 7-3
The General Preferences dialog box

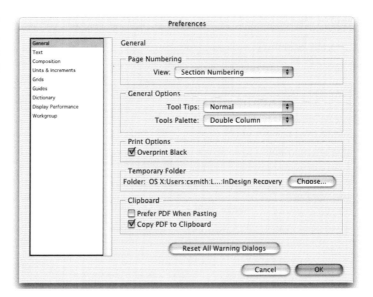

- **Clipboard.** These settings control whether objects are copied or pasted in the PDF file format. If you copy and paste objects from Adobe Illustrator, you probably want to leave Prefer PDF When Pasting turned off.

Text Preferences

Like in QuarkXPress, you can set the size applied to superscripted, subscripted and small-capped characters (for fonts that don't have these characters built-in) in the Text preferences section (see Figure 7-4).

You can also define whether InDesign should use typographers' quotes and, important for QuarkXPress users, whether leading is applied to the entire paragraph. By default InDesign applies leading only to selected lines within a paragraph, not to the entire paragraph—a very unusual option for QuarkXPress users, though a familiar one to some traditional typesetters and PageMaker users. If you prefer the QuarkXpress shortcut of being able to click three times to select a line, select this option.

Correct Optical Size lets users of Multiple Master fonts have the correct optical size be used at a certain size. Multiple Master fonts may include this feature which varies the appearance of the typeface for improved readability at various sizes. The Adjust Text Attributes When Scaling option changes how text values are displayed within the Character palette. With this option enabled, when you increase a text frame with 12 pt type and it is then displayed as 24 pt. You can disable this option and the display in the Character palette is then listed as "12pt(24pt)".

Figure 7-4
With Text Preferences you can establish guidelines for text appearance and editing.

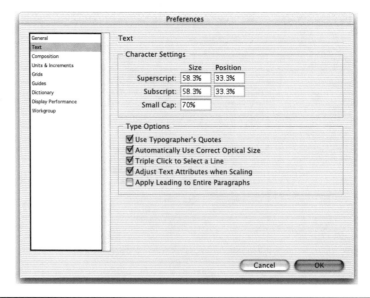

Composition Preferences

Using the Composition preferences (see Figure 7-5) you can ask InDesign to alert you to missing fonts or poorly composed text that violated hyphenation and justification rules that are applied to paragraphs.

Unlike QuarkXPress, InDesign lets you decide whether text should justify around a wrapped object or remain ragged. You can set this by clicking the Justify option in the Text wrap section of this dialog box.

Figure 7-5
The Composition Preferences indicate when InDesign should alert you if text can not be composed using hyphenation and justification guidelines.

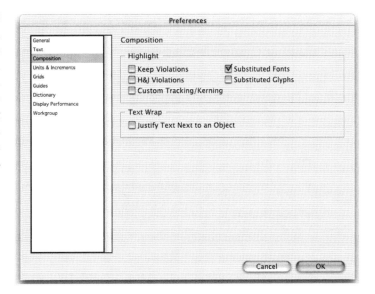

Units & Increments

The Units & Increments panel lets you pick the vertical and horizontal forms of measurement used by InDesign. It supports all the same measurement systems as XPress, and even allows you to establish your own form of measurement.

You can also define what values the Arrow keys nudge objects, and how much kerning, baseline shifting and type sizes are affected when using keyboard shortcuts.

Grids & Guides Preferences

With the Grids preferences you can define the frequency, starting point and color of both the document grid and the baseline grid (see Figure 7-6). You can also define the view threshold for the baseline grid, which determines the magnification at which the baseline grid becomes visible or invisible. QuarkXPress either displays the preference or it doesn't based

Figure 7-6

The Grids and
Guides Preferences
dialog box

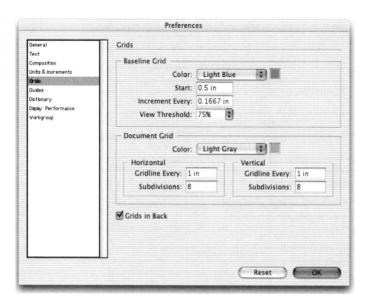

upon the View setting selected. InDesign enables or disable the viewing automatically based upon what view magnification is being used. Like QuarkXPress, grids are placed either in front of or behind page objects based upon preference settings, with InDesign you can set this in the grids preferences.

Guides preferences let you define their color and the snap zone within which objects are pulled to them.

Dictionary Preferences

You can define the look of single quotes and double quotes under the Dictionary preferences (remember that the choice for whether to convert straight quotes to curly quotes is found under the Text preferences, though).

If you are using a third-party dictionary for spell checking and hyphenation, you can select them in this section (Figure 7-7). We discuss InDesign's language and dictionary capabilities in Chapter 42.

You can also set complex composition options, including which dictionaries are used to flow the document. By default the user dictionary and the document dictionary are both used for hyphenation exceptions, so this should not need to be modified unless you want only one or the other to be used for composing purposes.

By default user dictionaries are merged into documents, but you can disable this if you desire. You can also set all documents to be recomposed

Figure 7-7
Using the InDesign
Dictionary
Preferences you
can set which
dictionaries are used
for spell checking and
hyphenation.

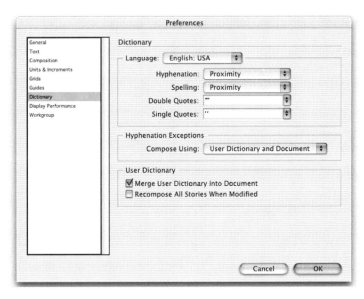

(reflowed) if the user dictionary is modified. You would use this if you set specific rules for hyphenating words in your user dictionary and need them to retroactively apply to stories that have been previously flowed into a document.

Display Performance

We've found many users who commented on poor performance with InDesign have had their Display Performance preferences set to operate inefficiently. InDesign is capable of displaying all images, including imported Photoshop or Illustrator files, at their native resolution. But just because InDesign can do this does not mean that this is a good thing in every case.

If you have many placed images and you set your images to display them all at their maximum resolution, InDesign will operate more slowly. The more images it must display at high resolution, the slower it operates.

You can still get high quality images when you need them but not overload your system to a point where it becomes unbearably slow. The Typical radio button in the Adjust View Settings portion of the Display Performance preferences (see Figure 7-8) gives you similar quality settings to QuarkXPress. When you need higher quality settings, choose the High Quality Display from the Display Performance context menu.

Figure 7-8

The Display Performance settings impact both the display quality and the speed at which pages are displayed. Higher quality settings display more slowly.

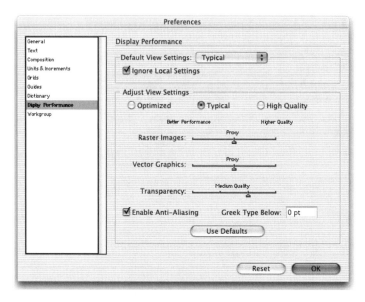

Workgroup Preferences

You can select the Enable Workgroup Functionality option to allow you to check files out from a workgroup file server, such as a WebDAV server. This allows for centralized management of who is working on what files. If you are not using a WebDAV server, you can ignore this feature, which has no QuarkXPress counterpart. But if file management is a problem in your workflow, you may wish to investigate this feature further.

Preference File

You may wish to make a backup of your preferences files to save all of your default settings, or you may wish to delte them if InDesign is behaving erratically as they may have become corrupt. They are located in the folder specified under the Temporary Folder within the General Preferences. This is usually the InDesign Preferences folder, and its location varies based upon the operating system in which you operate. These files are similar to the XPress Preference files that careful users back-up regularly or delete when they become corrupt.

8

Adobe Online

The cool picture of a butterfly on the top of the Tools palette (see Figure 8-1) is more than just a reminder of InDesign's application icon and splash screen. Clicking once in this area activates Adobe Online in older versions of InDesign or Adobe Product Update, which is the replacement for Adobe Online. If you see an Adobe Online dialog box after clicking the icon at the top of the tools palette, click the Adobe Online Preferences button and then click Updates, which downloads the most recent files and replaces Adobe Online with Adobe Product Update.

After updating to the most recent version of Adobe Product Update, clicking the butterfly icon takes you directly to the Adobe InDesign product information Web page where you can learn about product updates and bug fixes, locate training resources and learn about additional InDesign plug-ins. While this feature is vaguely useful, it is pretty annoying if you overshoot the selection tools and somehow end up in your Web browser waiting for a page to download.

Using Adobe Online

While you can visit the Adobe web site for information, the Downloadables feature in the Help menu tells InDesign to check for product updates. If you wish to download any updates, select the update and click the Download button. Oddly enough, some updates will display as a warning dialog the next time you restart the software, rather than allowing you to download immediately.

Figure 8-1
Adobe Online

*Click here to go to the
InDesign product Web page.*

Setting Online Preferences

You can make InDesign automatically check for updates to your InDesign software in the Online Settings Preferences dialog box (choose Online Settings from the Preferences submenu). By default, the program will not check for updates automatically (see Figure 8-2). In this case, you'll need to either select Downloadables from the Help menu or click the Updates button in the Adobe Online Preferences window to check for updates.

Figure 8-2
The Adobe Online
Preferences
dialog box

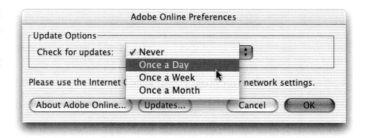

9

InDesign Plug-ins

When deciding to switch to InDesign, you might have wondered if your existing QuarkXPress XTensions would work with InDesign. The answer is no, because XTension and plug-ins are different, each being customized for a particular software program.

What Are Plug-ins?

InDesign may not be able to do everything you'd want, such as the ability to easily create mathematical equations for textbook publishing, arrange pages in printers spreads for offset printing, or interact with databases. Fortunately, you can buy third-party plug-ins that add these additional capabilities.

Most people don't realize that, unlike XPress, most of the features in InDesign are actually plug-ins written by Adobe, and that the application itself is sort of a glorified plug-in manager! This underlying technology has some advantages, like the ability for Adobe to update individual features easily. Some third-party software developers are even customizing InDesign by replacing Adobe's plug-ins with their own for specific publishing needs, such as newspaper or magazine publishing.

Managing Plug-ins

XPress lets you turn on and off XTensions using the XTensions Manager; InDesign can do the same thing with the Configure Plug-ins dialog box (which is available from either the application menu or the File menu, depending upon your operating system). If you never use Adobe Online (see Chapter 8) or the Indexing feature (see Chapter 90), then you can turn off those plug-ins, making the program launch and run slightly faster.

To enable or disable a plug-in in the Configure Plug-ins dialog box, click in the column to the left of the plug-in name (see Figure 9-1). Plug-ins with a lock icon are required by InDesign and may not be disabled. To make things even more confusing, some plug-ins are required by other plug-ins; if you try to turn one of these off, the program alerts you (and if you still agree to turn it off, the other plug-ins will be disabled, too).

After making changes you must quit and restart the program for the new settings to become active.

Figure 9-1
The Configure
Plug-ins dialog box

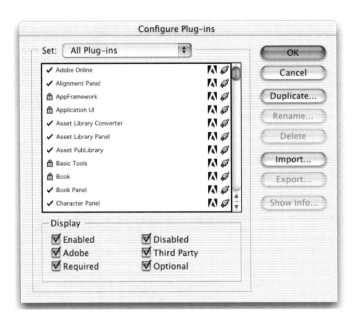

Plug-in Sets

You can create a new plug-in set by clicking the Duplicate button and then giving the new set a name. Then turn off the plug-ins that you don't need—for example, if you do not expect to use the Book feature for long documents or InScope for connecting into a central file management database you can disable these plug-ins. You might save different sets of plug-ins for different types of work, such as one set for long documents and another set for one-page ads. You can also save sets to disk and load them back in using the Import and Export buttons.

Third-Party Plug-ins

Your Adobe InDesign CD includes a free plug-in from A Lowly Apprentice Productions (*www.alap.com*) called InModify. It adds a Modify dialog box similar to the one found in QuarkXPress. You can install this plug-in by dragging it into the Plug-ins folder, located within the Adobe InDesign application folder on your computer (and then launching InDesign).

Several dozen plug-ins have been created by third-parties. When you want to expand your capabilities with advanced tools, check out the plug-ins from Gluon, Em Software, and other developers. The Power XChange is a great source for plug-ins (you can find this company on the Web at *www.thepowerxchange.com*).

PART 2

Building Pages

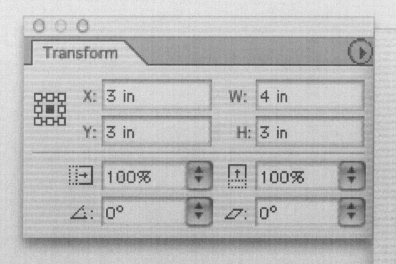

10

Creating Frames

The basic elements of an InDesign page are the same as they are in a QuarkXPress page—boxes, lines and text paths. But since you're now working in a new "country," you have to learn the language of your new land, which is a little different than the kingdom of QuarkXPress.

Understanding the Lingo

InDesign calls the basic elements of a page *frames,* instead of boxes. As in XPress, frames are used as the container for text or graphics, or they may have no content at all.

QuarkXPress uses the word *frame* to mean the border around a box. It calls the thickness of a frame its *width.* When you want to change the background, you change the *box color.* InDesign, on the other hand, follows Illustrator's terminology, and calls the border of a frame the *stroke.* When you change the thickness of a stroke, you change its *stroke weight.* Similarly, when a frame has a background color, InDesign calls it the *fill.*

The other basic element of a QuarkXPress page is a line. InDesign again borrows from Illustrator calling these *paths.* Note that we also call the edge around a frame a path.

Flexibility with Frames

When you work with QuarkXPress boxes, you have one workflow: First, you draw a text box or a picture box, then you fill it with content. InDesign offers more flexibility to the process: You can continue to use the same method you learned with XPress, or you can learn to create frames on-the-fly.

Placeholder Frames

When you want to use the XPress method, you can use InDesign's frame tools (see Figure 10-1). There are three basic tools to create a frame in the shape of a rectangle, an ellipse, and a regular polygon. (We'll show you how create squares, circles and stars from these tools in Chapter 12. And you can make fancier boxes with corner effects, which we describe in Chapter 15.)

Figure 10-1

The Rectangle, Ellipse and Polygon Frame tools

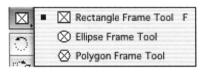

Note that there aren't separate frame tools for text and pictures, as there are in XPress; you use the same tool to create either a text or picture placeholder. By default, these tools create graphic placeholders (also called "picture frames"), indicated by the "X" in them (see Figure 10-2). However, you can turn them into text frames by clicking in them with the Type tool or selecting the frame and choosing Text from the Content submenu (under the Object menu). As in XPress 4 or 5, you can change the content of a frame at any time. You can recognize text frames by their in and out ports, used for connecting the frames. Unassigned frames have neither an "X" or ports.

Frames On-the-Fly

InDesign also offers the choice of creating frames on-the-fly. To place a graphic when no frame has been created, you can simply choose Place from the File menu (or press Command-D/Ctrl-D). After selecting a graphic to place, you'll see the loaded graphics cursor (see Figure 10-3). If you click, InDesign automatically creates a frame and places the graphic in it, at the point where you click. You can also click-and-drag on the page with the loaded graphics cursor, which places the picture inside a frame with one corner where you clicked and another corner where you let go of the mouse button.

You can make text frames on the fly just as easily. For example, if you just want to make a quick caption there's no need to make a frame first.

Figure 10-2
Three selected frames
with graphic, text and
unassigned content

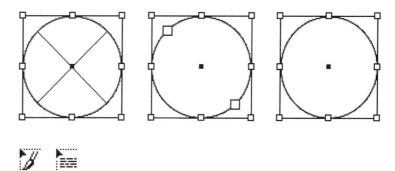

Figure 10-3
The loaded graphics
and text cursors

Just choose the Type tool (or press T), and drag out a rectangular frame with that tool. After dragging out the shape, the text insertion point is flashing, ready to accept your text.

Or, when you want to place text without first making a frame, choose Place from the File menu (or press Command-D/Ctrl-D) and select a text file to place. InDesign changes the cursor to the loaded text cursor (see Figure 10-3), with which you can drag out a frame to the size you wish. When you release the mouse, text flows into the frame.

Dragging and Copying Shortcuts

InDesign has two more frame creating shortcuts up its sleeve. First, when you paste graphics or text from the clipboard (select Paste from the Edit menu or press Command-V/Ctrl-V), InDesign creates a frame in the center of your current page. We discuss copying graphics from Adobe Illustrator and Macromedia Freehand in Chapter 63. Be warned, however, that when you copy a bitmapped image, it is becomes an embedded object and is not linked to a file on disk (we don't recommend doing this).

The second trick is a truly amazing way to add text or graphics to a page: You can select one or more text or graphic files on the Windows or Macintosh system desktop or in Windows Explorer and drag the files into InDesign! On the Macintosh, drag the files into an InDesign window until you see a black outline around window, then release the mouse. In Windows, drag the files over a minimized InDesign window and, when the window opens, release the mouse. InDesign creates a frame for each file (they're stacked if you're dragging several files), and the frames are linked to their external files. What a time saver!

11

Tools for Selecting

While it may seem obvious, before you can work with objects on a page, you have to select them. While QuarkXPress has the Item and Content tools for selecting, InDesign uses three tools: The Selection tool, the Direct Selection tool, and the Type tool. Selecting objects in InDesign is one of the most frustrating tasks for someone used to the way XPress does it.

The Selection tool (press V) selects an entire object; you can also use it to move or resize a frame or path (see Figure 11-1). The Direct Selection tool (press A) selects or edits *part* of an object, such as a single point on a path or a graphic frame's content. At first glance it appears that the Selection tool is like XPress's Item tool and the Direct Selection tool is like XPress's Content tool, but the similarity breaks down in several ways. For instance, to select or edit the content of a text frame, you must use the Type tool (press T). (Because text is handled so differently than other objects, we'll discuss the use of this tool in Part 4.)

Note that you can switch between the Selection tool and the Direct Selection tool by pressing Control-Tab.

We discuss basic selections in this chapter, but we cover more complex selections (like when objects are grouped or nested) in Chapter 20.

Figure 11-1
The Selection, Direct Selection and Type tools

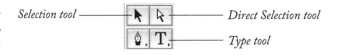

Selection tool ——————— Direct Selection tool

Type tool

Bounding Boxes and Anchor Points

InDesign is engineered from the ground up to allow shape editing. The appearance of a selected frame changes depending on the tool you are working with. When the Selection tool is active, a selected path or frame shows eight bounding box handles, just like in XPress (one on each corner, one on each side; see Figure 11-2). A solid, non-printing center point also appears which is handy for selecting objects that have no content.

When the Direct Selection tool is active, you see the the *anchor points* which make up the shape of the path or frame (see Figure 11-3). It's as though XPress's Edit Shape feature were turned on automatically. A non-printing center point is also displayed. We'll describe how to edit the shape of frames in the next chapter.

Selecting Multiple Objects

When selecting multiple objects, InDesign works almost identically to QuarkXPress. If you're working with the Selection tool, you can select more than one frame or path by Shift-clicking; you'll see the bounding boxes of each selected object. If you're working with the Direct Selection tool, you can Shift-click to choose more than one anchor point in frames and paths. With either tool, to deselect an object or anchor point, just Shift-click again.

Figure 11-2
Path and frame with the Selection tool active

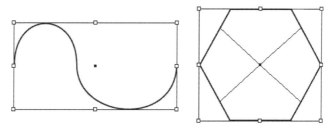

Figure 11-3
The same objects with the Direct Selection tool active

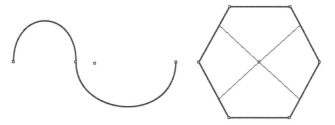

Dragging a marquee in InDesign also works similar to XPress. With the Selection tool, the marquee rectangle selects any objects whose shape falls within the marqueed area, no matter how little they are included. Marqueeing with the Direct Selection tool chooses any anchor points within the selection rectangle.

Lastly, you can select all of the objects on a page or spread by choosing Select All from the Edit menu (Command-A/Ctrl-A). InDesign also has a handy deselect command—Deselect All from the same menu (Command-Shift-A/Ctrl-Shift-A). We use Deselect All very frequently, such as before creating a new color in the Colors palette (so that the new color won't be applied to any accidentally-selected objects).

12

Creating and Editing Shapes

Now that you know how InDesign works with frames and paths, and how to select them, we'd better show you how to create some. As you might expect, there are tools available to create simple, freeform and precise shapes. Later in this chapter, we'll also explain how to reshape these objects once you've made them.

Simple Shapes

Simple shapes are the ones we create the most, so InDesign has specialized tools for making specific shapes.

Line Tool

Unlike QuarkXPress, there is only one tool dedicated to creating straight lines in InDesign. (You can also create creates lines with the Pencil or Pen tools, described below.) You use the Line tool exactly like QuarkXPress's tool of the same name. When you finish dragging, you'll see the bounding box of the line (unless the line is horizontal or vertical, in which case you only see the two end points). Dragging while holding down the Shift key is the equivalent of drawing with XPress's Orthogonal Line tool—it constrains your line horizontally or vertically. Plus, if you hold down the Option/Alt key while you drag, you can draw the line from the center.

Rectangle, Ellipse and Polygon Tools

When you want to make a background tint rectangle—a frame with no content—the Rectangle tool (press M; see Figure 12-1) is the one for you.

Figure 12-1
The Rectangle,
Ellipse and
Polygon tools

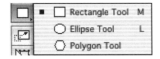

You can also use the Ellipse (press L) and Polygon tools to make content-less frames. What about a rounded corner rectangle? We show how to make these in Chapter 15 using corner effects.

There are several modifier keys already familiar to Illustrator users which work with these three tools:

- Holding down the Shift key constrains the shape to have the same height and width, just like in XPress.

- Holding down the Option/Alt key draws the shape from the center.

- Holding down Shift-Option/Shift-Alt draws a proportional shape from the center.

- Holding down the Space Bar when drawing lets you move the shape while still drawing it.

The Polygon tool is even more versatile—you can even use it to draw starbursts! After selecting this tool, double-click on the tool icon in the Tools palette to open the Polygon Settings dialog box. Here you can set the number of sides for a polygon. The default Star Inset is 0% which creates a polygon, but if you choose a positive value, you create stars. Increasing the percentage moves the inner vertices of the star inward, creating a spikier star (see Figure 12-2).

Freeform Shapes

As with QuarkXPress, InDesign offers two types of tools to create Bézier shapes—freeform and precise tools. If you haven't learned to use the Pen

Figure 12-2
Adjusting the
Star Inset

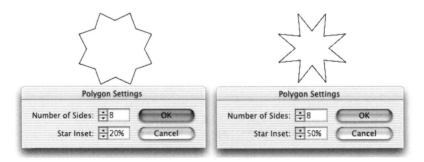

tool in another application, the freeform tools are the easiest to use, and InDesign's tools definitely give more control than those of XPress. Let's take a look at the three freeform drawing tools first.

Pencil Tool

The Pencil tool (press N) works analagously to QuarkXPress's Freehand Box and Line tools (see Figure 12-3). To create a line, you simply draw with it like you would on a piece of paper. But InDesign's Pencil tool not only draws, it redraws: if, after drawing a line, you draw over part of the line, InDesign deletes from that point to the end and the redraws using the new path you specified. If you want to use the Pencil to create a frame instead of a line, draw the shape, then hold down the Option/Alt key when you get close to the starting point, and a tiny circle cursor appears. Release the mouse button first, then the key, and you make a closed shape.

Figure 12-3
The Pencil, Smooth and Erase tools

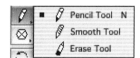

Smooth Tool

You may use the Smooth tool to smooth out a freeform shape. Dragging the Smooth tool over a path reduces the angularity of curves (helping to compensate for your shaking hand!) and produces a curve with fewer anchor points. You can also choose to smooth by holding down the Option/Alt key when using the Pencil tool.

In InDesign, you can control how accurately the Pencil and Smooth tools follow your mouse movements by double-clicking on each tool, opening the Pencil Tool Preferences dialog box (see Figure 12-4) or a similar dialog box for the Smooth tool. The Fidelity slider controls how much your mouse movements affect the path: Low pixel values produce more angles, and high values produce smoother curves. The Smoothness slider controls whether smoothing is automatically applied as you move; the default is 0%, meaning no smoothing.

Erase Tool

Finally, drag with the Erase tool to delete part of the freeform shape you created. It works like a real world eraser, erasing anchor points and the line segments between them.

Figure 12-4
The Pencil Tool
Preferences

Figure 12-4
The Pencil Tool
Preferences

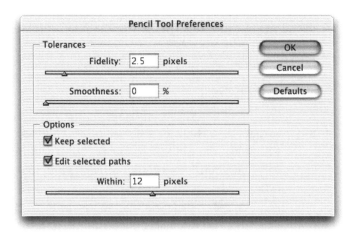

Precise Shapes with the Pen Tool

When we're creating a frame or path which isn't a simple shape, we always use the Pen tool (press P; see Figure 12-5), not the freeform tools. The reason: Despite the freeform controls we just told you about, it's almost impossible to create a precise path with those tools. InDesign uses a Pen tool and other path editing tools which are similar to those in XPress, and virtually identical to those in Illustrator or Photoshop. If you've learned to use the Pen tool in another Adobe product, you're home free! This section doesn't pretend to be a complete course in making precise paths (*Real World InDesign 2* covers the drawing tools in more detail). Instead we'll focus here on how InDesign's path creation tools are similar to and different from those of XPress.

Figure 12-5
The Pen tool and
associated tools

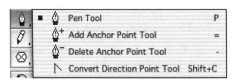

First, a little terminology review when you're working with precise paths (see Figure 12-6): The tiny squares which control the shape of a curve are called *anchor points*. InDesign uses *smooth points* and *corner points* like QuarkXPress, but it doesn't have *symmetrical points* (they exist in InDesign, but there's no special control to create them automatically like there is in XPress). The handles that extend out from anchor points are called *control handles*. Smooth points have two handles which move in

Figure 12-6

Curve terminology

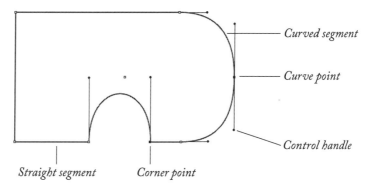

Curved segment

Curve point

Control handle

Straight segment   Corner point

unison around an anchor point. Corner points have either one, two, or no control handles, and their handles move independently of each other. The lines which connect the anchor points are called *segments*, which can be either curved or straight.

Similarities and Differences

While QuarkXPress uses different tools to create Bézier lines, text boxes, etc., InDesign has only one Pen tool. Creating most paths with the Pen tool works the same as in XPress:

- Clicking makes straight segments

- Shift-clicking constrains line segments to 45- or 90-degree angles

- Dragging creates smooth points

- Shift-dragging constrains control handles to 45° or 90° angles

- Moving over a path starting point always closes the path (in QuarkX-Press this only works with boxes, not lines)

- Clicking on the Pen tool after drawing a path lets you end one path begin a new one

As in QuarkXPress, it's a good idea in InDesign to watch how the cursor changes when you're working with the Pen tool. Table 12-1 shows several different Pen cursors, most of which are the same as in Illustrator and Photoshop.

Corner Point Tip

Here's one InDesign Pen technique which can be a big time saver: making corner points as you're drawing (see Figure 12-7).

1. Select the Pen tool and draw a smooth curve.

Table 12-1	If you want to...	Look for this cursor...
The Pen cursors	Make a new path	
	Continue an existing path	
	Close a path	
	Merge two paths	
	Add an anchor point	
	Delete an anchor point	
	Make a corner point	
	Convert a point	
	Snap a point to a guide	

Figure 12-7

Creating a corner point when drawing

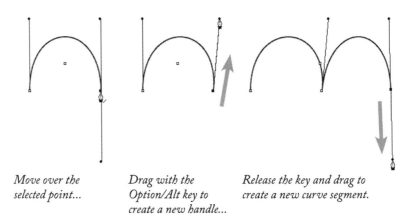

Move over the selected point...

Drag with the Option/Alt key to create a new handle...

Release the key and drag to create a new curve segment.

2. After dragging out the second anchor point (producing the curve segment), move your Pen over the second (selected) anchor point. You'll see a tiny V-shape cursor.

3. Hold down the Option/Alt key and drag to create a control handle moving in a different direction from the previous control handle. After dragging, release the key.

4. Drag again to create a second curve segment.

Reshaping Paths and Frames

InDesign uses the Direct Selection tool and several other dedicated tools for reshaping and editing the paths and frames which you've created with the Pen tool or any other method. You can use them immediately on any object without having to go into a special editing mode like QuarkXPress forces you to do.

Direct Selection Tool

Use the Direct Selection tool, not the Pen tool, to edit paths or frames. You can even use it while drawing: With the Pen tool selected, holding down the Command/Ctrl key gives you temporary access to this tool so you can move an anchor point as you're drawing.

When working with the Direct Selection tool, watch the cursors to see what part of an object you'll be affecting (see Table 12-2):

Table 12-2
Direct Selection tool icons

If you want to...	Look for this cursor...
Move or modify a point	▹□
Move or modify a segment	▹╱
Move or extend a control handle	▹◇

Add Anchor Point Tool

The Add Anchor Point tool, hidden under the Pen tool, is a tool dedicated to adding anchor points to an existing path or frame. When using this tool, to add an anchor point, simply select a path or frame and move over a straight or curved segment. When you see the small + cursor, click the tool. However, we never actually select this tool. It's much faster just to use the Pen tool. Whenever you move the Pen over a selected path or frame and see the same + cursor, clicking adds a point.

Delete Anchor Point Tool

The Delete Anchor Point tool, also hidden under the Pen tool, deletes anchor points on a frame or path. When you move this tool over an anchor point, you'll see a small – (minus) cursor. Just click the tool to delete the anchor point. You can do the same thing with the Pen tool when you move over an anchor point.

Convert Direction Point Tool

The last in this group of tools hidden under the Pen tool is the Convert Direction Point tool. It's a very versatile tool which changes corner points into smooth points and vice versa, and which you can use to manipulate handles.

This tool has three modes:

- Clicking over a smooth point turns it into a corner point (it sucks in the control handles).

- Dragging from a corner point drags out control handles, making it a smooth point.

- Dragging on the control handles of a smooth point converts it to a corner point with independent handles.

Scissors Tool

Finally, almost as an afterthought, InDesign has hidden one more path editing tool, the Scissors tool (press C; see Figure 12-8), under the Gradient tool, of all places!

You can use the Scissors tool to split a path or a frame, whether or not the frame has any content. When you click on a segment of a path or frame, InDesign creates two anchor points at the cut, one on top of the other. If you want to cut a frame in two, you need to cut it twice; otherwise, you'll just create an single path which has a gap.

Figure 12-8

The Scissors tool

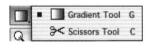

What's Missing—Merge and Shape Commands

With all these tools for creating and editing shapes, there are two sets of shape editing commands found in QuarkXPress which are missing in InDesign. First, there are no features in InDesign to combine shapes (the Merge commands in QuarkXPress, or the Pathfinder features in Illustrator). And there are no commands to automatically switch the shape of a frame or path to another shape.

13

Think Outside the Box: Nesting Objects

QuarkXPress allows you to anchor graphics and text boxes in a text flow. You can do the same in InDesign, but it calls them *inline objects*; we'll tell you about creating them in Chapter 69. But InDesign goes much further than this: Any object—text frame, graphics frame or path—can contain another object. This concept is called *nesting*, and it can give you great freedom in combining objects on your page.

Parent and Child Objects

To nest an object in another object, just choose the first object, which we'll call the "child," with the Selection tool, and Copy or Cut it to the Clipboard. Then select the second object, which we'll call the "parent," and choose Paste Into (not just Paste!) from the Edit menu (see Figure 13-1). You can only nest one object in another object at a time, but a group of objects counts as a single object—so if you want to nest more than one object in a frame, group them first. (We discuss the Group command in Chapter 19.)

You can even create a hierarchy of objects nested in objects—grandchildren and great grandchildren of the original object—by copying or cutting the parent object and using Paste Into to nest it into some other object.

Selecting Nested Objects

Making a nested object is pretty easy. The trick is how to *select* the nested object later. If you choose the Selection tool, it selects the parent object and its content (the child) at the same time. To select the child object so you can manipulate it, you must do it in two steps: First, click the edge of the child object with the Direct Selection tool (don't click one of its anchor points). Second, switch to the Selection tool (the easiest way is to press V), and you'll see the child object bounding box (see Figure 13-1). To move it, you can either drag it by its non-printing center point, or move it numerically with the Transform palette which we talk about in Chapters 17 and 18.

To remove a nested object from its parent, use the same two-step process to select the child object's bounding box. Then press Delete, or cut it to the Clipboard if you want to use the object again.

Figure 13-1

Nesting a circular graphic frame into another frame

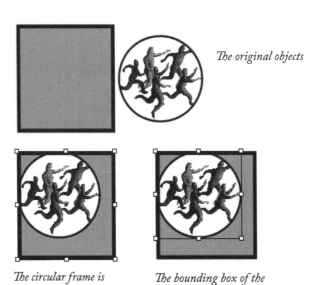

The original objects

The circular frame is now the child object

The bounding box of the child object is selected

Using Text as a Background

Suppose for artistic effect you'd like to use some text as the background for one or more very large letters. Here's how you can do it with nesting (see Figure 13-2):

1. Create a text frame that contains the large letters in a heavy weight. Choose the frame with the Selection tool and then select Create Out-

Figure 13-2

Nesting text as a background

lines from the Type menu. The letter is turned into a path. Give it any fill and stroke you wish.

2. Use the Selection tool to select a second text frame which contains the text which you want to be the background. Copy it to the Clipboard.

3. Now select the letter paths with the Selection tool, and choose Paste Into from the Edit menu (or Command-Option-V/Ctrl-Alt-V). Reposition the content if necessary as described above.

14

Fills and Strokes

As we mentioned in Chapter 10, InDesign uses a different dialect than QuarkXPress when it comes to describing page objects: QuarkXPress works with a box's background color, while InDesign lets you manipulate a frame's fill color. What XPress calls a box's frame InDesign calls a stroke. Every object on a page has a fill and a stroke, even if the color is "None" (transparent) or the stroke is set to zero points.

In QuarkXPress you can apply a background color and frame width using the Modify dialog box; to change text you can use the Style menu. In InDesign, however, you usually change an object's fill or stroke color with the Swatches palette (which looks sort of similar to XPress's Colors palette). We'll discuss in detail the use of the Swatches palette and other methods of applying color in Part 8, *Color and Transparency*. To change an object's stroke width, you use the Stroke palette.

The part that confuses many XPress users is that before you apply a color to an object, you have to choose whether the color should apply to the stroke or the fill. The easiest way to select between the fill and stroke attributes is at the bottom of the Tools palette (see Figure 14-1). The two largest buttons select the fill and stroke: Clicking the square one selects the fill attributes; choosing the outlined one selects the stroke attributes. The one in front is the active attribute. Clicking the small double-headed arrow swaps between the two (or press the letter X with no text selected). Clicking the small icon below the fill/stroke controls (or pressing D) returns you to the default—a black stroke with no fill. If you apply the color to the stroke when you meant to apply it to the fill (or vice versa), don't fret: just press Shift-X to swap them.

Figure 14-1
Fill and Stroke controls on the Tools and Swatches palettes

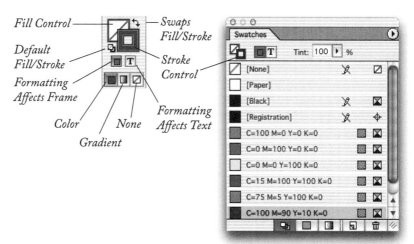

Fill Control — — *Swaps Fill/Stroke*

Default Fill/Stroke — *Stroke Control*

Formatting Affects Frame

Color *None*

Gradient

Formatting Affects Text

Note that when text is selected, you have to make one more choice here: Click the Formatting Affects Frame or the Formatting Affects Text button in order to choose which of the two (frame or text) will have the color applied to it. Also, below these buttons are controls that let you apply the last used color (or press period) or gradient (or press comma), or to apply "None" (no color; press /). For convenience, the fill and stroke controls are duplicated on the Swatches palette.

Fills

As in QuarkXPress, the fills of InDesign's frames can be transparent (None), a color, or a gradient. However, while XPress doesn't let you fill paths, InDesign does (see Figure 14-2). If you haven't closed a path, InDesign connects the starting and ending points and then fills the inside of the shape. (If the path is more complex, the fill will be less predictable.)

Figure 14-2
Filling an open path

XPress users are familiar with applying color to text, but InDesign lets you fill your text with a color, a gradient, or even None (no color). Of course, filling text with None doesn't make any sense unless you have also applied a stroke to the text (see below).

As noted above, the Tools palette's fill and stroke controls are also where you choose whether you're working with the color of a text frame or the color of the text within the frame.

Strokes

QuarkXPress and InDesign have similar ways of setting a frame's stroke (or frame thickness): in XPress, you set the frame to anything more than zero, in InDesign you set the stroke to anything more than zero thickness. However, InDesign not only lets you apply a width and color, you can even apply a gradient. And while QuarkXPress doesn't allow strokes around type, InDesign not only permits you to outline type and keep it editable, but the stroke can be either a solid color or a gradient.

Note that the weight of a stroke in InDesign is centered on its path, just like in Illustrator: Half of the stroke extends outward, and half inward (see Figure 14-3). However, when you stroke type, InDesign is very smart: Rather than cutting into the shape of the letterform when the stroke weight is increased, it applies the entire stroke weight to the outside of the character, preserving the character's integrity (see Figure 14-4). Behind the scenes, InDesign is actually stroking the text shape and then filling a non-stroked version (as though there were two characters on top of each other, one stroked and one filled).

The default behavior is for the bounding box of a stroked frame to be preserved, as the stroke gets thicker or thinner—as though the stroke were being applied to the inside of the frame. This matches the way QuarkX-Press handles changes to frame width. However, if you turn on the Weight

Figure 14-3
When stroking a path, the stroke centers on the path.

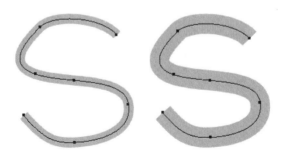

Figure 14-4

When stroking a type character, the stroke applies to the outside.

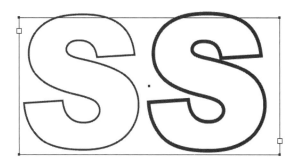

Changes Bounding Box option in the Stroke palette menu, InDesign maintains the shape of paths and changes the bounding box instead (as though the stroke were actually centered on the frame path). We tend to avoid this option, though it can be helpful when you need the shape of an path to remain exactly the same after applying a stroke.

The Stroke Palette

The control center for working with strokes in InDesign is the Stroke palette (see Figure 14-5). To see all the choices for the Stroke palette, choose Show Options from the palette menu.

The Weight control lets you either choose from a popup menu of preset stroke weights or type in an arbitrary weight from 0 to 800 points. As in XPress, stroke weight is always measured in points. (You can type in other units, like .25 in, but they will be converted to points.)

InDesign borrows some stroke controls—notably *Cap* styles and *Miter* styles—from Adobe Illustrator. The Cap style affects the appearance of both ends of an open path (see Figure 14-6). The cap style choices are:

- A *butt cap*, which creates square ends (the default).

- A *round cap*, which creates rounded ends.

- A *projecting cap*, which extends the ends of the path beyond the end points by half the thickness of the stroke.

Figure 14-5

The Stroke palette

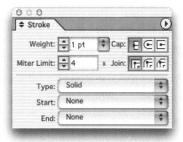

The Join styles control the appearance of a path at a corner point (not smooth curves; see Figure 14-7). There are also three choices:

- A *miter join* (the default) creates a crisp, pointed corner. However, InDesign may crop the corner, depending on the Miter Limit value described below.

- A *round join* creates a rounded corner.

- A *bevel join* creates cuts off the end of the point on the corner.

Finally, the Miter Limit controls when a sharp miter join is cropped to become a bevel join. In the star example (Figure 14-7), the Miter Join was set to 100 to ensure that the first star had sharp points.

Dashes, Stripes, and Path End Shapes

The bottom section of the Stroke palette gives you the controls for working with dashes, preset stripes, and path end shapes (like arrowheads).

The Type popup menu lets you choose between different path styles. You can choose between a solid path, preset stripes (like Thick-Thin), and dashed paths. There are two preset dashed styles and one dotted style, but you'll get the most control if you select the Dashed choice. Then the appearance of the palette changes to allow you to enter dash and gap values (see Figure 14-8). You might use this to create the dashed path for a special

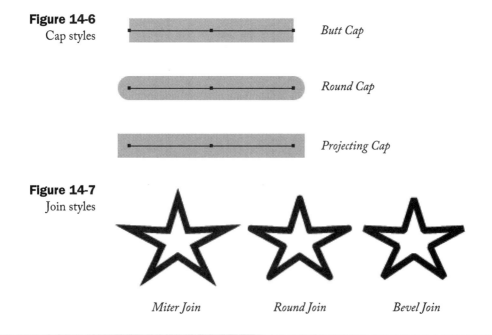

Figure 14-6
Cap styles

Butt Cap

Round Cap

Projecting Cap

Figure 14-7
Join styles

Miter Join   Round Join   Bevel Join

Figure 14-8
Cap styles

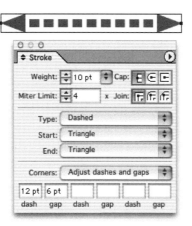

coupon border, for example. Unfortunately, InDesign has no Dashes and Stripes editor like you'll find in QuarkXPress 4 and 5. There is no way to expand beyond the built in stripe choices.

The Start and End popup menus have choices for path endings for the beginning point and end point of a path. You can choose between arrowheads, bars, circles, and so on, but the choices aren't editable. The endings are sized in proportion to the stroke weight, and their angle depends on the angle of the path's endpoint control handles. While the other choices on the Stroke palette apply to both frames and open paths, the Start and End styles only appear on open paths.

15

Corner Effects

Perhaps you think that Adobe left out rounded-corner frames because you can't find them in the Tools palette. Not so. InDesign has merely put rounded corner (and other special effect corners) in a different place. David thinks rounded-corner frames are a sure giveaway that you're creating your design on a desktop computer, and he avoids them. Steve and Christopher, however, think that special effect frames have their uses, provided you use them with moderation.

Finding the Corners

While InDesign's Tools palette only shows three built-in frame shape tools—Rectangle, Ellipse and Polygon—you can actually easily create any of the other shapes QuarkXPress has to offer. The key is to select Corner Effects from the Object menu. The Corner Effects dialog box lets you apply five different preset corner effects to your path or frame. Table 15-1 shows how they match up with QuarkXPress' box tools.

You'll notice two InDesign effects which aren't available in QuarkX-Press—the Inset and Fancy effects (see Figure 15-1).

Editing Effects

In the dialog box, the Size field is the equivalent of XPress' Corner Radius attribute. It controls the radius of the corner effect from each corner point. While QuarkXPress box shapes only apply to rectangles, InDesign's corner effects can apply to any path or frame—even polygons and Bézier shapes.

The effect only appears on corner points, however. For instance, you could apply a rounded effect to a startburst made with the Polygon tool to make each spike rounded.

Unfortunately, other than changing the Size (radius), you can't edit these effects. When you select the path with the Direct Selection tool, you'll see the anchor points of the underlying path shape, not the points on the effect itself. You can change the appearance of a corner effect by varying the path's stroke weight, by changing the Size setting, or by editing the underlying path. In Figure 15-1, the fancy effect rectangle has been edited to create the same effect applied to a parallelogram.

	To create this XPress shape...	Use this corner effect...
Table 15-1 Corner effects	Rounded corner	Rounded effect
	Concave corner	Inverse rounded effect
	Beveled corner	Bevel effect
	Oval	Ellipse tool
	[No QuarkXPress equivalent]	Inset effect
	[No QuarkXPress equivalent]	Fancy effect

Figure 15.1
Inset and Fancy
corner effects

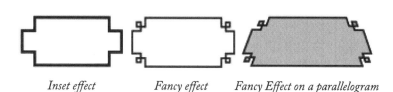

Inset effect   *Fancy effect*   *Fancy Effect on a parallelogram*

16

Compound Paths

QuarkXPress' Merge features can combine shapes into a *compound path*—a shape made up of two or more *subpaths,* which usually contains holes when one subpath is contained within another. For instance, when you convert text to outlines, you get a compound path made of individual paths (letter shapes). While InDesign doesn't have Merge commands yet, it does give you the same ability to create frames with holes. In fact, it has controls over creating and releasing compound paths identical to those you find in Adobe Illustrator.

How to Make Holes

If you haven't used compound paths before, you may wonder why they're necessary. You need a compound path whenever you want to put a hole in an object—like the middle of a bagel or the inside counters of the letter "g" after converting it to paths (see Figure 16-1; we discuss outlining fonts in Chapter 72). You also need a compound path when you want several frames on your page to act as a single frame, whether or not they're overlapping.

Figure 16-1
Letters turned into
compound paths

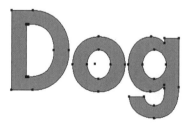

You can create compound paths in InDesign using two or more paths or frames, which can be either open or closed. It usually works best if you use closed shapes and position the largest shape behind the rest. Select all the objects with the Selection tool, then choose Make from the Compound Paths submenu (under the Object menu). The objects will be combined into one compound path (see Figure 16-2).

Figure 16-2

Creating a compound path when objects overlap

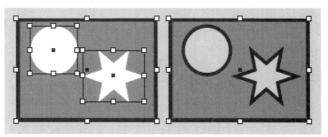

Three paths are selected...   *After applying the Make Compound Path command, they are combined*

In Figure 16-2, a white circle and star are placed on a dark gray rectangle. After applying the Make Compound Path command, the circle and star become holes in the rectangle. (The only way we can show this is by placing them over a different colored background.) Notice also that the holes now have taken on the same stroke attribute as the outside subpath, the backmost object. When you change the fill and stroke of a compound path, it affects all the subpaths together.

However, if the original white objects only partially overlap the backmost object, you can get somewhat unpredictable results when creating a compound path (see Figure 16-3).

Figure 16-3

Creating a compound path when objects only partially overlap

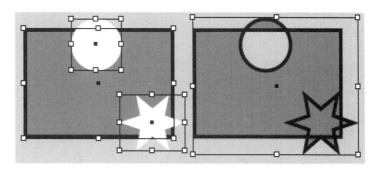

Editing Holes

When you want to edit the subpaths of a compound path, there are a few tricks which may help you:

- To work with a subpath or part of a subpath, use the Direct Selection tool

- There is a hidden tool, the Group Selection tool, which allows you to easily select an entire subpath. To select a subpath, first use the Direct Selection tool to click on its edge; you should see hollow anchor points. Then hold down Option/Alt key (you'll see a tiny plus sign beside the cursor) and click again, and the entire subpath is selected.

- Sometimes when you create a compound path, a hole may not open up. You aren't doing anything wrong; you just need to change the subpath's direction. (Holes are actually created by subpaths going in alternating directions. Unfortunately, InDesign never explicitly tells you the direction of a path; you just have to infer it from how the compound path acts.) To change the path's direction, select one anchor point on the subpath that is closed with the Direct Selection tool. Then choose Reverse Path from the Object menu. The hole will open up (or close up, if you're trying to get rid of a hole).

Releasing Holes

When you want to break a compound path back into its component objects, choose it with the Selection tool, then choose Release from the Compound Paths submenu (under the Object menu). Each of the resulting paths will have the same attributes; they won't return to their original appearance (see Figure 16-4). After the shape we created is released, the three paths take on the attributes of the compound path.

Figure 16-4
After releasing a
compound path

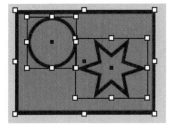

17

Moving and Resizing Objects

Apart from selecting objects or editing text, most of us probably spend more time moving and resizing objects on the page than any other activity. That makes this is a particularly important chapter. Fortunately, most of the ways moving and scaling work in XPress also work in InDesign—with the addition of a new palette and a couple of powerful new tools.

The Transform Palette

One of the first things QuarkXPress users notice first when they start using InDesign is the absence of a Measurements palette. Instead, InDesign lets you move and resize objects in the Transform palette (see Figure 17-1). Like the Measurement palette, the Transform palette provides two essential functions: The first is informational, providing precise data about an object's position, size, angle, and so on. The second is the ability to numerically transform these attributes.

Information on the Palette

What InDesign displays on the Transform palette when an object is selected depends on several things. The values shown are in the current ruler units (which we discuss in Chapter 7) and are relative to the position of the ruler origin. InDesign's default ruler origin is the upper left corner of the page, the same as in XPress.

When selecting an object which is nested inside another object, or when a selecting the content in a graphic frame, by default the Transform

Figure 17-1

The Transform
palette

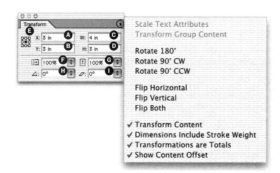

A *Horizontal (X)*
   position
B *Vertical (Y) position*
C *Width*
D *Height*
E *Proxy displays*
   transformation origin
F *Scale X percentage*
G *Scale Y percentage*
H *Rotation angle*
I *Shear (Skew) X angle*

palette displays the offset of the object from the containing frame (similar
to how XPress shows the Offset values for pictures inside picture boxes).
This is controlled by Show Content Offset on the Transform palette menu
(see Figure 17-1).

Setting the Transformation Origin

The Measurements palette and Modify dialog box in XPress always base
measurements in relation to the upper left corner of the object. InDesign—like PageMaker—is much more flexible, letting you pick the transformation point. This can be useful when you'd like to resize a frame from
its center, for example.

The Transform palette adds a small icon called the *proxy*, where you
can select the transformation origin. Clicking a point on the proxy sets
the origin. Figure 17-2 shows the center proxy point selected; when you
use one of the resizing methods described below, you enlarge the polygon
frame's shape outward from the center.

Figure 17-2

Resizing a frame
from the center

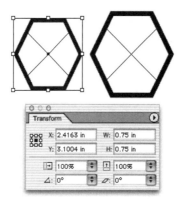

When using the Scale, Rotate and Shear tools (described in this chapter and the next) the proxy point also shows up in the document window itself—you can see the transformation point as a small nonprinting target icon. You can use these tools to drag the transformation point someplace else—even outside the object itself. If you drag near one of the center or corner points, the proxy snaps to that point and InDesign updates the proxy icon in the Transform palette.

Pay Attention to What's Selected

When doing any kind of transformation in InDesign, pay attention to which tool you're using to select the object. Use the Selection tool to select the frame or path when you wish to transform the object and its content. You can use the Direct Selection tool to transform only part of a path. For example, when you use this tool to select one anchor point, you can use the Transform palette to move it as described below. We discuss more about scaling content in Chapter 64 when we talk about resizing graphics.

Moving Objects

In QuarkXPress when you want to move a box or line, you use the Item tool, the Measurement palette, the Modify dialog box, or the Arrow keys on the keyboard. InDesign's methods are similar.

By Dragging

When you want to move a path or frame interactively, choose the object with the Selection tool and just drag it. (Holding down the Command/Ctrl key gives you temporary access to the Selection tool if another tool is selected.) For an object that has a fill, you can drag from anywhere inside the shape. However, unlike QuarkXPress, if it has a stroke and no fill, you must click it on its outline to move it. If the outline is difficult to select, you can also drag the object by its nonprinting center point.

When you drag an object quickly, you'll only see the outline of your object. If you pause a second before dragging, you'll see the object previewed as you drag. (This also true of the other transformations we describe in this chapter and the next.)

Using the Transform Palette

A second way to move an object is by changing the values of the Position fields (X and Y) in the Transform palette. Imagine that you have a text frame which is located 1 inch down and 1 inch across from the ruler origin, and you're using the upper-left proxy point. In the Transform palette, the position appears as "X = 1" in and "Y = 1" in. If you want to move the frame one inch to the right, you can change the X value to either "2 in" or "1 in + 1", then press Enter. Like XPress, InDesign can do addition, subtraction, multiplication, and division in any field that shows a number. Positive values move to the right and down, so the frame shifts one inch to the right.

Using the Move Dialog Box

InDesign borrows a third method of moving objects from Illustrator—the Move dialog box. You can get to it by selecting Move from the Transform submenu (under the Object menu). But we never do it that way. It's much faster simply to double-click the Selection tool (see Figure 17-3).

Figure 17-3
The Move dialog box

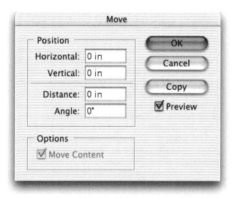

The fields in the Move dialog box tell InDesign how much and in what direction you want to move the frame.

- If you want to move the object horizontally or vertically, enter numbers in the Horizontal and/or Vertical fields, and press Enter (or click OK). Positive values move the object to the right and down, negative values to the left and up.

- If you want to move the object a specific distance and angle, enter numbers in those fields, and press Enter. InDesign measures angles from the horizontal. Positive angles rotate counterclockwise, negative angles clockwise.

You can preview your move by clicking the Preview checkbox. We'll discuss the Copy option in Chapter 21.

Using the Arrow Keys

Finally, you can move paths and frames with the Arrow keys on the keyboard. Each time you press an Arrow key, your object moves one point, by default. Holding down the Shift key while pressing an arrow key moves by 10 points. But you can change these amounts in the Cursor Key field in InDesign's Units and Increments preferences (see Chapter 7).

Resizing Objects

Resizing a path or frame changes its horizontal or vertical dimensions. As you'll see below, resizing is generally done in InDesign the same way as in QuarkXPress. But InDesign offers a few additional ways to resize—or *scale* as Adobe prefers to call it.

There are both interactive and numeric ways of scaling in InDesign. When using the numeric methods described below (the Transform palette and Scale tool), whether or not the content of a frame also changes depends on whether the Transform Content option is on or off in the Transform palette's menu. This feature is turned on by default, so any transformation applies to both frame and content; when turned off, the scaling applies only to the frame.

Dragging the Bounding Box

To resize an object interactively you need to see its bounding box, so you must select it with the Selection tool rather than the Direct Selection tool. You can drag the bounding box handles just as in XPress: When you drag a side handle it resizes it in one dimension—horizontally or vertically. When you drag a corner handle, you resize it in both dimensions.

To maintain proportions with when resizing a path or frame, hold down the Shift key while dragging the handle. (This is different than in XPress.) However, if you're working with a graphic frame (or a frame with a nested object) and you want the frame's contents to be scaled as well, hold down the Command-Shift/Ctrl-Shift keys when dragging. (This doesn't work for scaling text, though.) See Chapter 64 for more on working with scaling graphics.

Using the Transform Palette

If you know exactly the new size you want the object to be, you can enter either new Height and Width values (in the W: or H: fields) and press Enter, and the object changes immediately. Here's a handy trick to maintain proportions: Type either the Height or Width value, hold down the

Command/Ctrl key and press Enter. The other value gets proportionately changed, and the width/height ratio of the object is maintained.

If you want to scale the object to specific percentages, you can enter the new values in the Scale X Percentage and Scale Y Percentage fields, then press Enter. The new scaling percentage appears in the percentage fields. You can use the same trick mentioned above to maintain proportions: Enter a new value in either of the percentage fields, hold down the Command/Ctrl key and press Enter.

Another way to scale by percentage is to use math in the Width and Height fields: just type an asterisk (*) after the current width or height, then type the percentage as a decimal. For instance, 25 percent would be "*.25" and 140 percent would be "*1.4".

Dragging with the Scale Tool

While XPress has no Scale tool, if you're an Illustrator user, you're already familiar with this InDesign feature. InDesign's works almost identically. It has two modes—you can use it to scale by dragging, or you can use the Scale dialog to scale numerically. The Scale tool has one big advantage over other methods: If you want to track scaling changes for a graphic, empty frame, or a path, InDesign shows the scaling values in the Transform palette even after scaling; using most of the other methods, the scaling percentage reverts to 100 percent.

To scale a selected object interactively, position the Scale tool some distance away from the transformation point (see Figure 17-5). The farther from the transformation point you start, the more control you have. Drag in the direction you want to scale the object. Dragging away from the point will make the object larger; moving closer to the point makes it

Figure 17-5
Dragging with the
Scale tool

The transformation point can be moved with the Selection tool.

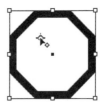

Dragging away from the point makes the octagon larger. The square is the outline of the scaled octagon.

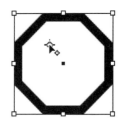

The scaled octagon.

smaller. Holding down the Shift key as you drag constrains to horizontal, vertical or proportional.

Using the Scale Dialog Box

To scale numerically, open the Scale dialog box. While you could choose the Scale command from the Transform submenu (under the Object menu), its much faster to simply double-click the Scale tool to open this dialog box (see Figure 17-6).

Figure 17-6

The Scale dialog box

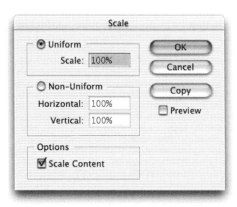

- To scale proportionately in the Scale dialog box, select Uniform, enter the scaling percentage, and click OK.
- To scale disproportionately, select Non-Uniform, enter horizontal and vertical scaling percentages, and click OK.
- You can move the object's transformation point and open this dialog box at the same time by Option/Alt-clicking on the page.

Other Ways to Scale

Amazingly enough, there are even two more ways to scale objects in InDesign. First, there is a keyboard shortcut to increase the size of an object in one percent increments (Command/Ctrl-. [period]); or to decrease the size (Command/Ctrl-, [comma]). To change the size in five percent increments also press the Option/Alt key. Note that these won't change the size of text within a text frame, but they do change pictures in graphic frames.

Finally, you can scale while using the Free Transform tool, a tool which lets you perform different kind of tranformations at the same time. We'll discuss that in the next chapter.

Stroke Weights and Scaling Objects

We said the Scale tool is *almost* the same as that in Illustrator. Unfortunately, there is one important command found in the illustration program which Adobe left out of InDesign: When you use the Scale tool in InDesign, stroke weights are always scaled with the object (Illustrator lets you turn off this "feature" if you wish). The result is that when you see a path or frame which has a stroke and the scaling percentage shows a value other than 100%, the stroke weight in the Stroke palette shows a value different than the actual stroke wieght on the object. This is very confusing, and we think this should be changed in the next version of InDesign.

18

Other Object Transformations

In the last chapter we discussed the two most common transformations on page objects—moving and resizing them. Now we'll discuss three other transformations: rotation, flipping (mirroring), and skewing (also called shearing). We'll also talk about a special tool borrowed from Photoshop and Illustrator, the Free Transform tool, which allows you to perform multiple transformations (see Figure 18-1).

Figure 18-1

Transform tools in the Tools palette

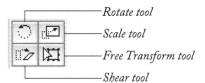

Rotate tool

Scale tool

Free Transform tool

Shear tool

In case you're jumping around in the book, here's a quick review of a few things you need to know about the way InDesign does transformations, which also apply here.

- Transformations are displayed and can be numerically changed on the Transform palette (see Chapter 17).

- Transformations are performed in relation to the transformation point—displayed as a point on the proxy in the Transform palette, or as a target icon attached to the selected object when using the Scale, Rotate and Shear tools.

- By default, when you tranform a frame InDesign transforms the content of the frame, too. But the Transform Content item on the Transform palette menu lets you turn this off.

- Use the Selection tool to change an entire object, and the Direct Selection tool to change part of an object (like a picture within a graphic frame).

Note that just because InDesign can do something, doesn't always mean it's a good idea. For instance, you can easily transform bitmapped images in ways that will make your favorite printer very unhappy. If you like the effects of rotating, shearing, transforming, or dramatically scaling bitmap (scanned) images, you should probably make these changes in Photoshop. Your pages will print faster and more reliably.

Rotating

In QuarkXPress, a frame or path can be rotated numerically in the Measurement palette or Modify dialog box, or interactively with the Rotation tool. InDesign gives you similar choices—the Rotate tool and the Transform palette. You can also rotate with the Free Transform tool, described below. We tend to just use the Transform palette; simply enter an angle in the Rotation field, and press Enter. You can also choose from preset rotation values found in the popup menu to the right of the field.

Dragging with the Rotate Tool

To drag with the Rotate tool, first set the point of transformation in the Transform palette proxy or by dragging the target icon anywhere on your page (it looks like a little crosshair that is, by default, in the center of the object). Then position the Rotate tool away from the transformation point (the further away, the more control you'll have) and drag in the direction you want the object rotated. The rotation is a circular motion around the transformation point. The angle of rotation is displayed in the Transform palette. Holding down the Shift key while rotating, constrains the rotation to multiples of 45 degrees.

Using the Rotate Dialog Box

If you would rather type in a rotation angle, and you have an unnatural aversion to the Transform palette, double-click the Rotate tool, Option/Alt-click with the tool on the page, or choose Rotate from Transform submenu (in the Object menu). This opens the Rotate dialog box (see

Figure 18-2) in which you simply enter the angle of rotation (a positive number is counterclockwise, a negative number is clockwise, just like in QuarkXPress), and click OK. If you Option/Alt-click, InDesign rotates around the point where you clicked.

Figure 18-2
The Rotate
dialog box

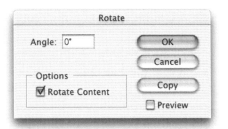

This dialog box also offers a checkbox which determines whether a frame's content is rotated and a button that tells InDesign to perform the rotation on a copy of the object (see Chapter 21).

Flipping

QuarkXPress lets you flip the contents of boxes using the Flip commands in the Style menu or the arrow icons on the Measurement palette, but it's relatively difficult to flip (mirror) object shapes. In InDesign, you can flip an object with or without its content with commands on the Transform palette menu: Flip Horizontal (which flips objects left-to-right, across the Y axis), Flip Vertical (which flips the object top-to-bottom, across the X axis), or Flip Both (to flip the object across both axes).

You can also flip objects with the Selection tool by dragging one of the object's bounding box handles across the object past the opposite side. Or, you can enter a negative value in the Scale X Percentage or Scale Y Percentage fields on the Transform palette. In all cases, InDesign flips the object based on the point of transformation (usually based on the Transform palette's proxy).

Note that InDesign does not have a Reflect tool for flipping, like in Illustrator.

Skewing or Shearing

Skewing (also called shearing) is technically the rotation of the two axes of an object differently. The result looks sort of like a 3D perspective effect. QuarkXPress only allows horizontal skewing, and lets you skew boxes or their content separately. InDesign also only skews horizontally, but it also fakes a vertical shear (or one on some other angle) by combining skewing and rotating. (However, InDesign can't shear text inside a frame without slanting the frame, which QuarkXPress can do.)

Skew With the Transform Palette

To horizontally skew an object in the Transform palette, enter an angle in the Shear Angle field, or choose one of the preset values in the popup menu. Both the object and its contents are slanted on the horizontal axis (unless you've turned off the Transform Content option). Note that a positive shear value angles the object *clockwise* (the top shifts to the right), unlike the rotation tools where a positive angle is counterclockwise.

For a vertical shear, enter the same angle in both the Shear Angle field and the Rotation field.

Using the Shear Dialog Box

You can make precise shearing tranformations by opening the Shear dialog box: Double-click the Shear tool, Option/Alt-click on the page, or choose Shear from the Transform submenu (in the Object menu). Here you have options for shearing on the vertical or horizontal axis, or on any angle you want (see Figure 18-3). If you Option/Alt-clicked, InDesign applies the transformation based on where you clicked.

Figure 18-3
The Shear dialog box and Text Transformations

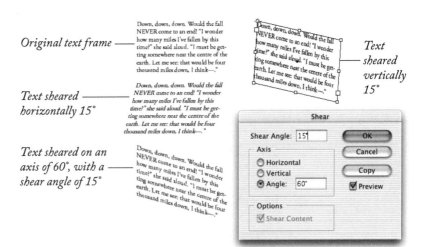

Original text frame

Text sheared horizontally 15°

Text sheared on an axis of 60°, with a shear angle of 15°

Text sheared vertically 15°

Dragging with the Shear Tool

If you insist on doing all your transformations by dragging the cursor, you'll be happy to know you can do that with the Shear tool as well. However, unless you're careful when dragging with this tool, you may find its results wild and unpredictable—don't forget to keep one hand on Command/Ctrl-Z to undo. Hold down the Shift key to constrain InDesign to shear horizontally or vertically.

The Free Transform Tool

InDesign has a Free Transform tool, similar to the ones in Photoshop and Illustrator (XPress doesn't have this tool). The advantage of this tool is that you can quickly perform multiple transformations with the same tool. While the Free Transform tool feels somewhat like the Selection tool, it doesn't work exactly the same. For example, you can't use it to select an object. You'll need to select the object to manipulate first, or hold down the Command/Ctrl key to temporarily get the Selection tool.

- To move a selected object, click anywhere within the bounding box and move it. Notice that, unlike the Selection tool, with the Free Transform tool you *can* move an object with no fill without clicking on its border).

- To scale a selected object, drag the bounding box handles as you would when dragging with the Selection tool. Holding down the Shift key while dragging constrains proportions. Holding down the Option/Alt key scales from the bounding box center. However, unlike the Selection tool, the content of a text frame scales with the object (unless you selected just the frame with the Direct Selection tool).

- To rotate a selected object, drag the cursor outside the bounding box until you see a double-headed arrow cursor, then drag clockwise or counterclockwise.

- To flip the selected object over the horizontal or vertical axis, drag one of the bounding box handles across the object past the opposite side.

- To skew the selected object, start dragging a *side handle* (not a corner), then hold down the Command-Option/Ctrl-Alt keys as you drag. Also holding down the Shift key constrains vertically or horizontally.

19

Grouping, Stacking, and Locking Objects

In the previous chapters in this part of the book, we've described how to create, edit and transform frames and paths in InDesign. This chapter focuses on some of the ways we can organize these objects when putting together a page or spread: grouping related objects, changing their *stacking order*, and locking them in position.

Grouping

Grouping is a way to select two or more objects so you can work with them as a single object—a group. The grouping and ungrouping of objects generally works the same as in QuarkXPress, though there are a few differences, which we cover below. To group objects, first select the various paths or frames, and then select Group from the Object menu (or press Command-G/Ctrl-G). To ungroup, select the group and choose Ungroup from the Object menu (or press Command-Shift-G/Ctrl-Shift-G). Of course, you can also group multiple groups together, forming groups of groups (if you're into that sort of thing).

Where Are Your Groups?

When you select a QuarkXPress group with the Item tool, you see a dashed line around the group's rectangular bounding box. InDesign doesn't provide such a visual indicator, but you can use two cues to tell whether you've clicked on a group. First, if you see a single bounding box surrounding more than one object when you click with the Selection tool, the objects are most likely grouped. (They could also be part of a compound path; see Chapter 16.) Second, see if the Ungroup command is available in the Object menu; it'll be dimmed unless you've selected a group.

Selecting the Members of a Group

The Direct Selection tool generally serves the same function as QuarkXPress's Content tool when working with a group. You use it to select a member or members of a group so you can manipulate them without ungrouping. This works with most objects, but because InDesign also uses the Direct Selection tool to edit paths or work with picture content, you should know some tips for selecting members of a group.

- For filled paths, text frames, or straight lines, you can simply click on the object to select the member.

- If you want to select more than one member, click on one with the Direct Selection tool, then Shift-click to select the others

- To select an entire path within a group, click once and then either click on its nonprinting center point, or hold down the Option/Alt key and click again (see Figure 19-1).

Figure 19-1
Selecting an unfilled
path in a group

Using the Direct Selection tool, click on the edge of the path...

Option/Alt-click on the path edge to select the group member

- For a graphics frame, click on the edge of the frame. (If you click on the center, you'll choose the content.) Press the letter V to switch to the Selection tool, and you'll see the bounding box of that graphic. Drag the center point if you need to move the graphic.

Stacking Order

Both QuarkXPress and InDesign let you stack objects on top of each other in two ways: stacking order and layers (XPress 3 and 4 do not offer layers). We'll discuss layers and the Layers palette in Chapter 24. Here we cover stacking order, the vertical arrangement of objects within a layer.

InDesign has the same four stacking commands for controlling the vertical order of page objects as in XPress (you can find these commands in the Arrange submenu, under the Object menu):

- Bring to Front—or press Command-Shift-] / Ctrl-Shift-]

- Bring Forward—or press Command-] / Ctrl-]

- Send Backward—or press Command-[/ Ctrl-[

- Send to Back—or press Command-Shift-[/ Ctrl-Shift-[

Another fast way of selecting these commands is to use the context menu: You'll see these same features if you right-click on an object in Windows, or Control-click it on the Macintosh.

Note that grouping affects stacking order: InDesign rearranges the grouped objects so that they're placed immediately below the topmost member of the group. We'll discuss how to select objects which are stacked on top of each other in the next chapter.

Locking

Many XPress users don't realize how fragile the Lock feature is in that program: While locked objects cannot be dragged with the Item tool, you can still change their position with the Measurement palette, the Modify dialog box or even by pressing the arrow keys on the keyboard. InDesign's implementation of the Lock feature is much better. To lock an object, select Lock Position from the Object menu or the context menu. When locked, an object can't be dragged, and can't be manipulated with the Transform palette or the transform tools. However, you can still change formatting attributes or edit text in a locked object. To unlock an object, select Unlock Position from the Object menu or context menu.

Another, even more powerful way of locking and unlocking is by organizing page objects on layers, and then locking layers (see Chapter 24).

20

Selecting with Complex Stacking and Nesting

Someday you will open up someone else's InDesign document, or perhaps one you created a long time before. And you won't be able to figure out how the layout is organized—how things are stacked, or grouped, or nested—or how to work with the complex organization that's there. That's when you need to pull out this chapter, in which we teach you a few tricks of the trade.

Clicking Through the Stack

QuarkXPress has a keystroke that lets you click through a stack of boxes or other items to get to the ones behind. InDesign has such a shortcut, too—in fact six of them!

- Hold down the Command/Ctrl key and click. The first click selects the top-most object, and successive clicks select objects *downward* below your cursor.

- Hold down the Command-Option/Ctrl-Alt keys and click. Successive clicks select objects below your cursor in an *upward* direction.

- You can select the bottom-most object on a page by pressing Option-Shift-Command-[/Alt-Shift-Ctrl-[(square bracket), or the top-most object on a page by pressing Option-Shift-Command-]/Alt-Shift-Ctrl-].

- You can select next object above the currently-selected one by pressing Option-Command-]/Alt-Ctrl-] or the next object below with Option-Command-[/Ctrl-Alt-[.

Note that the last four keyboard shorcuts select objects on the page in their stacking order and not necessarily if they're visually "above" or "below" other objects. For instance, the front-most object may be sitting by itself on the page, or even on a different layer.

Your Secret Weapon: The Group Selection Tool

You've created a complex page with groups inside groups inside groups. You've lost track of how things are organized. And you're missing QuarkXPress's dotted line border to see where the groups are. How do find out what's what?

Your answer is InDesign's secret weapon: The mysterious Group Selection tool. You can't see it on the Tools palette, but it's always at your disposal. Here's how it works: In Figure 20-1, we've created two groups—the circles and the squares—then we grouped these two groups together. Click once with the Direct Selection tool on a path segment (not anchor point). Then, to get the Group Selection tool, hold down the Option/Alt key (the + cursor shows you have the right tool) and click again. This time the entire path is selected. A third Option/Alt-click shows the first level of grouping. A fourth click shows the second level of grouping. Each time you click with the Group Selection tool, you get the next hierarchy of grouping.

Figure 20-1
Clicking through
the groups

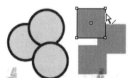

First click with the Direct Selection to choose the path segment...

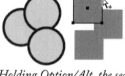

Holding Option/Alt, the second click selects the complete path...

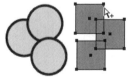

The third click selects the first group...

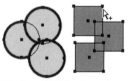

The fourth click selects the second level of grouping

Similarly, you could direct-select a picture inside a frame, and then Option/Alt-click the picture to select the next object "up"—the frame itself.

Once you've selected what you want with the Group Selection tool, you can press V to switch to the Selection tool and InDesign acts like you've selected the object (or objects) with the Selection tool. For instance, you could then switch to the Rotation tool to rotate these items.

Combining Groups with Nesting

In Chapter 13, we said that only one object could be nested in another object. The way to get around that limitation is to group objects before nesting them. For example, in Figure 20-2 we created four stars and a rectangle, then grouped the stars together. To nest the stars into the rectangle, select the group with the Selection tool, Cut them to the clipboard, select the rectangle, and choose Paste Into from the Edit menu (or press Command-Option-V/Ctrl-Alt-V).

Figure 20-2
Nesting stars
into the rectangle

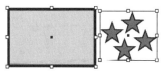 

Group the stars together.   *Cut the stars to the Clipboard and paste into the rectangle.*

Use the Group Selection tool to select the group of stars.   *Command/Ctrl-drag the bounding box to move them.*

When working with a group nested inside an object, the Direct Selection tool can be used to select individual stars. Click on the edge of a star's frame. If you then hold down the Command/Ctrl key, you can move the star around. To move the stars as a group, you need to use the Group Selection tool: Using the Direct Selection tool, click on the edge of a star, then Option/Alt-clicking twice selects the entire group.

Finally, to move the group of stars, hold down the Command/Ctrl key while dragging.

21

Duplicating and Deleting Objects

Making copies of things and getting rid of them: What could be easier? Yet, there's more to this topic than meets the eye. In this short chapter we'll show you some methods which aren't in the QuarkXPress vocabulary.

Duplicating Objects

QuarkXPress gives us three ways to make copies of its items—copying and pasting, Duplicate, and Step and Repeat. InDesign can do all this, of course, plus it has a few more options hidden up its sleeve.

Copying and Pasting

You can cut, copy, and paste objects in InDesign with the Selection, Direct Selection and Type tools. Like XPress, when choosing Paste from the Edit menu (or pressing Command-V/Ctrl-V), InDesign pastes the object in the center of the current page or spread. And, as with QuarkXPress, you may need to be careful about which page the object is copied to. InDesign places the object on the *targeted* spread—the one whose number is highlighted in the Pages palette and displayed in the lower-left corner of the document window—not necessarily the page that is visible on screen.

If you select a graphic (the content) in a graphics frame with the Direct Selection tool and copy it, pasting with either the Selection or Direct Selection tool automatically creates a new frame in the middle of the page or spread. This can drive XPress users mad because if they select another frame and choose Paste, they expect the graphic to be pasted into it. Not so in InDesign. Here, you must choose Paste Into (Command-Option-V/Ctrl-Alt-V) if you want the graphic to end up inside a selected frame.

If you select some text from a text frame with the Type tool and copy it, what happens when you paste depends on the tool you have selected. As you'd expect, if you have an insertion point in a text frame, the text is pasted there. However, if you have the Selection or Direct Selection tool selected (there is no text insertion point), InDesign creates a new text frame in the center of the targeted page or spread and pastes the text into it.

Finally, if you select a *part* of a path (one or more segments or points) with the Direct Selection tool and copy it to the Clipboard, pasting creates a duplicate of the partial path (including any fill or stroke attributes) in the center of the current page or spread.

Paste in Place

InDesign also offers an extra Paste command, already familiar to Page-Maker users: Paste in Place. This is handy when you want to copy objects to other pages. Choose the objects you want to duplicate, and copy as usual. Then jump to the page or spread where you want the copy and choose Paste in Place from the Edit menu (or press Command-Option-Shift-V/Ctrl-Alt-Shift-V). The objects are pasted in the same X/Y position on the spread. The only thing tricky about this command is that if you're using facing pages, it always copies to the same page on the spread. That is, you can't copy from a left-hand page and then paste in place on a right-hand page; the object will end up on the left-hand page.

Duplicating and Step-and-Repeating

InDesign's Duplicate and Step and Repeat commands (in the Edit menu) are almost exactly like the features of the same name in XPress, though the default keyboard shortcuts are different: Command-Option-Shift-D/Ctrl-Alt-Shift-D duplicates any selected object down and to the right of the original object. Unlike QuarkXPress, which bases the offset on the last-used Step and Repeat setting, in InDesign the amount of Duplicate offset changes, depending on screen magnification.

To duplicate with precise offsets, press Command-Shift-V/Ctrl-Shift-V) to open the Step and Repeat dialog box (see Figure 21-1). Like XPress, this feature lets you set the number of copies and the horizontal and vertical offset.

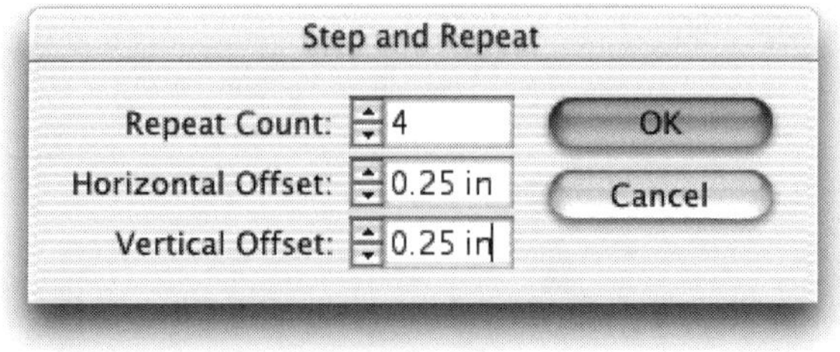

Figure 21-1
Step and Repeat
dialog box

Option/Alt-Dragging

Steve and Christopher's favorite method of duplicating is a feature borrowed from Illustrator and Photoshop, and involves holding down the Option/Alt key. Whenever you want to make a copy of something, you can hold down the Option/Alt key and drag with the Selection or Direct Selection tool to make a duplicate. If you have some other tool selected, then Command-Option/Ctrl-Alt-drag. A double-arrow cursor appears when dragging, indicating the duplication. Be sure to release the mouse button before releasing the Option/Alt key.

David says he hates this method because most of the time he wants that shortcut to be a grabber hand. (The Option/Alt key *is* a grabber hand when the cursor is blinking in a text frame.)

Copying While Transforming

The last method for copying objects is to make copies when transforming an object, which can be done when transforming either interactively (dragging) or precisely (in a dialog box). When you want to copy an object while dragging with the Scale, Rotate, or Skew tools, add the Option/Alt key modifier—the original object is left unchanged and the transformation is applied to the copy. However, you must press down the key *after* you start dragging. If you press before, you're using the key to set the transformation point instead.

If you use the Move, Scale, Rotate, or Skew dialog boxes (see Chapters 17 and 18), you can click the Copy button to apply the transformation to a duplicate, leaving the original unchanged.

Unfortunately, InDesign doesn't have Illustrator's Repeat Transform command to make extra copies once one of these transformations hasbeen performed. Oh well; maybe in the next version.

Deleting Objects

InDesign matches QuarkXPress's two methods of deleting page objects: the Clear command (from the Edit menu, or press Delete) and the Cut command. We're sad to report that InDesign does not sport a little martian that comes out to delete things. If you really love that little XPress "Easter egg," you'll have to use XPress.

Building Pages

22

Aligning and Distributing Objects

One of the more powerful and confusing dialog boxes in QuarkXPress is the Space/Align dialog box. It's powerful because it gives you great control over how selected boxes or lines are positioned in relationship to each other on the page. But the controls are confusing and so most users just ignore it. InDesign offers the very same abilities to align and distribute objects, using the Align palette, but we find its design is a great deal more intuitive.

To align or distribute objects, open the Align palette by choosing Align from the Window menu (or press F8), then show all its features by choosing Show Options from the palette menu. The Align palette is broken into five sections (see Figure 22-1). Remember that if you pause your cursor over a button, a tool tip provides a descriptive label.

Aligning Objects

Simple aligning is when you want two or more objects to align precisely along their sides or centers. In QuarkXPress, you choose this in the Space/ Align dialog box by turning on either Horizontal or Vertical, setting the Space value to 0, and choosing the side or center to align on. In InDesign, you just click on one of the six icons in the top row of the palette—there are three for horizontal and three for vertical alignment.

Where XPress always aligns to the top-most or left-most object, InDesign aligns along the most-obvious edge (top-most for top-aligning,

Figure 22-1
The Align palette

Horizontal Align options

Vertical Distribute Objects options

Distribute Objects Precisely option

Distribute Spacing Precisely option

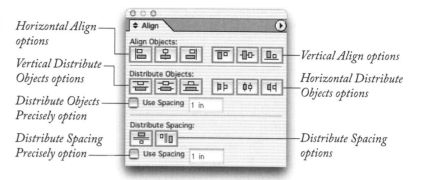

Vertical Align options

Horizontal Distribute Objects options

Distribute Spacing options

bottom-most for bottom-aligning, and so on). The one exception is when one object is locked; in that case, all the other objects move and the locked item stays put.

Distributing Objects

Distributing objects (placing equal space between them) requires that you first select three or more objects. InDesign lets you distribute items while maintaining the height and width of the bounding box (the invisible box which surrounds all the objects), or while ignoring the bounding box. XPress can do all of these distributions, but it would take four pages to explain how.

Maintaining the Bounding Box

To distribute while maintaining the bounding box means the left-most and right-most (or top-most and bottom-most) objects stay put while the other objects move. You can do this by choosing one of the six icons in the second row, labeled Distribute Objects. For this to work, make sure the Use Spacing checkbox just below these icons is turned off.

Alternatively, you can move the objects so that the space between them is equal (this is what we use most often) by choosing one of the two buttons marked Distribute Spacing—one for Horizontal and one for Vertical. Again, make sure the Using Spacing checkbox below the icons is turned off.

Distributing Using Precise Spacing

There are two more kinds of object distribution which don't maintain the bounding box of the selected objects. Here you're attempting to place a precise amount of space between selected objects. To do this, turn on the Using Spacing option and enter a value greater than zero in the Use Spacing field. (Typing zero make the Distribute buttons act just like the Align buttons.) As in XPress, the top-most or left-most object remains stationary, and the remaining objects space themselves in relation to that object. InDesign allows either positive or negative measurements; positive numbers move objects to the right or down, negative numbers to the left or up.

The last method of distribution specifies the spacing between object bounding boxes. You can do this by turning on the Using Spacing option at the bottom of the palette and choosing one of the two Distribute Spacing buttons. For example, if you select five frames and want to place two picas of space between each of them, you could type 2p into the Use Spacing field and click one of the buttons.

23

Making Objects Non-printing

You can make objects non-printing (that is, they appear on screen but don't print out) in XPress by turning on the Suppress Printout checkbox in the Modify dialog box. InDesign lets you do this, too, but because the feature is somewhat hidden, many people don't even know the feature exists. There are many reasons you might want non-printing objects in your document. For instance, you might want to add a note you want someone else handling the document to see, but which you don't want to appear when you print out the page that it's on.

To make an object non-printing in InDesign, open the Attributes palette (from the Window menu), select the object, and turn on the Non-printing checkbox (see Figure 23-1).

Figure 23-1
The Attributes palette

This checkbox sets the nonprinting attribute

InDesign has two advantages and two disadvantages compared to how QuarkXPress handles non-printing objects. In InDesign, you can override the non-printing feature in the Print dialog box. In XPress, if you wanted to print everything on the page you'd have to change all the non-printing objects manually. InDesign also lets you preview the non-printing status of objects by selecting the Preview mode button on the Tools palette, or pressing W (when you don't have a text insertion point). Non-printing objects disappear in the preview.

On the other hand, QuarkXPress lets you suppress the printing of individual pictures, while still allowing their frames to print. InDesign can only do this globally to all pictures in the Print dialog box: Select None from the Images menu on the Graphics panel (see Chapter 95).

XPress also lets you turn on Suppress Printout for every object on a layer. To accomplish this in InDesign, Option/Alt-click on the layer in the Layers palette (to select all the objects on that layer) and then turn on or off the Nonprinting checkbox in the Attributes palette.

24

Layers

You may be familiar with using layers in Illustrator, Freehand, or Photo-shop. QuarkXPress 5 and InDesign both let you work with layers, but the feature is missing from QuarkXPress 3 and 4. Artwork can be placed on different layers, and the layers can be shown or hidden, locked or unlocked, rearranged in the stacking order, and so on. Layers are particularly useful when creating multiple versions of a layout, or when you want to isolate elements like graphics and text in a complex layout.

It's important to realize that InDesign's layers (and XPress's) are document-wide, so changing a layer applies to all the pages in your document.

Both QuarkXPress 5 and InDesign control layers with a Layers palette (see Figure 24-1). The palettes in each application look and work in many similar ways, but there are important differences as well; notably, where InDesign's Layers palette has commands in a flyout palette menu, XPress offers controls in a context menu.

Basic Layer Operations

You can create a generic new layer (without naming it) by clicking the New Layer button on the Layers palette. InDesign automatically assigns a color and selects the layer so that objects you draw or place will be assigned to it. To create a layer and set its attributes (like its name) at the same time, either choose New Layer from the palette menu, or hold down the Option/Alt key while clicking the New Layer button. The Layer Options dialog box (see Figure 24-2) appears. You can also open this dialog box by double-clicking on any layer in the palette.

Assigning Objects to Layers

Whenever you create a new object on your page, InDesign assigns it to the the layer which has the pen icon on the Layers palette—called the *target layer*. To make a layer the target, just click on the layer's name.

Figure 24-1
The Layers Palette

Selected layer. These are the layers which would be affected by a Layers palette menu command—for example, Merge Layers. Shift-click or Command/Ctrl-click to select multiple layers.

New objects are assigned to the target layer. Click a layer to make it the target.

Objects selected on the page belong to these layers. You can drag the square to another layer to move the objects to that layer.

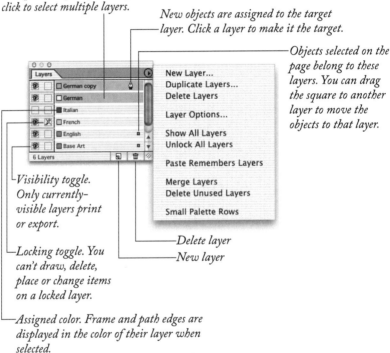

Visibility toggle. Only currently-visible layers print or export.

Locking toggle. You can't draw, delete, place or change items on a locked layer.

Delete layer
New layer

Assigned color. Frame and path edges are displayed in the color of their layer when selected.

Figure 24-2
The Layer Options
dialog box

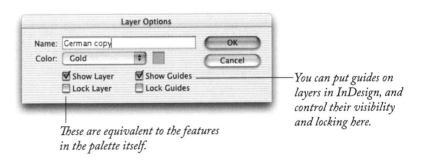

You can put guides on layers in InDesign, and control their visibility and locking here.

These are equivalent to the features in the palette itself.

InDesign doesn't have QuarkXPress's Move Item to Layer command. Instead, if you want to move an object to a different layer, first select the object. (Note that Option/Alt-clicking the layer name selects all the objects on a layer.) You'll see a small square appear beside the name of the layer (or layers) the objects are on. Drag this square to the layer where you want to move the objects. The color of the objects' frame and selection handles will change to the new layer color. You can also duplicate the selected objects to another layer by holding down the Option/Alt key while dragging the square icon. Secret tip: If you want to drag to a locked or hidden layer, hold down the Command/Ctrl key when dragging.

Rearranging and Combining Layers

The order in which you see the layers in the Layers palette indicates their stacking order in the document. A layer at the top of the palette is "higher" in the stacking order than the layers below it, so its objects will obscure objects that are on layers "below" it. (The stacking commands discussed in Chapter 19 only apply to the stacking order *within a layer*.)

To rearrange the stacking order of layers, simply drag the layer up or down within the palette (see Figure 24-3).

Figure 24-3
Moving a layer in the
Layers palette

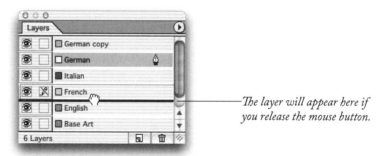

The layer will appear here if you release the mouse button.

You can also combine the elements of two or more layers onto one: In the Layers palette, select the layers which you want to combine by Shift- or Command/Ctrl-clicking their names. Then choose Merge Layers from the palette menu.

Duplicating and Deleting Layers

Duplicating a layer makes a copy of the layer and all of the objects on it. You can do this by selecting the layer and choosing Duplicate Layer in the palette menu. Or, bypass the Layer Options dialog box by simply dragging the layer on top of the palette's New Layer button.

When you delete a layer in XPress, the program gives you the option of moving objects on that layer to another layer. You have no such luck in InDesign, which simply deletes all the objects on that layer. To delete a layer, select it and click the Delete Layer button (or choose Delete Layer from the palette menu). If you have a bunch of layers you're no longer using (there are no objects on them), you can select the Delete Unused Layers command on the palette menu to delete them.

Differences from QuarkXPress 5 Layers

If you've worked with layers in QuarkXPress 5, there are a few other important points to consider.

- When you group objects which are on different layers in InDesign, all of the objects move to the frontmost layer on which you selected an object. (QuarkXPress 5 allows groups to incorporate items from different layers.)

- You can place guides on specific layers, which you can't do in XPress.

- InDesign lets you assign master page objects to different layers (XPress's layers are off-limits on master pages). Master page objects on a particular layer appear behind other objects on the same layer unless you override the objects (see Chapter 33 for more about working with master page objects).

- InDesign won't let you suppress the printing of objects on an individual layer, while XPress can. You can, however, accomplish this by hiding the layer.

- There is no way to turn off the text wrap (runaround) of objects on layers, even when the layer is hidden (XPress offers this as an option).

- When you select objects on different layers and paste them elsewhere in your document, InDesign retains their layer assignment. You can do this by first turning on the Paste Remembers Layers option in the Layers palette flyout menu. When this option is not selected, all pasted objects are placed on the target layer. QuarkXPress 5 always pastes to the target layer.

- There is no way to import layering from a QuarkXPress 5 file. InDesign only imports QuarkXPress 4 files, and if you save a QuarkXPress 5 file into the QuarkXPress 4 format, its layers will be flattened into one.

25

Object Libraries

An *object library* is a special kind of InDesign file which can contain any of the objects which InDesign can work with—text frames, pictures, rules, groups of objects, and more. In this way, it's basically the same as what QuarkXPress calls a *library*. However, InDesign's object libraries go far beyond what you can do in XPress, letting you add guides or entire pages, label objects with keywords, and perform complex searching to find just the library object you're looking for.

Figure 25-1

A Library palette

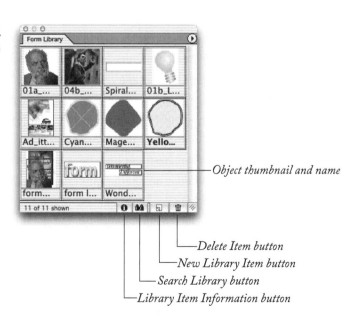

Object thumbnail and name

Delete Item button

New Library Item button

Search Library button

Library Item Information button

Creating and Managing Libraries

You create an object library in InDesign as in XPress: choose Library from the New submenu (under the File menu). The library file appears on screen as a small palette (see Figure 25-1).

Adding Objects to a Library

We find the easiest way to add objects to a library is to just to drag them in. Use the Selection tool to select the object or objects, then drag them over the library palette. When you see Add Item cursor (it looks like a hand with a plus sign), release the mouse, and the objects are copied into the library. Alternatively, you can select objects and either click the New Library Item button on the library palette or choose Add Item from the palette menu. You can't drag guides into the library palette, so you'll have to use these other methods. If you want to add all the items on a page, you can dispense with selecting anything and just choose Add All Items on Page from the palette's flyout menu (the objects become a single library item).

InDesign usually displays library items with a little thumbnail. However, if you prefer, you can choose List View from the palette menu to see the item names and an icon which represents the object type.

If you have more than one library palette open, you can copy an item from one to the other by dragging it. Or, if you want to move an item (rather than copying it), hold down the Option/Alt key while dragging.

Note that as in QuarkXPress, when you add a linked picture the library only stores a thumbnail of the graphic; you still have to maintain the separate full-resolution file on disk.

Opening and Closing Libraries

You can open an object library from disk the same way you open any InDesign document (select Open from the File menu, or double-click on the library from the desktop). Similarly, you may close an object library by either clicking the palette's Close box or choosing Close Library from the palette menu. Note that once you have opened a library, InDesign places its name at the bottom of the Window menu, even after you close the library. If you want to reopen it, just reselect it here.

By the way, there is no Save feature with object libraries because they are automatically saved whenever you add items to them or close them.

Using Library Items on a Page

It's easy to use a library item in an InDesign document: Simply drag the item from the palette over your page, and the object or objects will appear. You can also select one or more items in a library and choose Place Item(s) from the palette menu, and they will be added to the currently selected page. Note that Place Item(s) is like Paste in Place—it remembers *where* on the page the object was, and puts the library object in exactly the same place. This means an object might end up on a left hand page (because that's where it originally was) instead of the right hand page at which you're staring.

Also, if you have Paste Remembers Layers turned on in the Layers palette, layer information is retained for page items.

Deleting Library Items

If you want to delete library items, select them in the palette by clicking (or use Shift-click or Command/Ctrl-click to select multiple items). Either click the Delete Item button, or choose Delete Item(s) from the palette menu. If you want to avoid the annoying "Are you sure you want to delete these" alert, add the Option/Alt key.

Asset Management

InDesign's libraries act like little asset management utilities, letting you label each item and sort or search for items that match various criteria.

Adding Information About an Item

Each library item has a name. If it's a graphic, InDesign gives the item the graphic's file name by the default. If it's a text frame or a page object, it will be untitled. You can always add or change information about an item (like its name) by double-clicking it in the Library palette. Or, you can click the Library Item Information button or choose Item Information from the palette menu (see Figure 25-2).

The Item Information dialog box lets you enter a name for the item and add keywords in the Description field which you can use later for searching. The Object Type choice is selected automatically, depending on the nature of the object contained; we can't think of any good reason you'd want to change this.

Figure 25-2

The Item Information dialog box

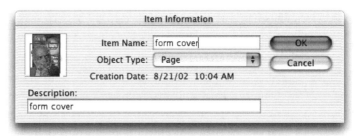

Finding Library Items

Adding more than a handful of objects to libraries would be useless unless you could find the items again when you need them. Fortunately, InDesign's organizational features are quite robust. The most basic method of finding library content is to use the Sort submenu (in the Library palette's flyout menu) to sort the items by name, date, or type.

If sorting isn't enough, you can search for one or more items by either clicking the Search Library button on the palette or choosing Show Subset in the palette menu (see Figure 25-3). The Subset dialog box lets you search by Item Name, Creation Date, Object Type, or keywords in the Description field.

Figure 25-3

The Subset dialog box

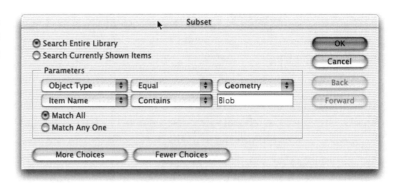

If you want, you can click the More Choices button to add other criteria to search on at the same time, or Fewer Choices to remove criteria. When you click OK, the results are displayed in the palette, and all items except the ones you find are hidden. To return to displaying all the library items, choose Show All from the palette menu.

PART 3

Building Documents

○ ○ ○

Pages

[None]

A-Standard

B-Inside Content

C-Gate Fold Master

D-Master Template Page

26

Creating New Documents

One of the easiest parts of switching to InDesign is starting a new document. The process is about the same as it is in QuarkXPress, with only minor variations. In fact, when you first look at InDesign's New Document dialog box you might think that you're just in a newer version of QuarkXPress. In the New Document dialog box (see Figure 26-1), you can define the following.

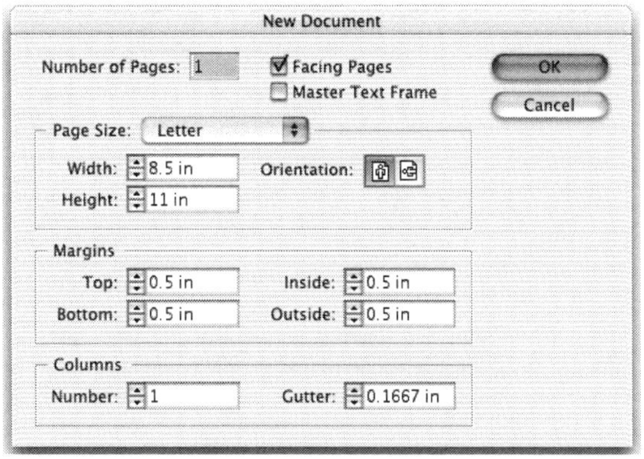

Figure 26-1
The New Document
dialog box

- **Number of Pages.** You can enter your final document size here or your can add pages later (we cover this in Chapter 28), up to 9,999 pages long.

- **Facing Pages and Orientation.** As in QuarkXPress, determine whether your document will use left-and-right-page spreads and whether it should be created in either portrait or landscape mode.

- **Master Text Frame.** This option is similar to the Automatic Text Box option in XPress's New Document dialog box. It creates a default text frame within the margins of the default master page, so that you can flow text from page to page without making a text frame first.

- **Page Size.** Use any of the preset page sizes from the popup menu or type in a custom size, ranging from a minimum size of ⅙-inch per side to a maximum size of 18-feet per side.

- **Margins.** Enter the distance from the page edge where these non-printing page guides should appear.

- **Columns.** As with XPress, you can enter the number of columns and the gutter (the space between the columns), which can be overridden on either document or master pages.

Here's a feature you won't find in QuarkXPress: You can bypass this dialog box by typing Command-Option-N/Ctrl-Alt-N. In this case, InDesign uses the default document settings (see Chapter 7).

Changing Page Size and Orientation

You're not stuck with a page size and orientation. To change these, do as you would in XPress: select Document Setup from the File menu. Here you can change the number of pages, the page size and orientation, and whether you're using facing pages. (Margin and column guides can also be changed, but elsewhere; we discuss that and how page objects are affected by these changes in Chapter 35.)

27

Opening and Saving Files

There are only subtle differences between QuarkXPress and InDesign in the way they open files, and the save options are virtually identical.

Opening Files

To open an InDesign file, choose Open from the File menu, double-click on the file on the desktop, or drag the file's icon onto the application icon. You can also open QuarkXPress and PageMaker documents with InDesign (see Appendix A). When opening InDesign files you can select from three options in the Open dialog box (see Figure 27-1).

- **Open Normal.** This is the default option and the one you'll use when you just want to edit an existing file. If you open a file saved as a template (see below), this option opens a new, Untitled document based on the template.

- **Open Original.** Use this option to open and edit a template file itself, instead of opening an Untitled file based on the template.

- **Open Copy.** With this option you can use any document as a starting point for a new document. To achieve the same result in QuarkXPress, you'd need to manually duplicate a document and then open it.

Saving Files

Use the Save As dialog box to specify whether a InDesign should save your file as a document or template (Figure 27-2). This choice has the

Figure 27-1

The Open dialog box

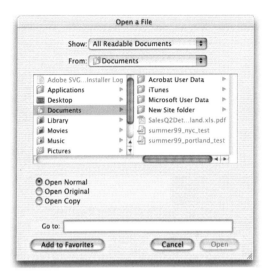

same effect as choosing Document or Template in the Save As dialog box in QuarkXPress. The default, InDesign 2.0 Document, saves a normal InDesign 2.0 file; choose the InDesign 2.0 Template option to be able to create new, untitled InDesign documents that use the current file's settings and contents.

One difference between XPress and InDesign is that InDesign doesn't have an option to save files that are compatible with earlier versions of the software. And although InDesign can open XPress files, there's no built-in way to save InDesign files as XPress files (though Markzware has an XTension called ID2QX that lets you do this).

Figure 27-2

The Save As dialog box

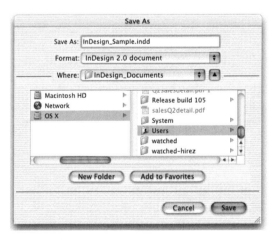

28

Adding, Deleting, and Arranging Pages

When you're looking for the Document Layout palette that you're used to in QuarkXPress, look at the Pages palette in InDesign.

The Pages Palette

You can access the Pages palette from the Window menu (or press F12). Like the QuarkXPress Document Layout palette, it displays master pages in one section of the palette and document pages in another (see Figure 28-1).

Figure 28-1
The InDesign Pages palette

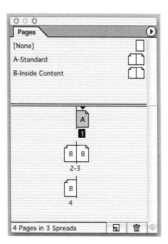

Unlike XPress, InDesign lets you customize the way the pages are displayed in the Pages palette. You can make it look like XPress if you want: Select Palette Options from the Pages palette menu and you'll see the Palette Options dialog box (see Figure 28-2), which contains the following options:

- **Icon Size.** Sets how large the icons appear.

- **Show Vertically.** Displays the sequence of page icons as columns like QuarkXPress, which is the default. Unchecking the option displays the pages horizontally.

- **Pages on Top/Masters on Top.** Determines which side of the Pages palette the pages and masters icons occupy. The default setting, Masters on Top, matches the arrangement in XPress.

- **Resize.** Determines how the page and master areas change when you resize the Pages palette. If you want the size of the pages section to stay the same and let the masters area resize, which is the way XPress works, choose Masters Fixed. If you want it the other way around, choose Pages Fixed. Choose Proportional to let both areas resize proportionally as you resize the palette.

Figure 28-2
The Pages palette
Options dialog box

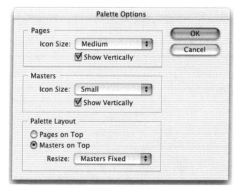

Adding Pages

As with QuarkXPress, you can add pages by dragging a master page icon from the master page section of the Pages palette to the document page section of the palette.

If you drag an individual page from the master to the document section of the Pages palette, InDesign creates one page. You can also select and drag a multiple-page spread from the masters section of the Pages palette into the pages section by dragging the page numbers under the spread.

In addition, you can use the New icon at the bottom of the Pages palette to add more pages to a document (the pages are added following the currently-selected page in the Pages palette). You can use this button to add multiple pages in one step by holding down the Option/Alt key while clicking the New button. The dialog box that appears (see Figure 28-3) is the same one that appears when selecting the Insert Pages command from the flyout menu of the Pages palette. In this dialog box you can enter the number of pages to add, their location in the page sequence, and which master page should be used to format them.

Figure 28-3
The Insert Pages
dialog box

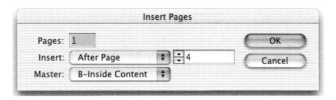

Arranging Pages

Like QuarkXPress's Document Layout palette, the InDesign Pages palette allows you to re-arrange pages by dragging page icons. A thin vertical line appears in the location where pages will move if they're placed between two spreads or between individual pages in a non-facing pages document.

You can also move a page so that it breaks apart an existing spread. Drag the page to be moved so that it is placed between the pages in a spread. An arrow appears showing the direction in which the spread pages will be relocated.

Deleting Pages

Deleting pages from the Pages palette is also similar to QuarkXPress. You can select a page or group of pages to be deleted and click the Delete icon at the bottom of the palette. (Select more than one with Command/Ctrl for non-contiguous pages, or the Shift key for contiguous page ranges.) With the flyout menu from the Pages palette you can also select Delete Page(s) or Delete Spread(s) depending upon what is selected in the palette.

29

Multipage Spreads

You can use InDesign to create spreads that span more than two adjoining pages, which are sometimes referred to as gatefolds because they open similar to a gate.

Creating a Multipage Spread

It's important to note that stand-alone gatefold documents, such as direct mail pieces with multiple folds, require a separate size for each fold so that inner pages fit inside the outer pages. Like QuarkXPress, InDesign requires all document pages to be the same size, so if you need these kinds of documents you should probably create them as one-page-per side and place fold marks where appropriate.

After determining which spread is to be expanded beyond two pages, select that page (for single-sided documents) or spread (for facing pages documents) and choose Keep Spread Together from the flyout menu within the Pages palette. The spread will then have brackets surrounding the page numbers (see Figure 29-1). You can then drag additional pages into the spread just as you would within QuarkXPress (either by dragging a master page icon next to it or dragging another page icon next to it in the Pages palette).

Creating a Multipage Master Page

Unlike QuarkXPress, you can create a master page for your gatefolds within InDesign. This is sometimes the easiest way to build a gatefold. Select New Master from the flyout menu in the Pages palette. Enter the

Figure 29-1
Multipage spreads
are displayed with
brackets surrounding
their numbers.

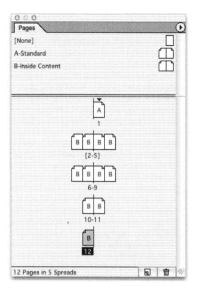

number of pages to be in the multipage spread and click OK. Then use this
master page (see Figure 29-2) to create as many groups of gatefold pages
as you need. This lets you bypass the process of selecting the Keep Spread
Together option and then manually dragging pages into the gatefold.

Figure 29-2
InDesign master
pages can contain
spreads up to nine
pages wide.

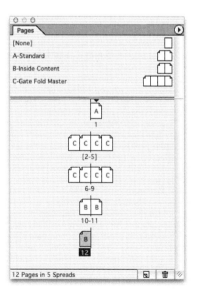

30

Creating and Applying Master Pages

As with QuarkXPress, you can create master pages with InDesign to eliminate the need for repetitive page formatting. InDesign also includes additional master page features like parent-child ("based on") master pages and selective overriding of master page items, which we discuss in this and the next few chapters.

Creating a New Master Page

Making a new master page in InDesign is probably different than you're used to. To make a master page, you must select New Master from the Pages palette's flyout menu. In the New Master dialog box (see Figure 30-1) you can then enter the number of pages in the master and identify if it is based upon another master page. We discuss creating multipage master pages in Chapter 29, and we cover basing one master on another in Chapter 32.

You can also open the New Master dialog box by Command-Option/Ctrl-Alt-clicking the new page button in the Pages palette.

Automatic Linked Text Frames

Like XPress, anything you put on a master page appears on any document page tagged with the master. However, note that InDesign handles automatic text-link boxes differently than XPress. In XPress, you link from the

Figure 30-1
The New Master
dialog box

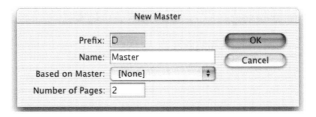

funny chain icons in the upper-left corner of the master page to the text box. You can achieve the same result in InDesign by simply linking the text frame on the left master page to the frame on the right. We cover linking text frames in more detail in Chapter 40.

Note that InDesign offers something that XPress does not: You can have more than one automatically-linked text frame per page. For instance, if you have two text frames per master page, you can link the first on the left page to the first on the right page, and the second on the left page to the second on the right page.

Duplicating a Master Page

If you want to create a master page that is very similar to an existing master, you can duplicate a master page by choosing the Duplicate Spread command from the Pages palette's flyout menu. Note that if you want a duplicate master page to dynamically update itself when the master you copied is changed, you should create a child master instead, as covered in Chapter 32.

Converting a Document Page into a Master Page

Everyone, sooner or later, thinks they're laying out a master page when they're actually placing objects and guides on a document page. There's little you can do to recover from this in XPress, but InDesign lets you turn a document page into a master page: Simply drag the document spread icon in the Pages palette to the master section of the Pages palette.

If the original document spread was based upon a master page, changes to that master page will still impact both the document page and also the new master page that was built from the document page. We discuss this in more detail in Chapter 32.

Applying Master Pages
to Document Pages

Applying a master page to a document page works similarly in both InDesign and QuarkXPress. You can drag a master page onto a document page (the page is highlighted), or you can drag a master over the numbers of a spread (an outline surrounds the spread to which you're applying the master). You can also select one or more document pages (remember to Command/Ctrl-click to select discontiguous pages) and Option/Alt-click on the master page you want to apply. As in XPress, each document page in the Pages palette is marked with the prefix of the master page applied to it.

There's one other way to apply a master page to document pages: Select Apply Master to Pages from the Pages palette flyout menu. InDesign lets you select a master to apply and a page range. For instance, you could apply B-Master to pages "2, 4-5, 11-16, 22".

31

Targeting versus Selecting Pages

InDesign makes a distinction between *targeting* a page or spread and *selecting* a page or spread. The distinction may be new to QuarkXPress users:

- A page (or spread) is *targeted* if it is the page onto which the next new objects will be placed, such as objects pasted into a document.

- A page (or spread) is *selected* if the next page action—like duplicating the spread—will affect that page or spread. The target page and the selected page can be different pages.

You may wonder why this distinction is useful. In XPress, the targeted page is whatever page is touching the upper-left corner of the screen. InDesign is more flexible, and if you're looking at your document at a lower magnification (a birds-eye view, showing more than one page at a time), you may still want to place an object onto a certain page or spread. By targeting a spread, you can be certain as to where objects will be placed.

Targeting a Page or Spread

By default, the target spread is the spread that's centered in the document window, but you may want another spread to be targeted. Before performing an action that depends on the targeted spread, double-check which page or spread is actually targeted by finding the highlighted page numbers in the Pages palette—note that the page numbers can be highlighted without the page icons being highlighted (Figure 31-1). Target a page by clicking on any element on a page or clicking on the page or pasteboard within the document window. You can also target a spread by double-

Figure 31-1
Here the target
spread (highlighted
page numbers) differs
from the selected
page (highlighted
page icon).

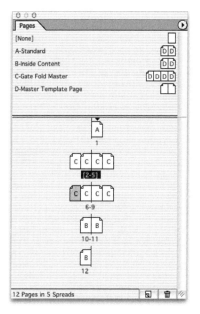

clicking the page numbers under the spread's page icons in the Pages palette (but this centers that spread in the window).

Selecting a Page or Spread

You can select pages or spreads in the Pages palette to identify which pages will be affected by page-editing commands. Clicking on a page icon in the Pages palette selects a page. Once a page or spread is selected you can use a command such as Margins and Columns on the Layout menu to edit the margins and number of columns on the selected page or spread.

You can select multiple pages or spreads by holding down the Shift key while selecting contiguous pages, or by holding down the Command/Ctrl key if they are discontiguous. Double-clicking on the page number beneath a page or spread will both target and select the page or spread.

32

Creating Parent/Child Relationships

InDesign introduces a great master page feature unavailable in XPress: You can base master pages on other master pages using a parent-child relationship. For example, many books and catalogs use several different-but-very-similar master pages. By creating one "parent" master page and then basing the other "child" master pages on it, you can later make changes to the parent that ripple through to all the child master pages.

Working with a Parent Page

The parent master page should contain all elements that are in common between it and its children. For example, let's say you have a book with ten chapters, and each chapter will use an identical layout with the exception of the chapter name as a running header. You can create one master page for the chapter content and then make ten master pages based on it. On each of the ten master pages you will only need to modify the running header, rather than having to build each master page from scratch. The difference between this relationship and simply duplicating the parent master is that making a change to the parent also affects the same elements on the child masters.

Making Child Masters

After building your parent master page, select the New Master command from the Pages palette's flyout menu. In the New Master dialog box, choose the parent master page from the Based On popup menu. When you click OK, the new master page will be a child master page (it'll be based on the parent master page; see Figure 32-1).

You can also drag one master page icon on top of any other master page in the Pages palette. The page you drag becomes a parent master, the page you drop it on becomes a child master. The prefix on the master page icon indicates the relationship.

Figure 32-1

A master page can be based on another master page.

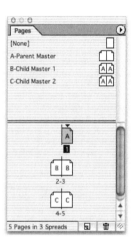

Here we named the pages to indicate the parent and child masters, although you can also tell from the parent prefix displayed on the child pages.

Overriding Parent Items on a Child Master

While the idea for creating a parent master page is to have it format all child pages in one simple step, there will be times when you want to modify parent elements on a child master page. By default, parent items on child master pages are inaccessible for editing. However, you can make them accessible by Command-Shift/Ctrl-Shift-clicking on an item. Just keep in mind that once you do this, those items will no longer update if you change the same items on the parent master. We discuss this more in the next chapter.

Overriding Master Items

QuarkXPress lets you select and modify any master page item while on a document page. This can cause problems because you may edit a master page item accidentally, breaking the link between the document page and the master page. In InDesign you cannot select a master page item by simply clicking on it while on a document page.

However, note that you don't actually need to select master page items when placing imported text or graphics (like you do in XPress). InDesign is smart enough to know that if you click a loaded Place icon on a master page frame, the master frame should accept the content. That means that you only need to override a master page item when you need to change something about the object.

Also unlike XPress, InDesign lets you turn off and on the visibility of master page items by choosing Display Master Items from the View menu.

Changing Master Items

If you need to select and modify a master item on a document page you must first Command-Shift-click/Ctrl-Shift-click with the Selection tool or the Type tool. (This also works to select parent items on a child master page.) After selecting a master page item, it then becomes a part of the local document page. This is called *overriding* the master page item.

When you override a master page item, you can make local changes to it, such as changing its frame thickness, fill color, position on the page, and so on. However, changing the frame thickness only overrides the frame thickness attribute; the fill color and so on is still linked back to the master page item. (That is, if you change the fill color on the master page, it *does* update on the document page, even though the object has been overridden.) If you don't want any link between an object and its original master page, then first override it and then (while it's selected), choose Detach Selection From Master from the Pages palette menu. *Detaching* means there's no longer a link to the master page item.

Note that the act of overriding an object always breaks the link to a frame's content. That is, even if you just override a text or graphic frame and then don't actually change anything else about it, the content (the text or the picture inside the frame) is no longer linked to the master page.

Removing Master Item Changes

In QuarkXPress, the only way to remove overridden master items changes is to re-apply the master. Fortunately, unlike XPress, InDesign can remove changes you've made to specific master items. You can remove changes to individual items or to all master items that have been modified on a spread.

To eliminate changes to a specific master item, select the item and choose Remove Selected Local Overrides from the Pages palette's flyout menu (see Figure 33-1). Or, if you want all the overridden master page items on a spread to revert back to their original state, first deselect all objects and then choose Remove All Local Overrides from the flyout menu.

Note that this only works for objects that have local overrides, *not* for objects that have been detached from the master page.

Reapplying Master Pages

Here's one of the most common problems people encounter in XPress: You add or remove a page in the middle of a facing-pages document and suddenly you have duplicate master page items on each subsequent page—the empty master page frame and the master page object that has content in it (like the text of a story). This problem does *not* go away in InDesign.

The reason this happens is that, as we said earlier, placing a graphic or text inside a frame on a document page automatically overrides the frame for you. When you delete or add an odd number of pages in the middle of a document, the subsequent left-hand pages become right-hand pages

Figure 33-1
Use the Remove
Selected Local
Overrides command
to eliminate changes
to selected master
page items.

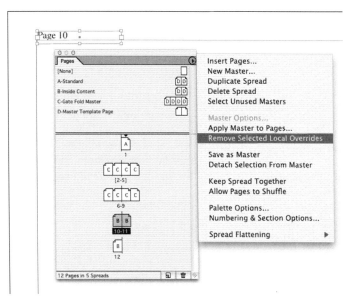

(and *vice versa*), and InDesign has to reapply the master page to the document page. Reapplying a master page creates duplicate master page items
wherever you have overridden the objects. The only solution is to always
add or remove an even number of pages at a time. We feel your pain.

34

Ruler Guides

At first glance, InDesign's ruler guides work in much the same way they do in QuarkXPress: Simply pull a guide from the vertical or horizontal ruler and drag it onto the page. Like XPress, ruler guides that are dragged and released over the page appear only on the page, while guides released with the mouse over the pasteboard extend over both the page and the pasteboard—across all pages in a spread.

However, that's where the similarities between the two programs stop. InDesign's ruler guides are much more powerful and much more flexible than XPress's. For example, InDesign ruler guides act just like page elements, so you can select one or more guides at a time, copy and paste them, and even position selected guides numerically using the Transform palette. Guides, like any other object, can be placed on a layer (by default, a guide belongs to the layer that was active when you created it), and using the Layers palette you can show and hide different ruler guide layouts.

Customizing Ruler Guides

InDesign gives you quite a bit of control over individual ruler guides in the Ruler Guides feature (see Figure 34-1)—it's on the Layout menu, but you can also get to it by Control/right-clicking a guide. The dialog box offers these options:

- **View Threshold.** Determines the magnification above which a guide is displayed and below which a guide is hidden. This is equivalent to when you Shift-drag as you create a guide in XPress.

- **Color.** Sets the guide color. A guide is displayed using this color when it isn't selected. When you select a guide, it appears in its layer's color.

Because InDesign works with guides as objects, you can change the settings for one or more guides simultaneously by selecting the guides before choosing the Ruler Guides command. Or, to change the default settings for future guides, choose the Ruler Guides command when no guides are selected.

Figure 34-1
The Ruler Guides
dialog box

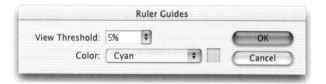

Guide Position

Because InDesign guides act like objects, you can use the Transform palette (or double-click on the Selection tool to display the Move dialog box) to numerically control the position of a selected guide, or use the arrow keys to nudge it slightly. If you need more than one guide, you might want to place one and then use the Step and Repeat command (on the Edit menu) to repeat it at regular intervals, or use the Create Guides command described below.

To convert a page guide into a pasteboard guide (one that extends onto the pasteboard), hold down the Command/Ctrl key while you drag it.

If you know where you want a pasteboard guide, you can place one quickly by double-clicking in the ruler at that point. For example, if you want a horizontal guide at 4 inches, double-click at the 4-inch mark on the vertical ruler. Even better, hold down the Shift key when you double-click and InDesign will snap the guide to the nearest ruler tick (so you don't have to worry that it's not positioned correctly).

Here's one more trick: You can place a horizontal and a vertical guide at the same time by Command/Ctrl-dragging from the intersection of the two rulers. Or, better, Command-Shift/Ctrl-Shift-drag to snap the guides to the nearest ruler ticks.

Locking Guides

Note that guides, like any object, can be locked in place by selecting Lock Position from the Object menu. You can also lock all the guides in the document at once with the Lock Guides feature in the View menu. Finally, you can lock one or more guides by placing them on a locked layer (see Chapter 24).

Copying Guides

When you copy and paste one or more guides, InDesign always remembers the guide's position on the page. For instance, you could draw four guides around the page, each .25-inch outside the page boundary ("bleed guides"), then select those guides, copy them, jump to a different page, and paste them—the guides will appear in exactly the same place. (You might need to do this because in InDesign, as in XPress, guides on the pasteboard—like any object on the pasteboard—around a master page don't appear on the document pages.) Note that you might get unexpected results when copying guides and then pasting them into a different-sized document.

Deleting Guides

XPress lets you delete a guide by dragging it outside of the document window. You can't do this in InDesign (the document window just scrolls!), so to delete a guide, just select it and press the Delete key.

Create Guides

The Create Guides feature (in the Layout menu) really should be called "create columns with guide rules." Use this feature when the Columns option in the Margins and Columns command (see Chapter 35) isn't adequate for the type of layout grid you are setting up, such as when creating multiple row or column variations. The Create Guides dialog box (see Figure 34-2) includes these options:

Figure 34-2
The Create Guides dialog box makes it easy to add more column and row variations to your InDesign layouts.

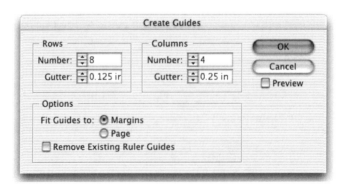

- **Number.** Sets the number of rows or columns you want to create using guides.

- **Gutter.** If the Gutter setting is larger than zero, InDesign places two guides in each location, rather than one; the amount of space between the two guides equals the Gutter value.

- **Fit Guides To.** Adjusts the row and column spacing based on the page edges or margins.

- **Remove Existing Ruler Guides.** Clears all page guides, useful when you want to remove guides you were using to roughly sketch out the layout.

Building Documents

35

Margin and Column Guides

One of the most common questions QuarkXPress users ask is, "How do I change my margin and column guides?" It's not intuitive at all. XPress does let you do this, but only on master pages. InDesign offers much more flexibility, though its method takes some getting used to for XPress users.

How InDesign Handles Margin Guides

Like XPress, the margin and column guides on each document page reflect those on the master page. However, unlike XPress, you can override the margin and column guides on individual document pages. Because of this capability, you have to be aware of whether you're on a master page or a document page before editing guides; consider locking your guides to prevent unintended modifications (see the previous chapter for more on locking guides).

By default, the margin guides are pink (magenta) and the column guides are violet. That's why in a normal, one-column document the top and bottom margins appear pink and the left and right margins appear purple (because the column guides are overlapping the margin guides). If you wish, you can change the colors by opening the Preferences dialog box and selecting Guides.

Hiding Guides

To turn off guide display, choose Hide Guides from the View menu (or press Command-;/Ctrl-;). Hiding a layer also hides all guides on that layer.

You can also turn on the Preview mode in the Tools palette (or press W when not editing text) to hide all non-printing objects, like guides.

Editing Margin & Column Guides

Before you edit your margin or column guides, select one or more pages in the Pages palette (see Chapter 31)—the page you're looking at on screen may or may not be the page that gets affected. If you select the master page in the Pages palette, the changes you make will affect the master page (and all document pages based on that master page), even if you're not currently looking at the master page!

Next, select the Margin and Columns command from the Layout menu and enter the desired values in the Margins and Columns dialog box (see Figure 35-1). We like to turn on the Preview checkbox so we can see the effect before clicking OK. Whether or not the objects on your page change (like text frames resizing to the new margins) after you click OK depends on the Layout Adjustment option (see below).

Figure 35-1
The Margins and
Columns dialog box

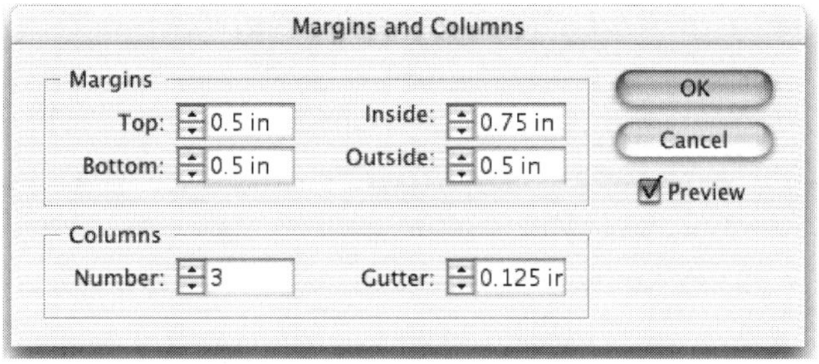

Yes, changing the values in the Margins and Columns dialog box while no documents are open establishes a new, default set of values for all future documents you create.

Of course, editing columns with the Margin and Columns dialog box always results in equally-sized columns. If you need unequal columns—like a larger column on the left—you can drag the column guides to where you want them. Unfortunately, there's no way to position these numerically other than just watching the value in the Transform palette.

Layout Adjustment

In QuarkXPress, any text box that reaches to the margin guides automatically resizes when you make changes to the margin guide values. To duplicate this in InDesign, you have to turn on the Layout Adjustment feature (choose Layout Adjustment from the Layout menu and then turn on Enable Layout Adjustment; see Figure 35-2).

Figure 35-2
The Layout
Adjustment
dialog box

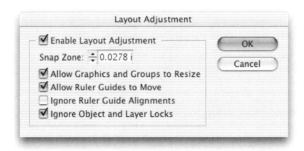

Notice that the Layout Adjustment dialog box offers other options, too. That's because InDesign provides more flexibility than XPress's automatic text box resizing. Layout Adjustment can resize or reposition any object that's aligned to a margin, column, or ruler guide. You can fine-tune the feature using these options:

- **Enable Layout Adjustment.** Lets layout adjustment happen. It's important to note that when this is on, layout adjustment won't happen as soon as you click OK—once it's on, layout adjustment happens whenever you change margin or column guides.

- **Snap Zone.** If an object is closer than this distance to a guide, it's considered aligned to that guide and may be moved or resized during layout adjustment.

- **Allow Graphics and Groups to Resize.** Enables graphics and groups to be scaled during a layout adjustment. Text frames are always scaled if needed.

- **Allow Ruler Guides to Move.** You might leave this on if you want ruler guides to be proportionally repositioned relative to the new margin or column settings.

- **Ignore Ruler Guide Alignments.** When this is on, objects won't be adjusted to stay aligned to ruler guide position changes.

- **Ignore Object and Layer Locks.** When this is on, locked objects are allowed to move to follow changes to guide positions.

Use layout adjustment with care. If it's what you want, it will save you tons of time when repurposing content for radically different page sizes or layouts, but if your layout isn't designed for it, you can end up with a disastrous mess. (Remember InDesign's multiple undo!) It works best when your layout was designed from the start with resizing and repositioning in mind, such as keeping all objects clearly aligned to column guides and margins and leaving space for adjustments. Note that layout adjustment applies to all pages, not just the page you're looking at.

Building Documents

36

Document and Baseline Grids

InDesign and QuarkXPress have similar baseline grids to which you can lock text. But InDesign also allows you to set up a document grid for aligning objects.

Baseline Grid

Like QuarkXPress, the baseline grid is used to align the baseline of text across multiple columns on a page or spread. Alignment is a paragraph attribute, and you can force text to align to the baseline grid in by clicking the Lock to Baseline Grid button in the Paragraph palette.

The starting point of the baseline grid, how frequently it is repeated and at what view percentage it become visible or hidden are defined by settings in the Grids Preferences dialog box (Figure 36-1). InDesign provides two additional options over XPress: grid color and view threshold. These options work the same way as they do for ruler guides (see Chapter 34).

You can make the baseline grid visible or invisible by selecting Show/Hide Baseline Grid from the View menu (or press Command-Option-'/Ctrl-Alt-'). The Show/Hide Baseline Grid command is also available in the context-sensitive menu when clicking an empty area of the document.

Here's a hidden trick: InDesign lets you lock the *first line* of a paragraph to the baseline grid, leaving alone the rest of the paragraph's spacing. To do this, select Keyboard Shortcuts from the Edit menu, choose Text and Tables from the Product Area popup menu, then search through the list of commands until you see "Only Align First Line to Grid." Select this feature and assign a keyboard shortcut to it (see Chapter 6). Now, select

Figure 36-1
Grids preferences

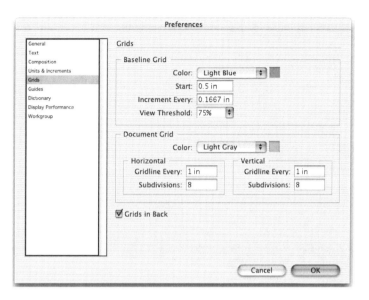

a paragraph, turn on Lock to Baseline Grid in the Paragraph palette, and then press the keyboard shortcut you defined. Cool, huh?

Document Grid

The document grid supplements margin and column guides and creates a grid across the entire document—like an enormous piece of graph paper. The grid makes it possible to align elements vertically and horizontally without having to build individual ruler guides. Some folks find the document grid to be too obtrusive and prefer to stick with ruler guides (see Chapter 34), but others just love the full-page grid.

You can set up the document grid by opening the Preferences dialog box and selecting Grids. In the Document Grid section, you can set the grid color, the measure between each horizontal and vertical gridline, and the subdivisions between the gridlines. Then, to make the document grid visible or invisible, select Show/Hide Document Grid from the View menu (or press Command-'/Ctrl-'). You can turn on and off whether objects snap to the grid by selecting or unselecting Snap to Document Grid from the View menu (or press Command-Shift-'/Ctrl-Shift-').

37

Numbering and Sectioning

QuarkXPress and InDesign can both handle multiple sections within a document. For example, the numbering scheme of a book's front matter, table of contents and index may be different from that of its body (perhaps A, B and C for the Table of Contents and 1, 2 and 3 for the body of the book). You control sections using the Pages palette (see Chapter 28 for an overview of the Pages palette).

Creating Sections

To create a section, select the page where you want the section to start in the Pages palette, then choose Numbering & Section Options from the palette's flyout menu. In the New Section dialog box (see Figure 37-1), turn on the Start Section checkbox to start a new section on the selected page.

Figure 37-1
Numbering and
Section Options

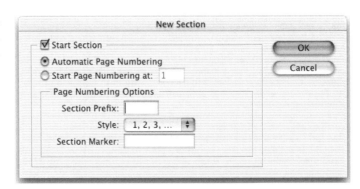

Section Options

If you want the section to begin with a specific page number, choose Start Page Numbering At and type the page number. Otherwise, if the page numbering simply continues from the previous section, use the Automatic numbering option.

Prefixes

As in XPress, you can enter a Section Prefix if you would like the page numbers to be preceded by a label of 5 characters or fewer. For example, enter "A-" if you want the pages within this section to appear as *A-1, A-2,* and so on.

Style

The Style popup menu lets you determine whether the pages within a section are numbered using Arabic page numbering (our usual counting method), Roman numerals, or letters.

Section Marker

InDesign's Section Marker option (XPress doesn't have this) lets you type variable text that will be inserted whenever you use the Section Name command from the Insert Special Character menu (see Chapter 51). For instance, if you lay out more than one chapter of a book within a single InDesign document, you could make each chapter a different section, typing the name of the chapter into the Section Marker field. Then, insert the Section Name character into a text box on a master page applied to the document pages. When you return to the document pages, you'll see the proper chapter name in each section. This is much faster than creating a different master page for each chapter.

Editing Sections

When you create a section, InDesign places a black triangle above the page icon in the Pages palette. To change the section's settings, double-click the section triangle icon. If you need to delete a section, open the Numbering & Section Options dialog box for the first page of that section and turn off the Start Section option.

By the way, if you're using many sections within a document, you can have InDesign display the absolute page numbers rather than the section numbering by changing this option in the General Preferences (see Figure

37-2). Absolute numbering displays all page numbers based upon their position from the start of the document, not the section number assigned to them. This affects only the displayed number for navigational purposes within InDesign, not the page numbers that print.

Figure 37-2
The General
Preferences dialog
box lets you display
absolute or section
page numbers.

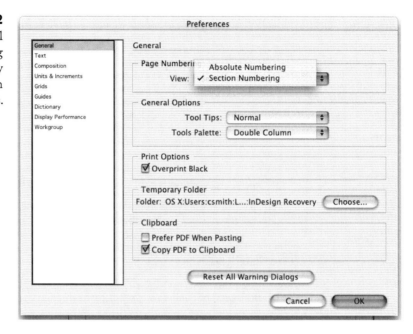

Typography

38

Typing and Editing Text

Most of the time, whether you're working with QuarkXPress or InDesign, you import text from a Microsoft Word file (or some other word processor). However, sometimes we need to type text in the program, or do heavy amounts of editing in InDesign after text has already been placed. This chapter gives you some tips on how to do this easily in InDesign. It assumes you already know the basics of text editing on either a Macintosh or Windows computer.

Unfortunately, InDesign doesn't have a Story Editor feature like Page-Maker (neither does XPress, of course). This makes editing text—especially small text in hard-to-read fonts—somewhat annoying, so we hope that we'll see a Story Editor in a future version of InDesign.

Selecting, Deleting, and Navigating

While text must always be placed in a text frame, remember that you can drag out a rectangular frame with the Type tool (press T). Once you have a frame, you can begin typing. In addition to the usual ability to select text by dragging the cursor, you can also use the same shortcuts as QuarkXPress for selecting text by clicking:

- Double-clicking selects a word.
- Triple-clicking selects a line.
- Quadruple-clicking selects a paragraph.
- Clicking five times (or pressing Command-A/Ctrl-A) selects all the text in your threaded text frames.

However, if you turn off the Triple Click to Select a Line option in the Text panel of the Preferences dialog box (see Chapter 7), then clicking three times selects a paragraph and four times selects the whole story.

One thing you may miss from XPress: If you make a selection and click outside of the frame, InDesign forgets the selection (QuarkXPress remembers it when you click back in the text box). Another feature which is missing in InDesign is drag-and-drop text. This is an option in XPress (and Microsoft Word) which hasn't yet made it into InDesign.

Deleting text works the same as in XPress: The Delete key kills the character to the left of the cursor, and Shift-Delete the character to the right of the insertion point.

Keyboard Navigating

If you like keyboard commands to navigate through text, rather than using a mouse, most of the commands you know from QuarkXPress work just the same. Using the Up, Down, Left and Right Arrow keys move you around in text as you'd expect. As in XPress, adding the Command/Ctrl key to the arrow keys moves by word or paragraph.

However, in InDesign the Home key takes you to the start of a line, and the End key to the end of the line. Command/Ctrl-Home takes you to the beginning of the story, and Command/Ctrl-End takes you to the end.

As in QuarkXPress, if you add the Shift key to each of these keyboard commands, InDesign selects all the text from the insertion point's location to the location where the command sends it. For example, Command-Shift-End/Ctrl-Shift-End selects from the current cursor location to the end of the text story (even if the end doesn't appear in the current text frame).

Hidden Characters

In QuarkXPress, characters which don't print—tabs, spaces, ends of paragraphs, and so on—are called *invisibles*. InDesign calls these *hidden characters*, and you make them visible (or invisible again) by selecting Show Hidden Characters from the Type menu or pressing Command-Option-I/Ctrl-Alt-I. (In XPress, the shortcut is simply Command-I/Ctrl-I.) The characters appear in the color of the current layer.

Speeding Up Editing

When you first start using InDesign, you may be disappointed that InDesign seems slower at text editing than QuarkXPress—especially on a slower computer, or when working on a long document. InDesign can slow down because it's doing much more work than XPress: Its high-resolution previews, and improved text composition require more processing power. Fortunately, there are couple of things you can do to improve editing speed.

- When you're editing text, turn off InDesign's High Quality Display mode: Choose Typical Display or Optimized Display from the View menu (see Chapter 66).

- Try selecting Adobe Single-Line Composer from the Paragraph palette's menu (we describe this in Chapter 46). InDesign responds slightly faster, and it doesn't rewrap the previous lines. When you're done editing, select the text and switch back to Paragraph Composer to get better composition when you're finished.

Typography

39

Importing Text

InDesign can import text files from recent versions of Microsoft Word and Excel, files in Rich Text Format (RTF—a common interchange format), and tagged text format files. Remember that you don't need to make a text frame first to import text: As we discuss in Chapter 10, all you need to do is choose Place from the File menu, or press Command-D/Ctrl-D. (Though, of course, you can make a frame first if you want.)

Import Filters

As with QuarkXPress, for InDesign to be able to bring in data from another file format, it must have an import filter for that format. The filter decides what information to bring in and what to leave out. There are also options which you can set which affect the import.

For text, word processing and RTF files, InDesign brings in most paragraph and character attributes and ignores most page layout information. It also imports paragraph and character styles if they're saved with the document (we describe working with imported styles in Chapter 58).

Unlike QuarkXPress, InDesign can directly import tables from Microsoft Word documents and Excel spreadsheets (we discuss how to create tables in Chapter 74). QuarkXPress imports tables as tab-delimited text. However, note that InDesign doesn't import Word or Excel files before version 8 (Office 97/98), nor does it import WordPerfect files. For these formats, you should save as RTF files, which should retain formatting attributes. We discuss tagged text in Chapter 60.

Import Options

When you choose the Place command, InDesign offers several import options (see Figure 39-1). Some of the features of the dialog box are specific to your operating system, but there are four checkbox options which are always available:

Figure 39-1

The Place dialog box

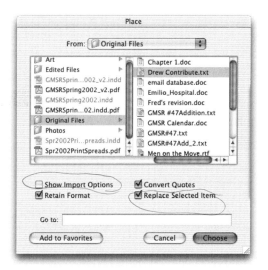

- **Show Import Options.** This tells InDesign to display the Import Options dialog box (after this dialog box closes), which offers different settings depending on the file format. Holding down the Shift key when you select a file does the same thing as turning on this checkbox.

- **Retain Format.** If you turn this on, character and paragraph attributes and styles are retained. If off, character and paragraph attributes are stripped out; however, word processing styles (like bold and italic) are still imported.

- **Convert Quotes** converts straight quotation marks to "curly" typographers' quotes.

- **Replace Selected Item.** When this is on, InDesign goes ahead and places the text (either at the current insertion point or replacing the text in any selected text frame); when off, the program displays the "Place gun."

Typography

Flowing Text

After making your import choices for one of the formats above, click Choose (Mac OS X) or Open (Mac OS 9 and Windows). Then, one of two things happens: If you don't have a frame selected, you'll see the loaded text cursor, which changes depending on where the cursor is and what modifier keys you're holding down (see Figure 39-2). If you have a frame (either text or graphics) selected and the Replace Selected Item option was turned on, InDesign fills the frame with the imported text. (If this was a mistake, just choose Undo Replace from the Edit menu, or press Command-Z/Ctrl-Z, which reloads the "Place gun.")

Figure 39-2

Text flow cursors

Loaded text   *Over frame*   *Semi-autoflow*   *Autoflow*

Manual Flow

You can manually flow text from one unlinked frame to the next by clicking the loaded text cursor anywhere on the page. If you click on a frame, the text is placed into it. If you click elsewhere on the page, InDesign creates a frame and flows the text from the point where you click to the bottom of the page (or to the end of the text, whichever comes first). If there's more text than can fit in that frame, you'll see a plus sign in the out port of the text frame (see Figure 39-3). Instead of clicking, you can also drag out a text frame with the cursor to create the shape of a rectangular frame.

Figure 39-3

Manual text flow

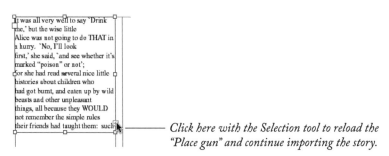

Click here with the Selection tool to reload the "Place gun" and continue importing the story.

To continue manually flowing text, choose the Selection tool and click the frame's out port. Again, you'll see the loaded text cursor, with which you can fill or create a frame elsewhere in your document. Note that you can change pages or scroll around while the loaded text cursor is showing. (You can also cancel further text flow by selecting any other tool in the Tools palette.)

Semi-Autoflow

Semi-autoflow works the same as manual text flow, except that after creating each text frame, the cursor automatically changes to the loaded text cursor so you can create another text frame or fill an existing frame without clicking on the out port. You can choose the semi-autoflow method by holding down the Option/Alt key when placing text. InDesign then displays the semi-autoflow cursor.

Autoflow

If you hold down the Shift key when you click with the loaded text cursor, InDesign flows your text automatically, creating new frames and pages, and linking them automatically (this is the default behavior of XPress). If you Shift-click on a frame from a master page, InDesign automatically adds new document pages and links from one master page text frame to the next (see Chapter 30).

Unfortunately, unlike QuarkXPress, InDesign can't automatically add pages and text frames when editing text—only when importing with the Shift key.

Pasting Text

While placing is usually the preferred way to import text, you can also paste text from another InDesign document, or from some other application. When possible, InDesign always retains character and paragraph formatting attributes and any word processing styling in the pasted text; there is no option to paste as plain text.

Unlinking Imported Text

When you place a text, Word, Excel or RTF file, InDesign creates a link to that file on disk which appears in the Links palette, just as it does when you place a graphics file. You can see the link in the Links palette (choose Links from the Window menu, or press Command-Shift-D/Ctrl-Shift-D to open or close the palette).

This is, of course, very different than XPress. Linking to text files is potentially cool, but in reality it's often just a hassle, and we almost always sever the link by selecting the name of the linked file in the Links palette and selecting Unlink from the palette's flyout menu (see Figure 39-4).

If you don't break the link to the file on disk, and later make changes to this file in your word processor or in Excel, when you reopen the InDesign

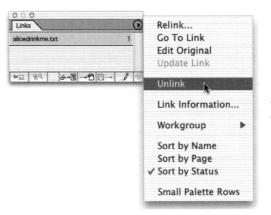

Figure 39-4
A linked text file

Choose Unlink to remove the link to the external text file.

file, the program alerts you that the linked file has been modified, and asks whether you want to update the link. If you click the button to Fix Links, you'll then get a second dialog box which says, "Edits have been made to this object. You will lose these edits by updating. Update anyway?" If you click Yes (the default), any formatting or edits you have applied to the story in InDesign will be lost. The moral of the story is: Don't update the links unless you haven't changed anything in InDesign or you don't mind repeating the changes you have made.

Creating Placeholder Text

InDesign makes it easy to create placeholder text when you're creating a preliminary layout: First, either place an insertion point in a text frame with the Type tool, or select one or more text frames with the Selection tool. Then choose Fill with Placeholder Text from the Type menu or the context menu. Dummy text fills the frames, and continues through any threaded frames.

Of course, this isn't as powerful (or cool) as Quark's Jabberwocky XTension. On the other hand, if you want to use text of your own for a placeholder, create it in any word processor and save it as a text-only file with the name "placeholder.txt" (with no quotes), in your InDesign application folder. The next time you use the Fill with Placeholder Text command, InDesign uses your text instead.

Threading and Unthreading Text Frames

What do you do when you have more text than can fit in one text frame? In this chapter, we'll explain *threading* and *unthreading* text frames. This is the equivalent of using the Link and Unlink tools in QuarkXPress to "chain" together text boxes.

Threading Terminology

InDesign has no text linking tools, like XPress. Instead, when you select a text frame with the Selection tool, you can see an *in port* at the upper left corner of the frame, and an *out port* on the lower right corner (see Figure 40-1). The in port of the first box in a thread is always empty. A red plus sign in the out port of a frame means there's more text than can fit (the text is *overset*). When a triangle appears in an in or out port, it's an indicator that the text thread is continuing: In an in port, there is text coming from another frame preceding this frame; in an out port, text continues in another frame following this frame.

The threading of text frames is indicated by a text thread—a line in the color of the current layer which connects the frames. To see the thread, select any frame in the thread and choose Show/Hide Text Threads from the View menu (or press Command-Option-Y/Ctrl-Alt-Y).

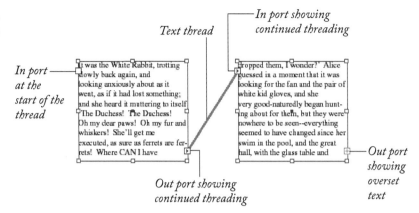

Figure 40-1
Threaded text frames

In port showing
continued threading

Text thread

In port
at the
start of the
thread

Out port
showing
overset
text

Out port showing
continued threading

Threading

It's easy to link text frames together: With the Selection tool, select a frame and then click its out port. You'll see the loaded text cursor (see Figure 40-2). Then you may either:

- Drag out a new text frame. InDesign automatically links the current frame to this new frame.

- Click on another text frame to link the current frame to that one.

If there's a lot of overset text in the first frame, you may also hold down the Option/Alt key to use semi-autoflow or the Shift key to use autoflow, as we described in the previous chapter.

Note that, unlike XPress, you can link two frames together even if they both have text in them. The text from the two frames merges together into a single text story.

Unthreading

To disconnect two frames in the text chain—stopping the text flow at that point—use the Selection tool to select the frame before where you want to make the break and click its out port. The unthreading cursor appears. Now click on either the selected frame or the following frame in the thread. The link is broken and the text will be overset.

You can also unthread in the opposite direction. Select the frame after where you want the break to occur, click the in port of that frame, and then click on the selected frame or the preceding frame.

Figure 40-2
Threading and
unthreading cursors

Loaded text   Threading   Unthreading

Removing a Frame from the Chain

Finally, you may want to remove one or more frames from a text chain. If you want to delete the frame, select it and press the Delete key. The frame is deleted, but the text flows on into the succeeding frames in the chain. (Text is never removed from the chain when a frame is deleted.)

If you want to cut the frame and use it elsewhere, choose Cut from the Edit menu (or press Command-X/Ctrl-X). The text flows into the succeeding frames in the chain. Then go to the page where you the frame to appear, and choose Paste from the Edit menu, or press Command-V/Ctrl-V. The frame appears with the text which was in the previous location, but it is now disconnected from the chain. You can also Option/Alt-drag the text frame with the Selection tool to duplicate it (text and all).

Typography

41

Checking Spelling

Whether you've imported text into your document or typed it directly, you'll probably want to check the spelling before you go to press. When InDesign checks spelling it highlights words which are misspelled or unknown, based on whatever language dictionaries you've assigned to your text (see Chapter 42). Unlike XPress, it also finds double words and capitalization errors—it even flags unknown single-letter words, which XPress ignores.

Picking a Search Range

Like QuarkXPress, InDesign can check the spelling of a word, a selection of text, your current story, or your current document. Unlike XPress, it can also search multiple selected stories and all of your stories in all open documents. It's not necessary to separately check your master pages, as you must do in XPress, since InDesign searches master pages whenever you search your document.

To select a word or a range of text, use the Type tool to make the selection. To select a story, either click within the story with the Type tool, or select the story's frame with the Selection tool (or one frame from a series of linked frames). To select multiple stories, Shift-select their frames with the Selection tool. To search one or more documents, make sure they're open.

After making your selection, choose Check Spelling from the Edit menu (or press Command-I/Ctrl-I). InDesign displays the Check Spelling dialog box (see Figure 41-1). Select the range to be checked in the Search popup menu: Selection, Story, Stories, To End of Story, Document, or All Documents.

Figure 41-1
Check Spelling
dialog box

Performing a Search

When you're ready to begin the spell-checking process, click the Start button. As InDesign searches the text, it highlights each suspect word at the top of the dialog box and displays one of these messages: Not in Dictionary, Capitalization Error, Duplicate Word or Unknown Word. Unlike XPress, InDesign shows replacement suggestions from its dictionary immediately.

- If you'd like InDesign to skip the word and not change anything, click either Ignore or Ignore All. Selecting Ignore skips the current instance of the word. Selecting Ignore All skips all instances of the word until you quit InDesign.

- If you'd like InDesign to replace the word, either type in the correct word in the Change To field or select a word in the Suggested Corrections list. Click Change to change that single instance of the word, or Change All to search the current range and change all instances. After a Change All command, InDesign displays a dialog box telling you how many replacements were made.

- If you'd like InDesign to add the word to your user-editable dictionary, click Add to open the Dictionary dialog box (we discuss this in Chapter 42). Note that it's not necessary to open an auxiliary dictionary first to add a word, as it is in XPress.

When InDesign has completed the search, it displays a Spell Check Complete message. If you want to stop the search before completion, just click the Done button.

42

Foreign Languages and Dictionaries

Many people in the United States are brought up with a pretty ethnocentric point of view, and we're only used to communicating in one language. But working in multiple languages is increasingly an everyday reality. In this chapter we discuss how InDesign compares with QuarkXPress in working with multiple languages, and in customizing the dictionaries used for checking spelling and hyphenation.

Foreign Languages

QuarkXPress is a single-language application. When you want to work in more than one language, Quark requires that you buy a more expensive version of the program called Passport. If you use Passport, you can set language as a paragraph attribute, and then use the application to spell check and hyphenate in the 12 supported languages. However, if you're exchanging a file with a regular QuarkXPress user, you must save the file in a single-language version, where you lose the language-specific spell checking and hyphenation.

InDesign takes a more international point of view: Out of the box, it includes 20 dictionaries for 12 languages which are used for spell-checking and hyphenation. (However, to use languages beyond those included—like Japanese or Hebrew—you must purchase a special language edition of InDesign.)

Figure 42-1

Applying a language
to text with the
Character palette.

The extra dictionaries are not installed by default. To use them, you must do a custom install from the InDesign 2.0 installer CD. On the Macintosh, when you get to the step where the default choice is Easy Install, instead select Custom Install and then turn on the Dictionaries option. In Windows, when you get to the step where the default is Typical, click Custom and then turn on the Dictionaries option. Then continue with the installation process. (Yes, if you've already installed InDesign, you can install the dictionaries by themselves.)

Applying Language to Text

InDesign sees language as a character attribute, not a paragraph attribute as in QuarkXPress Passport. That means you can select any amount of text you want with the Type tool and choose a language in the Language popup menu on the Character palette (see Figure 42-1). You can also set a character or paragraph style to a specific language. (Note that before you can include a language in a character or paragraph style, you must have already applied the language to text somewhere in the document. The styles dialog boxes and the Find/Change dialog box only lists languages that you've actually used.)

This means you can mix languages within the same paragraph, and when InDesign is either spell-checking or hyphenating, it uses the appropriate language dictionary for the text it is working with.

Adding or Removing Words

InDesign handles dictionaries for spell checking and hyphenation differently than QuarkXPress. In XPress, you can't add or change words in its standard dictionary. Instead, you must first create or open an auxiliary dictionary. Then, when spell-checking, XPress uses both dictionaries. To change the way QuarkXPress hyphenates words, you can enter words in its Hyphenation Exceptions dialog box; this information is stored in the XPress Preferences file and is applied globally to all documents.

In InDesign, you add or remove words using the Dictionary dialog box (see Figure 42-2), which you can get to by selecting Dictionary from the Edit menu or by clicking the Add button in the Check Spelling dialog box (see Chapter 41). If you have a word selected in your text or the Check Spelling dialog box, it appears in the Word field—or you can just type one in. Then fill out the other settings in the Dictionary dialog box:

Figure 42-2
The Dictionary dialog box

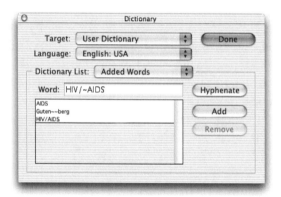

- Choose a language dictionary from the Language popup menu.

- When you add or remove words in a dictionary, InDesign actually adds the word to one of two lists: the Added Words exception list and the Removed Words exception list. For example, words added in the English (USA) language are stored in the ENG.UDC file. Select either Added Words or Removed Words from the Dictionary List popup menu.

- To change where the added or removed word is stored, use the Target popup menu. The default is the external user dictionary, but you can select any currently open document instead. The advantage of storing in the document is that this makes the change transportable. The advantage of storing exceptions outside the document is that you can use them with multiple documents.

- Finally, click the Add button to add the word to the exception list.

Hyphenation Points

You can examine InDesign's hyphenation break-points for a word, or change them if you like. In the Dictionary dialog box, when there is a word in the Word field, click Hyphenate to see that word's default hyphenation. InDesign's dictionaries rank syllable breaks for desirability. You can change these hyphenation points:

- Type one tilde (~) to indicate the best (or only) hyphenation point.

- Type two tildes (~~) for your second choice point.

- If necessary, type three tildes (~~~) for your last choice point.

- To prevent hyphenation, type a tilde before the first letter.

  When you're finished editing your added words, click Done.

Removing Words

To remove a word from one of the exceptions lists, choose Dictionary from the Edit menu. In the Target menu, choose the dictionary (external or document) from which you want to remove a word. Choose whether you want to modify the list of Added Words or Removed Words in the Dictionary List menu. In the word list, select the word and click Remove. When you're finished editing the lists, click Done.

Typography

43

Think Outside the Box: InDesign and Fonts

When it comes to fonts, QuarkXPress goes strictly by the book: It totally relies on your operating system for font selection and display. However, by sticking to that conservative approach, QuarkXPress users can't take advantage of recent advances in font technology. Furthermore, this approach means that there are differences between the way XPress handles fonts cross-platform. For instance, you can only access 256 characters from a font, and not the same ones on each platform. (Did you know that fonts often have more than 256 characters in them? Neither did we until we started using InDesign.)

Adobe applications—including InDesign—march to a different drummer. They share a core font technology called CoolType. This technology works with the Adobe Graphics Manager to rasterize PostScript and True-Type fonts for the screen and printers. Fonts render at high quality, even when highly magnified, without relying on the operating system or extensions like Adobe Type Manager (ATM). CoolType also creates InDesign's font menus and determines the characters (glyphs) which can be displayed. Adobe's approach applies cross-platform consistency to its font display and opens InDesign up to some important new font features.

InDesign's Font Folder

Look closely and you'll notice a Fonts folder inside the InDesign folder. Fonts in this folder are only available to InDesign, and you can add fonts (or even aliases or shortcuts to fonts) to the folder at any time, even while InDesign is running. Because the fonts in this Fonts folder are managed by InDesign rather than the system, even if you use a Macintosh you can put Windows fonts in here. Similarly, Multiple Master fonts are no longer supported in Mac OS X, but you can put old font instances that you built in OS 9 into InDesign's Fonts folder in OS X and use them in InDesign.

Font Menus

InDesign creates its own hierarchical font menus, organized by font family. (You can do this in XPress only with a third-party XTension or a system extension like the old Adobe Type Reunion.) Its menu scheme is quite sophisticated. The Adobe Garamond and ITC Garamond font families, for example, are alphabetized with other Garamond fonts in the "G"s (see Figure 43-1).

Figure 43-1
InDesign's font menus are arranged by family.

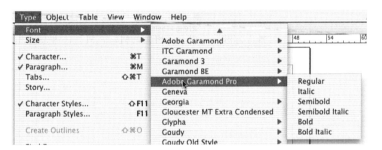

In QuarkXPress it's very easy to select a font and apply a type style (like Bold or Italic) that doesn't actually exist in the font. Onscreen, the font may be emboldened or obliqued, but if the font doesn't contain the style, it will print in an incorrect way to a PostScript printer. By contrast, InDesign's font menus only list the type styles which actually exist in the font, and it's not possible to pick a non-existing style.

QuarkXPress's Style menu and Measurement palette also include the Outline and Shadow type styles. XPress lets the operating system build these effects, and they print poorly on high-resolution printers. While InDesign doesn't include these styles, you can create a high-quality outline effect for type by adding a stroke to type and you can make much better shadows using the transparency effects we describe in Chapter 85.

Access to All Characters

In QuarkXPress, you only have access to the characters—also called "glyphs"—which are *encoded* for the operating system. (Encoding is the process of assigning glyphs in a font to numeric slots so they can be used by an application.) QuarkXPress and older versions of the Windows and Macintosh operating systems only support single-byte fonts, which can contain a maximum of 256 characters (in practice, since some positions in a font are reserved, about 224 glyphs). Fonts usually contain more glyphs than the system can display. For example, Macintosh users can type the *fi* and *fl* ligatures, but those using Windows cannot. Those running Windows can type a font's built-in ¼, ½ and ¾ fractions, but Mac users can't. Platform differences like this can cause font substitution in a cross-platform environment.

In addition, having so few characters in a font is a severe limitation if you work in a multilingual environment, and is impossible if you're using with Asian fonts. It's also very constricting if you want to create high-quality typography including correctly built fractions, ligatures, special ornaments, or true small caps, for example. To get around these limitations, some users purchase special "expert" sets of fonts, but using these requires extra manual work.

InDesign's font technology gives you access to all the characters in a font—even if there are thousands of glyphs. We describe this more in Chapter 51.

OpenType Font Support

The biggest advance in fonts in the past decade is the advent of OpenType fonts, a new font format developed by Adobe and Microsoft and introduced in 2000.

OpenType fonts have several advantages:

- They use a cross-platform format and store their data in a single file. The same font file can be used on either the Macintosh or Windows platforms.

- They use in an industry-standard double-byte encoding called Unicode which can support over 64,000 glyphs. As a result, a single font can now contain all the characters for several different languages—and also contain the glyphs used in fine typography.

- They support high quality typography through the use of standardized layout tables. This makes it possible for an Open Type-smart application like InDesign to automatically call out these typographic features without extra effort.

InDesign 2 comes with five OpenType font families: three Roman families—Adobe Garamond Pro, Adobe Caslon Pro, and Caflisch Script Pro—and two Japanese families—Kozuka Gothic and Kozuka Mincho. If these fonts aren't installed automatically, you can find them in the Goodies folder on the InDesign installation CD.

OpenType fonts work in in XPress, but you only get access to the first 256 characters, as though they were normal PostScript fonts. InDesign 2.0 gives access to all the glyphs of an OpenType font, which we also discuss in Chapter 51.

Typography

44

Character Formatting

In this chapter, we're beginning to consider the kinds of formatting which can be applied to text, and how that is done in InDesign. As in Quark-XPress, you can format text on a character level or a paragraph level. This chapter focuses on character-level formatting, including selecting such things as typeface, font size, type styling attributes, and so on. One big difference between the programs: InDesign treats leading as a character attribute, rather than as a paragraph attribute. Fortunately, we'll tell you about a preference that can change that.

Selecting Text for Formatting

As with many other functions, InDesign gives you more flexibility than QuarkXPress in how you select text for formatting. Besides the obvious method of using the Type tool to select a range of text in a text frame, you can also:

- Use the Selection tool to select one or more unlinked text frames. Formatting applies to all the text in the selected frames. This can be a very quick way of selecting several small text frames—captions, for example—and formatting them all at the same time.

- In addition, character attributes can be copied with the Eyedropper tool and applied to other type. You can choose which attributes are copied. We discuss this in Chapter 82.

Basic Character Formatting

It's worth mentioning that character formatting can be applied locally to selected text or text frames—which is what we're talking about here—or it can be applied using character styles (see Chapter 55). We'll start by considering the text attributes you change the most: typeface, font size, and leading.

Typeface

QuarkXPress lets you set the typeface with the Measurements palette, the Style menu, and the Character Attributes dialog box. InDesign uses the Character palette (see Figure 44-1) and the Type menu (see Chapter 43). As we mention in the previous chapter, InDesign creates its own hierarchical font menus based on font family, so the order of your fonts in the list may be different than you expect.

Figure 44-1
The Character palette

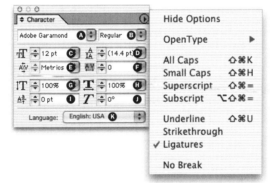

A	*Font family*
B	*Type style*
C	*Font size*
D	*Leading*
E	*Kerning*
F	*Tracking*
G	*Vertical scale*
H	*Horizontal scale*
I	*Baseline shift*
J	*Skew*
K	*Language*

If the Character palette isn't visible, you can choose Character from the Type menu. You can also press Command-T/Ctrl-T, which also activates the Font family field. As in XPress, you type the first few characters of a typeface name and the menu jumps to the proper font. Note that you can use the Up and Down Arrow keys on the keyboard to skip to the previous or next font in the list. You can also choose a typeface by selecting it from the Font submenu in the Type menu.

Font Size

You can choose type size in the Character palette or the Type menu. Like XPress, InDesign offers preset sizes and also lets you type your own. Unlike XPress, you can make text up to 1296 points (18 inches) large, and use the

Up and Down Arrow keys to adjust the size in 1-point increments. (Hold down the Shift key to change the size in 10-point increments.)

Finally, there are keyboard shortcuts similar to those in XPress for changing size incrementally: Command-Shift-period/Ctrl-Shift-period to increase, and Command-Shift-comma/Ctrl-Shift-comma to decrease the size by 2 points. However, InDesign allows you to set the increment in the Units & Increments Preferences (see Chapter 7). Adding the Option/Alt key to the keyboard shortcut multiplies the increment by five.

Leading

QuarkXPress users may wonder why InDesign considers leading a character attribute instead of a paragraph attribute. In fact, arguments can be made for either choice. (The real reason is probably that Adobe PageMaker, Illustrator and Photoshop do it that way!) What's important is that you can set it the way you want. If you like the XPress way of doing it, choose the Text Preferences (see Chapter 7), and turn on the Apply Leading to Entire Paragraphs option. Do this when no documents are open, and it will apply to all new documents you create.

In InDesign, you can set leading in the Character palette or with keystrokes. In the Character palette, use similar methods to those described above: select a preset value, type your own value, or use the up/down arrows to change the leading value. Leading can be set in .001-point increments from 0 to 5000 points. You can also change leading for selected characters (or paragraphs) by pressing the Option/Alt key and the up/down arrows. The default—2-point increments—can be changed in Units & Increments Preferences. Adding the Command/Ctrl key to the keyboard shortcut multiplies the incremental value by five.

InDesign doesn't have XPress's more arcane leading methods—relative leading or word processing mode. But it does let you set automatic (Auto) leading. If you see a number in the Leading menu surrounded by parentheses, that's the current Auto leading value. To select Auto leading, choose Auto from the Leading popup menu on the Character palette. Ironically, Auto leading—normally 120% of the font size of the largest character, the same as in XPress—is based on a setting in the Justification dialog box in the *Paragraph* palette menu!

Kerning and Tracking

Kerning and tracking remove or add space between character pairs. *Kerning* adjusts spacing between two characters. *Tracking* changes the spacing for all character pairs in a range of text (sometimes it's referred to as *range kerning*, as in Adobe PageMaker). Kerning and tracking are measured in units relative to the size of the typeface—in *ems*. Note that by default XPress defines an em as the width of two zeros next to each other in a given font and size. InDesign uses a more standard value: An em equals the point size, so in 24-point text, one em is 24 points wide.

QuarkXPress lets you manually kern character pairs or use the automatic kern values ("metrics") built into the font. It also lets you set up kerning tables with the Kerning Table Edit feature. InDesign supports both manual kerning and metrics kerning. It also introduces a new method called Optical kerning. Metrics and Optical kerning can be part of a paragraph or character style; manual kerning cannot. InDesign has no kerning table function; if you want to build kerning tables, you'll have to edit the font using a font utility such as FontLab or Fontographer.

Metrics Kerning

Normally, if you select a range of text you'll see the word "Metrics" on the Kerning popup menu in the Character palette. If you click an insertion point between two characters, the Kerning menu shows the value of the font kern pair in thousandths of an em: It will show a number like "0" (no kerning) or "(–70)" (which means that the current font has a kern pair that reduces the space by $70/1,000$ of an em). To apply Metrics kerning (removing any manual kerning), select a range of characters with the Type tool or one or more unlinked text frames with the Selection tool, then choose Metrics in the Kerning menu.

Manual Kerning

If you want to manually kern in InDesign, place the text insertion point between two characters. Then, in the Kerning field of the Character palette, either choose from the preset kerning values in the popup menu, type your own value, or use the up/down arrows to change the units of kerning (add Shift to increase/decrease in larger increments). You can also use keystrokes: Hold down the Option/Alt key, and press the Left or Right Arrow keys to decrease or increase the space—by default in $20/1,000$ of an em, though you can change this in the Units & Increments Preferences. Adding the Command/Ctrl key to the keyboard shortcut multiplies the value by five. Manual kerning overrides Metrics and Optical kerning.

Typography

Optical Kerning

If you choose Optical kerning, InDesign uses a different approach: It calculates the kerning values based on the optical appearance of the character shapes. This can often better handle situations where fonts and sizes are mixed (see Figure 44-2). To apply Optical kerning, select a range of characters with the Type tool (or one or more unlinked text frames with the Selection tool), then choose Optical in the Kerning popup menu. The menu displays "Optical," for the selected text, but if you click an insertion point between two characters, InDesign shows you the actual kerning value.

Figure 44-2
Optical kerning is great with mixed sizes or fonts.

Wonderful
Optical kerning off

Wonderful
Optical kerning on

Word Space Kerning

In addition, InDesign supports *word space kerning*. This adjusts kerning only for the space bands in a range of text. (You can do this in XPress only if you've installed the Type Tricks XTension and have an extended keyboard.) To add space between words, select a range of text, then press Command-Option-Shift-Backslash/Ctrl-Alt-Shift-Backslash. To tighten space, press use Delete rather than Backslash.

Tracking

Tracking in InDesign and XPress are almost identical. You can set tracking values in InDesign by selecting a range of text and using the Tracking menu in the Character palette or with keystrokes (hold down Option/Alt and press either the Left or Right Arrow keys on your keyboard). Tracking is measured in thousandths of an em, and can be used in a style. Note that InDesign lacks XPress's tracking tables function.

By the way, don't try the keyboard shortcuts for tracking, kerning, or leading if you've selected a text frame with the Selection tool; then Option/Alt plus the Arrow keys duplicates the frame!

Type Styles

QuarkXPress has 13 character-level styles which can be applied to type. These are applied using icons on the Measurement palette, with the Style menu, or with the Character Attributes dialog box. InDesign has direct equivalents for most of those attributes (see Table 44-1), though you apply some of them differently than in XPress. In addition, InDesign has two character-level attributes—ligatures and no break—which don't exist in XPress.

Table 44-1 Character styles

To create this style...	Do this...	Or use this keystroke
Plain text	Use Font Family popup menu	Ctrl/Command-Shift-Y
Bold	Use Font Family popup menu	Ctrl/Command-Shift-B
Italic	Use Font Family popup menu	Ctrl/Command-Shift-I
Outline	Stroke the type	
Shadow	Use the Drop Shadow feature	Command-Option/Ctrl-Alt-M
Strikethrough	Use Character palette flyout menu	Ctrl/Command-Shift-forward slash
Underline	Use Character palette flyout menu	Ctrl/Command-Shift-U
Word underline	Style not supported	
Small caps	Use Character palette flyout menu	Ctrl/Command-Shift-H
All caps	Use Character palette flyout menu	Ctrl/Command-Shift-K
Superscript	Use Character palette flyout menu	Ctrl/Command-Shift-Equals
Subscript	Use Character palette flyout menu	Command-Option-Shift-Equals/ Ctrl-Alt-Shift-Equals
Superior	Style not supported; use Superscript	

Font Styling

InDesign controls its own font menus, and only type styles which actually exist in the font appear in the Font Family menu on the Character palette and in the Font menu under the Type menu. To choose font styling (Plain, Bold or Italic), pick a typeface using one of these methods, or use a keyboard shortcut.

If you press the keyboard shortcut for bold or italic, InDesign will only apply the style if those font styles actually exist. However, these shortcuts may not work the same with every font. For example, Sumner Stone, the designer of Adobe's Stone Sans, Stone Serif and Stone Informal families, decided that the Bold command should call out the semibold weight of the font instead of the bold weight.

Underline and Strikethrough

InDesign uses the same Underline and Strikethrough type styles as QuarkXPress. The strikethrough thickness is ½ point, but the underline thickness varies with the font size. Unfortunately, there are no controls in InDesign for setting the line thickness or offset for either type style. There is no match for XPress's Word Underline style. You must create that manually by removing the Underline style from space bands (see Chapter 52 for a shortcut technique).

All Caps and Small Caps

InDesign includes the same All Caps and Small Caps type styles that QuarkXPress has, but InDesign's implementation is more sophisticated. These type styles are found on the Character palette's flyout menu. Applying the All Caps style does not change the case of the type, only its appearance (to change the case, use the Change Case command described below). Applying the Small Caps style calls out the small cap glyphs if they exist in the font (as is the case with many "pro" OpenType fonts). If they don't exist, InDesign does the same thing as XPress: It synthesizes them using the settings in Text Preferences, reducing the text size.

If you apply the All Caps and Small Caps styles to OpenType fonts, it applies more typographically sophisticated changes. For example, if you apply All Caps, it shifts certain punctuation marks vertically so their appearance in improved.

Changing Case

In addition to the type styles described in the previous section, InDesign has Change Case commands in the Type menu. These aren't really type styles; they're more like functions you can use to change text characters. There are four Change Case commands:

- Uppercase actually changes the characters to the uppercase characters, rather than simply changing their appearance. We'd rather just use the All Caps style.

- Lowercase changes all characters to lowercase characters.

- Title Case capitalizes the first letter of each word.

- Sentence case capitalizes the first letter of each sentence.

Changing Position

QuarkXPress has three type styles for offsetting a character from the baseline and optionally scaling it smaller: superscript, subscript and superior. InDesign has two: superscript and subscript, both of which are found on the Character palette flyout menu. You can set the preferences for the size and position for each of these in the Text panel of the Preferences dialog box.

If you're using an OpenType font which contains real superscript and subscript glyphs for the characters you're using, you can instead choose Superscript/Superior or Subscript/Inferior from the OpenType submenu (in the Character palette's flyout menu).

Ligatures

A *ligature* is a character that combines two or more characters into one. The most common examples are the *fi* and *fl* ligatures which are part of the Macintosh font encoding (but not Windows). Unlike QuarkXPress, InDesign applies ligatures as a character attribute. (For XPress it's a document preference which is applied globally.) Ligatures can also be included in a character or paragraph style.

When you turn on ligatures (from the flyout menu in the Character palette) with an OpenType font, InDesign uses any standard ligatures which the font designer has included in the font. Additionally, however, you can choose Discretionary Ligatures on the OpenType submenu, and turn on additional discretionary and historical ligatures which may be defined in the font (see Figure 44-3).

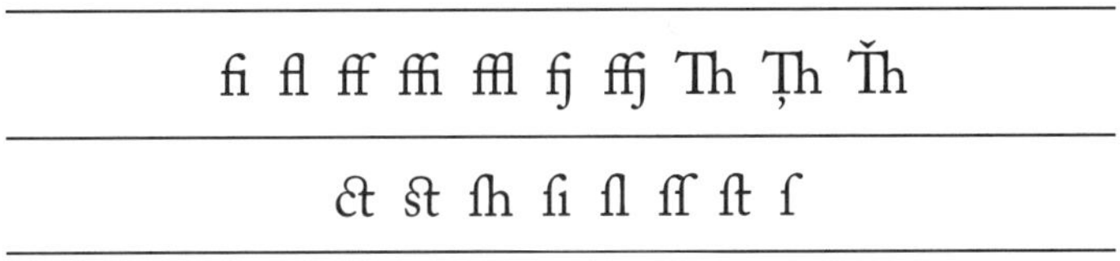

Figure 44-3
Standard and
discretionary ligatures
in the OpenType font
Adobe Caslon Pro

No Break

When you want to keep a word or words from breaking in QuarkXPress, you can either use a discretionary hyphen or non-breaking spaces and hyphens. InDesign lets you use those methods, but also adds another option: You can keep a range of selected characters from breaking by applying the No Break type style, found on the Character palette menu; this can also be included in a character or paragraph style. When you use it, InDesign attempts to keep the selected characters on the same line. It's not a good idea to apply this to more than one or two words because if all the characters can't fit on one line, the rest of the story gets overset!

Other Character Formatting

As long as the list of character formats which we've already covered is, there are still a few more to add. Several of these are familiar to XPress users: applying horizontal and vertical scaling, color and shade, and baseline shift. Two are new: InDesign lets you skew type, and apply a language attribute. All of these attributes can be included in character and paragraph styles.

Horizontal and Vertical Scaling

Horizontal or vertical scaling artificially compresses or expands characters, distorting their shapes. In QuarkXPress, when you want to apply horizontal or vertical scaling, you choose the command from the Style menu or the Character Attributes dialog box. There you may set either a horizontal or vertical scaling value, but not both.

InDesign allows you to set horizontal and vertical scaling for type independently using controls on the Character palette. There is no keyboard shortcut for horizontal/vertical scaling, as there is in XPress.

Color, Tint, Gradient and Stroke

QuarkXPress gives you the ability to set character color and shade using the Style menu or the Color palette. InDesign provides similar character formatting controls to apply color and shade (InDesign calls it "tint") in the Swatches palette and the Color palette. In addition to applying color to text, InDesign also supports applying a gradient, and stroking text characters. We discuss these features in Part 8, Color and Transparency.

Baseline Shift

Baseline shift moves characters above or below the baseline, the imaginary line on which your type sits. In XPress, you choose this feature from the Style menu, in the Character Attributes dialog box, or with a keystroke. In InDesign, you choose a value in the Baseline Shift field on the Character palette. Positive values shift characters above the baseline; negative values shift them below the baseline. To baseline shift selected text, either type in a value in points, or click the up/down arrows to increase or decrease the offset value in 1-point increments. You can also use a keyboard shortcut: hold down the Option-Shift/Alt-Shift keys and press the Up or Down Arrow keys to increase or decrease the baseline shift in 2-point increments (you can change this in the Units & Increments Preferences dialog box). Adding the Command/Ctrl key to the keyboard shortcut multiplies the incremental change by five.

Skew

The *skew* type style lets you create a false italic effect in a font which lacks that feature (see Figure 44-4). It distorts the characters in the process, similar to the way horizontal or vertical scaling does. You can apply this type style in InDesign by choosing a value in the Skew field on the Character palette. Enter a skew angle in degrees, or click the up/down arrows to increase or decrease the angle in 1-degree increments. Holding down the Shift key while clicking the arrows uses 4-degree increments. A positive angle slants forward; a negative angle slants backward.

Figure 44-4

A font with skew applied (above), compared to a true italic font (below).

How doth the little crocodile
Improve his shining tail

How doth the little crocodile
Improve his shining tail

Language

You may assign language as a character attribute to text at the bottom of the Character palette. This is useful when you want to check spelling or hyphenate based on another language's dictionary (see Chapter 42).

Typography

45

Paragraph Formatting

As you work with text, you organize characters into words and words into paragraphs. When you work on a paragraph level, you shape the way text looks by defining its horizontal alignment, spacing, indents and tabs, baseline grid, text composition, hyphenation and justification, and you create attributes like drop caps and rules. We begin to discuss how InDesign controls paragraph formatting in this chapter. The discussion continues in succeeding chapters: We discuss composition in Chapter 46, hyphenation and justification in Chapter 48, and tabs in Chapter 49. We cover paragraph rules in Chapter 70.

Selecting Paragraphs

InDesign provides several ways to select text when you're using paragraph formatting:

- As in XPress, you can place the text insertion point anywhere in the paragraph; you don't have to select the whole paragraph. Similarly, you can select a range of text in a text frame with the Type tool. Formatting applies to paragraphs included in the range, even if you don't select all the text in a paragraph.

- Unlike XPress, you can use the Selection tool to select one or more unlinked text frames. Formatting applies to all the text in the selected frames.

- In addition, paragraph attributes can be copied with the Eyedropper tool and applied to other type (see Chapter 82).

Alignment and Spacing

Some alignment and spacing choices are tied to the text frame. These include inset spacing, first baseline, and vertical alignment; we discuss these in Chapter 50. For now, we'll discuss how to control space within and around paragraphs.

The control center for paragraph alignment in InDesign is the Paragraph palette (see Figure 45-1). If the Paragraph palette isn't open, you can choose Paragraph from the Type menu (or press Command-M/Ctrl-M, which also selects the Left Indent field in the palette). To see all the palette's choices, choose Show Options from the palette menu.

Figure 45-1
The Paragraph palette

A *Align left*
B *Align center*
C *Align right*
D *Justify with last line aligned left*
E *Justify with last line aligned center*
F *Justify with last line aligned right*
G *Justify all lines*
H *Left indent*
I *Right indent*
J *First line indent*
K *Do not align to baseline grid*
L *Align to baseline grid*
M *Space before*
N *Space after*
O *Drop cap number of lines*
P *Drop cap number of characters*
Q *Hyphenate checkbox*

Leading

If you're expecting us to talk about leading as a paragraph attribute here, you're looking in the wrong place! InDesign, by default, considers leading to be a character attribute, although you can make it apply to an entire paragraph (see Chapter 44).

Horizontal Alignment

Five of the seven horizontal alignment buttons in InDesign's Paragraph palette duplicate the alignments in XPress. The last two offer new options: setting the last line of justified text center aligned or right aligned. We usually use the keystrokes we know from QuarkXPress: You can hold down the Command-Shift/Ctrl-Shift keys, and press L for left, C for center, R for right, J for justified (last line aligned left). The only difference is the shortcut for force justifying all lines: Command-Shift-F/Ctrl-Shift-F.

Left and Right Indents

InDesign shares the same basic paragraph indent commands as Quark-XPress—left indent, right indent, and first line indent—each of which you can set in InDesign's Paragraph or Tabs palettes.

By default, indent values are displayed in the units shown on the horizontal ruler, but you may use any measurement units InDesign supports: Type *i*, *in*, or " for inches, *pt* for points, *p* for picas, *mm* for millimeters, *cm* for centimeters, or *c* for ciceros. If you're typing in a number, press Tab or Enter to make the indent take effect. You can also press the arrow buttons or the Up/Down Arrow keys to nudge the amount smaller or larger; the increments are bigger if you press the Shift key.

We'll discuss different methods of creating hanging indents when we talk about hung punctuation in Chapter 47.

If you like working interactively rather than numerically, you can set your indents on InDesign's Tabs palette (see Figure 45-2). To open the palette, choose Tabs from the Type menu or press Command-Shift-T/Ctrl-Shift-T. We explore the Tabs palette in detail in Chapter 48; here we'll just discuss its indent features. Use one of these methods to position indents:

Figure 45-2
The Tabs palette showing the first line indent set at 0.5 inches.

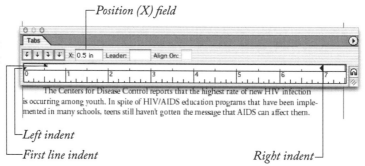

Position (X) field

Left indent

First line indent

Right indent

- Drag the top marker on the left side to indent the first line. Drag the bottom marker on the left to move both left markers and set the left indent for the paragraph. Drag the right marker to set the right indent. As you move these markers, InDesign displays their numeric position in the Position (X) field.

- Click on one of the indent markers to select it, type an indent value in the Position (X) field, then press Enter.

Space Before and After

Both XPress and InDesign let you set space before and after paragraphs. In InDesign you can use the Paragraph palette's Space Before and Space After fields. Either type a value into the fields and press Enter, place the cursor in one of these fields and press the Up/Down Arrow keys, or click the up/down arrows next to the field. As in XPress, Space Before has no effect at the top of a column of text and Space After has no effect at the bottom of a column of text.

Baseline Grid

InDesign supports using a document-wide baseline grid to align paragraphs, just as QuarkXPress does. We rarely uses baseline grids because we think that you can get the same quality—and more flexibility—with careful use of leading and the Space Before/Space After values.

However, should you wish to use this feature, the settings which control the baseline grid are in the Grids Preferences dialog box (see Chapter 7). There you'll find choices for the grid color, start value, and increment, which normally should match the document's leading. While XPress has all those, InDesign adds a twist: You can set a View Threshold value. For example, if you set this to 100%, the baseline grid is invisible at magnifications lower than 100%, but appears when you are zoomed in.

If you want to anchor a paragraph to the baseline grid, click the Align to Baseline Grid icon on the Paragraph palette (or press Command-Option-Shift-G/Ctrl-Alt-Shift-G to turn it on or off). To remove the anchoring, click the Do Not Align to Baseline Grid icon. You can display or hide the baseline grid from the View menu or by pressing Command-Option-'/Ctrl-Alt-' (quote mark).

Note that InDesign also includes a secret, hidden baseline alignment feature (which XPress does not have): You can align just the first baseline of a paragraph to the grid. Open the keyboard shortcuts editor (see Chapter 6), select Text and Tables from the Product area popup menu, and scroll down the feature list until you see Only Align First Line to Grid. Assign a shortcut to this, and then you can use it on any paragraph for which Align to Baseline Grid is turned on.

Drop Caps

Drop caps work identically in InDesign and XPress, though here you set them in the Paragraph Attributes palette. The palette contains two drop cap fields: Number of Lines and Number of Characters. While a drop cap usually consists of a single character, you can also create a multi-character drop cap for special effects (see Figure 45-3).

Figure 45-3
This multi-character drop cap has been created using options on the Paragraph palette.

By the way, the old XPress tip for adjusting the space between a drop cap and the text which follows also works in InDesign: Adjust the kerning between the drop cap and the next character.

Keep Options

InDesign's Keep Options dialog box helps you eliminate widows and orphans in text as well as control how paragraphs stay together. You can find these choices by choosing Keep Options on the Paragraph palette's flyout menu, or by pressing Command-Option-K/Ctrl-Alt-K (see Figure 45-4). QuarkXPress has two similar features—Keep with Next ¶ and Keep Lines Together—but InDesign also adds a handy Start Paragraph feature. Notice there is also a Preview checkbox in this dialog box which is similar to XPress's Apply button.

Figure 45-4
The Keep Options dialog box

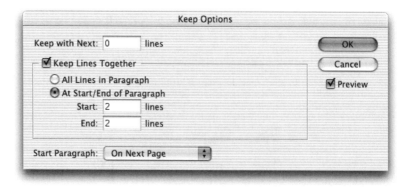

Keep with Next

The Keep with Next option lets you specify how many lines (up to five) of the following paragraph must stay with the current paragraph. (XPress only lets you keep with one subsequent paragraph.) Usually you'll use this to keep a heading with the paragraph which follows it.

Keep Lines Together

The Keep Lines Together feature has identical choices to those in XPress: All Lines in Paragraph and Lines At Start/End of Paragraph. By using these options you can control orphans and widows by deciding whether all lines in a paragraph are kept together, or just a couple of beginning and ending lines.

Start Paragraph

The Start Paragraph menu (there's no equivalent XPress feature), you can force a paragraph to begin in the next column, frame, page, or even the next odd or even page.

Typography

46

Composition

Composition is the complex process of fitting words into lines by weighing the hyphenation and justification settings (which we talk about in Chapter 48) and the break-points specified in hyphenation dictionaries (which we discuss in Chapter 42). Steve, who worked as a typesetter a long time ago, remembers using dedicated systems to compose the high-quality justified text demanded by art directors. But when graphic designers started using QuarkXPress and PageMaker to set type themselves, they lost some of the quality of the type composition because these applications used simpler ways of calculating line endings than the dedicated systems. Justified type didn't look as good any more so more type was set flush left (ragged right) to compensate. The difference was in the quality of the composer—the software which decides where lines break.

Single-line vs. Paragraph Composers

Single-line composers—like the ones in QuarkXPress and Adobe Page-Maker—only sets one line of type at a time, ignoring the lines above and below it. The result of this process is that, while many lines may look fine, some lines in a parargraph will be looser or tighter, giving an overall unevenness to the "color" of justified type.

InDesign includes a single-line composer, too, but it also has a "paragraph composer" which almost always sets better-looking type.

Paragraph Composition

A paragraph composer has a more complex job: While it uses the same rules for hyphenation and justification as the single-line composer (based on the Hyphenation and Justification dialog boxes; see Chapter 48), it looks through all the words of the paragraph in deciding how lines should end. It evaluates a complex network of choices—sometimes looking backward—and moves words up and down between lines until the best overall appearance is reached (see Figure 46-1). You can see this process when typing in InDesign. As you type, words you already have typed are shifted up and down, or hyphenated.

Figure 46-1

Single-line and Paragraph composer

So she was considering in her own mind (as well as she could, for the hot day made her feel very sleepy and stupid), whether the pleasure of making a daisy-chain would be worth the trouble of getting up and picking the daisies, when suddenly a White Rabbit with pink eyes ran close by her.

There was nothing so *very* remarkable in that; nor did Alice think it so *very* much out of the way to hear the Rabbit say to itself, "Oh dear! Oh dear! I shall be late!" (when she thought it over afterwards, it occurred to her that she ought to have wondered at this, but at the time it all seemed quite natural); but when the Rabbit actually *took a watch out of its waistcoat-pocket,* and looked at it, and then hurried on, Alice started to her feet, for it flashed across her mind that she had never before seen a rabbit with either a waistcoat-pocket, or a watch

Single-line composition in QuarkXPress

So she was considering in her own mind (as well as she could, for the hot day made her feel very sleepy and stupid), whether the pleasure of making a daisy-chain would be worth the trouble of getting up and picking the daisies, when suddenly a White Rabbit with pink eyes ran close by her.

There was nothing so *very* remarkable in that; nor did Alice think it so *very* much out of the way to hear the Rabbit say to itself, "Oh dear! Oh dear! I shall be late!" (when she thought it over afterwards, it occurred to her that she ought to have wondered at this, but at the time it all seemed quite natural); but when the Rabbit actually took a watch out of its waistcoat-pocket, and looked at it, and then hurried on, Alice started to her feet, for it flashed across her mind that she had never before seen a rabbit with either a waistcoat-pocket, or a watch to take out of it, and burning with curiosity, she ran

Paragraph composition in InDesign

Most of the time, you'll probably want to compose your type using the Adobe Paragraph Composer, which is InDesign's default choice. Occasionally, you may want to try the single-line composer. For example, type set with the single-line composer usually takes up slightly more space, so you might want to choose this to match the copyfitting of a legacy document.

You can choose among the two composers in the Paragraph palette's flyout menu, or when creating a paragraph style.

Composition Preferences

InDesign has a Composition Preferencees dialog box where you can flag lines which have composition problems (see Chapter 7). For instance, if you turn on H&J Violations and Keep Violations options, lines that exceed the limits set in the Hyphenation and Justification dialog boxes, or in the Keep Options dialog box, are displayed in a shade of yellow.

Hanging Indents and Punctuation

This chapter hangs together (pardon the pun) two ways of forming the shape your text columns take. Attributes which shape your text are usually applied at the paragraph level. That is the case with one of the options we discuss here: hanging indents. However, we'll also discuss a feature long prized by typesetters, and one that XPress does not have: the ability to hang punctuation outside the margins of a text frame. InDesign makes this attribute a property of the *story*, not the paragraph.

Hanging Indents

Creating hanging indents is one of the most common ways of formatting text: It's used whenever you want to create a numbered or bulleted list, for example. InDesign and QuarkXPress both let you create hanging indents in the same two ways: by using left and first-line indents, or by using a special Indent Here character.

Hanging in the Paragraph Palette

The first way to create a hanging indent effect is by typing a negative number in the First Line Indent field of the Paragraph palette. For example, if you want to create a hanging indent where a bulleted list hangs in .25 inch, set the Left Indent value to ".25 in" and the First Line Indent to "–.25 in" (see Figure 47-1). You can only use a negative first-line indent when there is an equal or greater left indent.

Figure 47-1
A hanging indent created with the Paragraph palette. With hidden characters showing, you can see the tab after the bullet.

- » Create·with·the·Paragraph· palette.¶
- » Or,·create·with·the·Tabs·pal-ette.¶
- » Or,·you·can·even·create·with· the·Hanging·Indent·character#

Hanging with the Tabs Palette

You can also create a hanging indent with the Tabs palette (see Chapter 45 for more on setting indents with the Tabs palette). In the Tabs palette, either drag the indent markers, or type indent values in the Position (X) field with a negative value for the First Line Indent. If you're dragging, first drag the lower left marker to set the Left Indent value, then drag the top left marker back to the margin to create the effect.

The Indent Here Character

QuarkXPress has an invisible Indent Here character which lets you quickly format hanging indents, and InDesign has also adopted this feature. Typing Command-backslash/Ctrl-backslash causes the text on the remaining lines of the paragraph to indent to the same horizontal position as the Indent Here character. You can use the Indent Here character to create a type effect like a hung initial cap, for example, or to make a quick bulleted or numbered list. Unfortunately, while hanging indents created with the Paragraph or Tabs palette can be included in paragraph styles, those using the Indent Here character cannot.

Hanging Punctuation

People who love well-set type are always concerned about the "look" of the type. One high-quality "look" which has largely disappeared over the past decade of desktop publishing is when the edges along each side of a column of text appear even. Normally, when some punctuation marks—periods, commas, dashes, and quotations marks—and the edges of some letters (like a capital A) touch the left or right edge of a text frame, they appear to be very slightly indented from the edge. *Hanging punctuation* makes subtle adjustments to the position of these characters, moving them slightly outside the frame, making the column appear straighter and cleaner.

InDesign calls this feature *optical character alignment,* and it implements it as an attribute of the story. To apply this effect to your text, select a text frame with the Selection tool or click an insertion point with the Type tool, open the Story palette (choose Story from the Type menu), and turn on the Optical Margin Alignment option. The hanging effect applies to all linked frames in your story (see Figure 47-2).

Figure 47-2
Optical margin alignment turned on (left) and off (right)

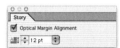

"Curiouser and curiouser!" cried Alice (she was so much surprised, that for the moment she quite forgot how to speak good English); "now I'm opening out like the largest telescope that ever was! Goodbye, feet!" (for when she looked down at her feet, they seemed to be almost out of sight, they were

"Curiouser and curiouser!" cried Alice (she was so much surprised, that for the moment she quite forgot how to speak good English); "now I'm opening out like the largest telescope that ever was! Goodbye, feet!" (for when she looked down at her feet, they seemed to be almost out of sight, they were getting so far off). "Oh, my poor little feet, I wonder who will put on your shoes and stockings for

The Font Size menu in the Story palette can be used to adjust the amount of the hang (though it actually adjusts other indenting, too). Your type usually looks best when you set it to match the size of the font you are using.

Typography

48

Hyphenation and Justification

Hyphenation and justification—usually called "H&J" by those who love fine typography—are the controls (along with the dictionaries we talk about in Chapter 42) which your composition engine uses to decide how much text to fit on a line. We discuss composition in Chapter 46. In QuarkXPress, these settings are created and saved in the Edit Hyphenation and Justification dialog box. InDesign uses two separate features to control H&J—Justification and Hyphenation—which are found on the Paragraph palette's flyout menu. The two applications share similar settings, but InDesign adds a couple of new features to the process.

Applying H&J Settings

For both QuarkXPress and InDesign, H&J is controlled at the paragraph level, but the way the settings are applied differs between programs. In XPress, you create named H&J settings which are saved with the document and which you can then apply to selected paragraphs in the Paragraph Attributes dialog box. InDesign doesn't let you save H&J settings. Rather, you apply H&J settings in the following ways:

- To apply settings to particular paragraphs, select the paragraphs and make your choices in the two dialog boxes.

- To create default settings within a document, make choices in the Hyphenation and Justification dialog boxes with nothing selected. All subsequently created text frames will use these settings.

- To create default settings which apply to all new documents, make the choices in these two dialog boxes with no document open.

- The most efficient way to apply multiple H&J settings in a document is to include them in paragraph styles. All of the settings in these two dialog boxes are available when you are creating styles (see Chapter 54).

Hyphenation Settings

If you simply want to turn hyphenation on or off in InDesign, just select your paragraphs with the Type tool or choose text frames with the Selection tool, and then check or uncheck the Hyphenation option in the Paragraph palette. However, to fine-tune the settings InDesign uses for hyphenation, choose Hyphenation from the Paragraph palette's flyout menu. With one exception, InDesign's Hyphenation dialog box mirrors the left side of XPress's Edit Hyphenation and Justification dialog box (see Figure 48-1).

Figure 48-1
The Hyphenation dialog box

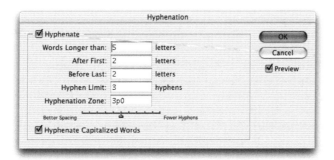

InDesign's Words Longer Than, After First, and Before Last fields match XPress's Smallest Word, Minimum Before, and Minimum After. What XPress calls Hyphens in a Row, InDesign calls Hyphen Limit. Both have a Hyphenation Zone control and an option to hyphenate capitalized words.

Hypenation Penalty Slider

The new feature which InDesign introduces to control hyphenation is a *hyphenation penalty slider*, affectionately known internally at Adobe as "Nigel." As InDesign's composition engines work, they can use adjustments in word and letter spacing settings and hyphenation to break lines. If you move the slider to the left toward Better Spacing, the composer relies more

Typography

on hyphenation and less on adjusting spacing. If you drag the slider to the right toward Fewer Hyphens, it makes more adjustments with spacing, and use fewer hyphenation break-points. Be sure to turn on the Preview checkbox so you can see the effect on your selected paragraphs.

Note that Nigel works on justified, left-aligned, and right-aligned paragraphs. You can use this in left- and right-aligned text to adjust the "rag"—how the right or left edge of the column flows.

(Why do they call this feature Nigel? Adobe evangelist Tim Cole recalls that he asked the engineer for 11 marks on this slider, remembering that Nigel Tufnel—the guitarist in the movie *Spinal Tap*—loved his amplifier because the volume knob went all the way to 11.)

Justification Settings

Justification controls the spacing of letters and words across the text column by setting a range of acceptable spacing which the composition engine can use. You can adjust these settings in the Justification dialog box, also found on the Paragraph palette's flyout menu (see Figure 48-2). It is similar to the right half of QuarkXPress's Edit Hyphenation and Justification dialog box, with one more and one less feature.

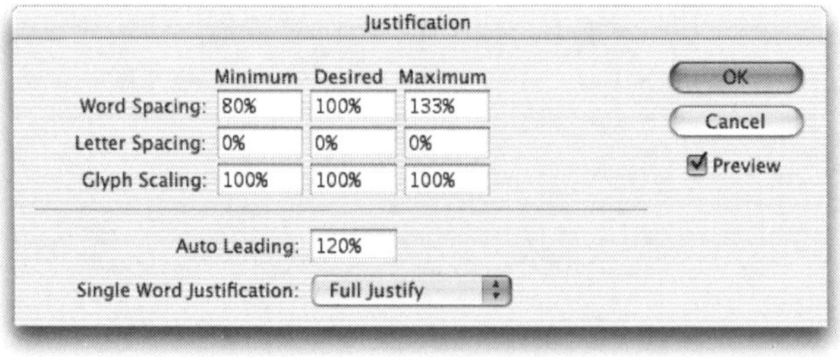

Figure 48-2
The Justification
dialog box

Word, Letter, and Glyph Spacing

QuarkXPress lets you set Minimum, Optimum, and Maximum values for Space (word spacing) and Character (character spacing), all set as a percentage of a normal space character. InDesign has equivalent controls, called Minimum, Desired, and Maximum Word Spacing and Letter Spacing, each also set as a percentage.

In addition, InDesign gives you the ability to alter Glyph Scaling, which lets you subtly change the width (horizontal scaling) of the characters. If you set a modest Glyph Scaling value—like Minimum 98-percent and Maximum 102-percent—the difference in letterform shapes probably won't be distinguishable. It's also useful to use the Preview option to test out spacing alternatives before applying them or including them in a paragraph style.

InDesign lacks XPress's Flush Zone setting, the value which controls whether the last line of a paragraph gets forced justified. The Single Word Justification choice matches XPress's Single Word Justify command. This controls what happens in a text frame with a narrow width (like a newspaper column) when a word falls on a line by itself. Inexplicably, InDesign also puts the control for Auto Leading default in this dialog box as well.

Flush Space Character

While we discuss special characters in Chapter 51, it makes sense to mention one other new feature which InDesign adds to control how lines are justified: the *flush space* character.

The flush space character can add a variable amount of space to the last line of a paragraph when the alignment is set to Justify All Lines. In a paragraph where the line is set to be flush left, center or right, the character only takes up the width of a word space. In a fully-justified paragraph, it adjusts its width to take up all the extra space on the line where it appears. It works best at the end of a story between the last word and the end-of-story character which is often used to end a magazine article (see Figure 48-3). You can insert the flush space from the Insert White Space menu (under the Type menu or in the context menu).

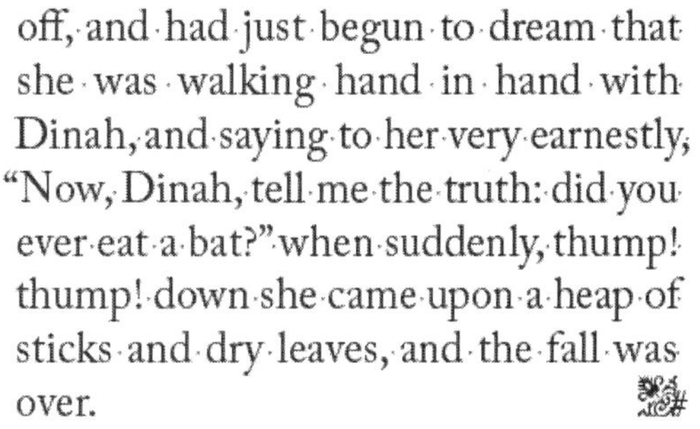

Figure 48-3
A flush space character inserted between the last word of the story and the dingbat

off, and had just begun to dream that she was walking hand in hand with Dinah, and saying to her very earnestly, "Now, Dinah, tell me the truth: did you ever eat a bat?" when suddenly, thump! thump! down she came upon a heap of sticks and dry leaves, and the fall was over.

Typography

49

Setting Tabs

Tabs are characters which cause text to jump to a horizonal position across a text column. InDesign and QuarkXPress use similar methods to handle the tab stops that position the text, except that InDesign uses the Tabs palette instead of a dialog box. In both applications, tabs are a paragraph attribute, and if you don't set your own tabs, each program creates default tabs which are spaced every one-half inch across the frame.

We suggest that you consider another way of positioning text which in many cases may give you more flexibility—by creating tables. InDesign's powerful table features let you create cells that can grow as text is added, and can include borders, background color, graphics, and many other attributes. We discuss tables in Chapters 74 through 78.

You can also use the Tabs palette to set indents; we discuss this in Chapter 45.

Working with Tabs

To work with tabs in InDesign, open the Tabs palette by choosing Tabs from the Type menu (or press Command-Shift-T/Ctrl-Shift-T; see Figure 49-1). Unlike XPress, which affixes a temporary ruler at the top of the text box whenever the Tab dialog box is open, InDesign's Tabs palette contains a ruler. If you want the ruler to align with the text frame, change your view to show the top of the text frame at its full width, select the frame with the Selection tool or the Type tool, and then click the magnet button on the right side of the palette. The palette should jump into position at the top of the frame. However, note that you don't have to align the ruler in order set tab stops.

Figure 49-1

The Tabs palette

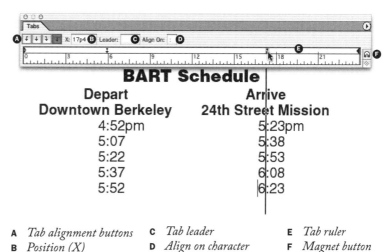

| A | *Tab alignment buttons* | C | *Tab leader* | E | *Tab ruler* |
| B | *Position (X)* | D | *Align on character* | F | *Magnet button* |

Creating Tab Stops

To add a tab stop, first select the paragraphs which you want to affect (either use the Type tool to select one or more paragraphs or use the Selection tool to choose an unlinked text frame). Next, click one of the four tab alignment buttons in the Tabs palette to set the alignment of the tab stop. Then do one of the following:

- Click in the tab ruler where you want the tab stop to appear (click in the narrow space just above the ruler).

- Type a value in the Position (X) field and press Enter.

- To type values for a series of tab stops in the Position (X) field, complete each value by pressing Command-Enter/Ctrl-Enter (this applies the tab stop but keeps the field active).

- To set a number of equally spaced tabs, select a tab stop, then choose Repeat Tab from the Tabs palette's flyout menu. Tabs stops will be repeated across the text frame. The distance between tabs will be based on the space between the selected tab and the left indent (or the previous tab).

In addition, if you click in the Position (X) field, you can press the Up or Down Arrow keys to move the tab stop to the right or left. Unfortunately, you cannot move more than one tab stop at a time).

By the way, you don't have to align the Tabs palette with the text frame because when you click and drag a tab stop in the palette, InDesign displays a vertical line over the text frame reflecting the position of the tab stop. It's a little thing, but it saves so much time. Try it!

Tab Alignment

Tab stops can either be aligned by pressing one of the tab alignment buttons before creating a tab stop, or by selecting a tab stop and clicking a button. You can also Option/Alt-click the tab stop to cycle through the alignment options.

While QuarkXPress uses seven types of tab stops, InDesign combines these into four: Left, Center, Right, and Align On. The Align On button can handle alignment on a decimal point (period), comma, or any other character. Type or paste the character you wish to align on into the Align On Character field and press Enter.

Tab Leaders

What QuarkXPress calls fill characters, InDesign calls tab leaders. As in XPress, to add a one or more characters to fill the space created by the tab, select a tab stop and enter one or more characters in the Tab Leader field, then press Enter. XPress is limited to two fill characters, but InDesign allows as many as eight. Like XPress, you can select the tab character with the Type tool and format it in the Character palette or Type menu to change the appearance of the tab leader.

Changing and Deleting Tabs

Once you have created tab stops, you can change or delete them in similar ways to the methods used in QuarkXPress. To move a tab stop, select it on the tab ruler. Then either drag it to a new position, or type a new value in the Position (X) field and press Enter. To remove a tab stop, drag it off the tab ruler. If you want to remove all the tabs, choose Clear All from the Tabs palette's flyout menu.

Right Indent Tab

Both QuarkXPress and InDesign have a special character called the Right Indent Tab. When the character is typed in text, all the rest of the text on the line is aligned against the right edge of the frame (you don't have to set a tab stop there). If you later change the frame's width, the right indent tab automatically moves, too. You can insert this character by typing Shift-Tab or by choosing it from the Insert Special Character submenu (under the Type menu or in the context menu). However, unlike XPress, in InDesign the Right Indent Tab character can't be used with a tab leader.

Typography

50

Text Frame Properties

While most text attributes are controlled on the character and paragraph level, there is a third way you can change text appearance—by setting the properties of the frame which contains the text. For example, you can do this in QuarkXPress on the Text tab of the Modify dialog box, in which you can control properties which are particular to the text box: the number of columns, the inset of the text from the box, and so on. There are similar settings in InDesign.

Fitting a Frame to Its Text

Before we discuss those controls, let's introduce a useful technique for fitting text in its frame which XPress doesn't have. Text frames are often larger than they need to be. You can ask InDesign to automatically fit the frame to the size of the text contained in it. First, either select the frame or frames with the Selection tool or click an insertion point with the Type tool. Then choose Fit Frame to Content from the Fitting submenu (under the Object menu), or press Command-Option-C/Ctrl-Alt-C.

The frame's size is reduced to the size of the text, but how it happens depends on what it contains.

- If the text is only one line, InDesign changes both the height and width of the frame (this is useful for captions!)

- If the text is more than one line, InDesign reduces the height, but not the width of the frame.

- If the frame contains only a table, InDesign reduces or expands the text frame to fit the table.

The Fit Frame to Content command will be unavailable if the frame is linked to other frames or if text is overset (the frame will not be made larger). We discuss similar commands for working with fitting graphics in Chapter 64.

Text Frame Options

To set text frame attributes, either choose the frame or frames with the Selection tool, or place the text insertion point in the frame with the Type tool. Then choose Text Frame Options from the Object menu (or press Command-B/Ctrl-B; see Figure 50-1). Throughout the dialog box, you can either type in values, click the tiny up/down arrows, or press the Up or Down Arrow keys to increase or decrease the values—the amount of change depends on the ruler unit selected.

Figure 50-1
Text Frame Options
dialog box

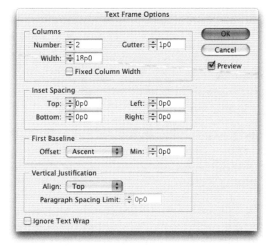

Columns

InDesign, like QuarkXPress lets you set the number of columns in a text frame and the gutter width (width between columns). But InDesign also lets you define the width of a column. If you do this, as you adjust column and gutter widths, the width of the text frame changes, too. If you want to make sure the text column width doesn't change, you can turn on the Fixed Column Width option. With this on, resizing the text frame leaves the column width unchanged, but changes the *number* of columns (see Figure 50-2).

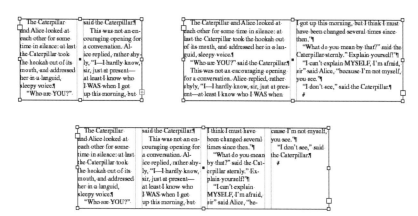

Figure 50-2
Adjusting column widths. Top left, the original text frame; top right, resizing the frame with Fixed Column Width deselected; bottom, when resizing with Fixed Column Width selected, extra columns are created.

Inset Spacing

Text inset defines the amount of space from the edge of the frame to the text in the frame. QuarkXPress 3 and 4 let you define one text inset for all four sides of the text box; QuarkXPress 5 allows different insets for each side of a box. InDesign also allows you to set the Top, Bottom, Left and Right inset values independently. InDesign's default is an inset value of 0 (zero), rather than the 1-point value in XPress which has always annoyed us. As in XPress 5.0, when it comes to non-rectangular frames, you can specify only one inset value.

Vertical Text Alignment

QuarkXPress has two ways of adjusting text vertically in a box: by setting the First Baseline Offset and by choosing a Vertical Justification option in the Modify dialog box. InDesign closely matches these choices in the Text Frame Options dialog box.

You can set the distance from the top of the frame to the the first baseline of text by choosing the Minimum amount for baseline offset, and then choose between Cap Height, Ascent, Leading (the text's leading value), x Height (the height of the "x" character of the font), or Fixed.

Both XPress and InDesign also let you choose between Top, Centered, Bottom and Justified vertical alignment within a text frame. XPress has a choice to set the Inter ¶ Max when Justified is selected—the maximum distance between paragraphs. In InDesign, the same option is called Paragraph Spacing Limit. As with XPress, vertical justification isn't allowed when a frame isn't rectangular.

Special Characters

To produce high quality type in a layout application, you need to use a variety of special characters. Some of them appear visibly in the text—a bullet or a section mark, for example. Other special characters are normally invisible but produce formatting results—em spaces or page-break characters, for instance.

Calling Out Characters

To insert a special character in QuarkXPress, you're forced to memorize particular keystrokes, or perhaps rely on a crib sheet taped near your computer. By contrast, InDesign gives you several ways of calling out special characters—including two menus and a palette. However, you can still use keystrokes if you prefer. In addition, if you're using OpenType fonts, some special characters can be inserted in your text automatically.

Insert Character Menus

InDesign offers three special character submenus under the Type menu: Insert Special Character, Insert White Space, or Insert Break Character. The menus list all the white space and break characters and many common visible special characters. Instead of going to the Type menu, you can insert special characters with the context menu: Use the Type tool to place the text insertion point, then Control-click/right-click and select a character from one of the three submenus (see Figure 51-1).

Figure 51-1
Insert Special
Character, Insert
White Space
and Insert Break
Character menus

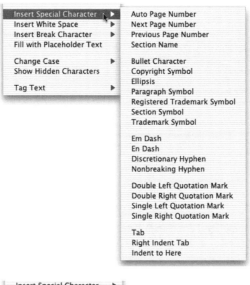

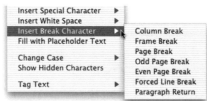

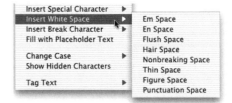

Glyphs Palette

The Glyphs palette gives you access to all glyphs in a font. You can open the palette by placing the text cursor in a frame and choosing Insert Glyphs from the Type menu (see Figure 51-2). The palette displays the glyphs from the current font, though you can choose a different font from the Font Family and Type Style menus at the bottom. Click the Zoom buttons to enlarge or reduce the size of the glyphs. Then scroll through the palette to see all the characters. To insert a glyph you see in the Glyphs palette, double-click on it.

When viewing an OpenType font, the Show menu also lets you see a subset of the glyphs, such as Small Capitals or Oldstyle Figures. To replace one character with an alternate glyph, select the character in your

Figure 51-2

Glyphs palette

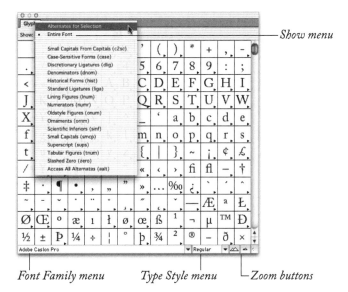

Show menu

Font Family menu   Type Style menu   Zoom buttons

text, then choose Alternates for Selection from the Show menu. If there are alternate glyphs, they are displayed. Double-click a glyph to replace the selected character.

Be careful when changing fonts in the Glyphs palette; if you have text selected, this is the same as changing its font in the Character palette.

Keystrokes

Of course, the fastest way to get a special character is to memorize and type a keystroke. Many special characters already have shortcuts defined (see Chapter 6 for more on how to set, view, and edit shortcuts).

OpenType Fonts

The OpenType submenu in the Character palette's flyout menu provides controls for turning on and off features which may be available in OpenType fonts (see Figure 51-3). When you turn on a feature, such as Contextual Alternates, the special characters are applied automatically. If you see a feature listed in square brackets, like "[Swash]," that feature isn't available in the current font. The OpenType User Guide, also included in the Goodies folder of the installation CD, gives detailed suggestions for using Adobe OpenType fonts. Some examples of fine typography produced with these fonts are shown in Figure 51-4.

Figure 51-3
The OpenType
submenu

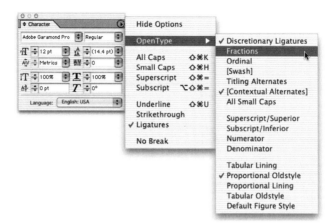

Fractions

In QuarkXPress, there are several ways to work with fractions—none of them pretty. You can fake fractions using character styles or with the Type Tricks XTension, but the results are usually spindly and of only marginal quality. You can use expert set or other specialized fonts which include true fraction characters, but this is time-intensive.

InDesign has no macro like the Type Tricks XTension, so making fractions with non-OpenType fonts is a hassle. (You can use the Superscript and Subscript styles and the fraction-bar character, or use specialized fonts.) However, many OpenType fonts support some pre-built fractions, and some (mostly the Pro fonts) even support the creation of any arbitrary fraction (like $355/113$). To use this feature, select any two numbers separated by a slash character—for example, 3/4—then select Fractions from the OpenType menu on the Character palette. The fractions will be correctly built using numerator and denominator characters included in the font.

Typographers' Quotes

Both QuarkXPress and InDesign have preferences that control the appearance of single and double quotation marks in text. By default, InDesign converts quotes to typographers' ("curly") quotes, but you can turn this off in the Text panel of the Preferences dialog box. Or, in the Dictionary Preferences panel, you can choose the appearance of single and double quotes for each of the languages which you have installed. You can also toggle this option (turning it on and off) by pressing Command-Option-Shift-'/ Ctrl-Alt-Shift-' (quote).

Figure 51-4 Faked styles (left) versus OpenType features (right)	CURIOUSER AND CURIOUSER	CURIOUSER AND CURIOUSER	*Small caps*
	$1\frac{1}{8}$ $3\frac{1}{2}$ $5^{11}/_{12}$ $8^{234}/_{567}$	$1\frac{1}{8}$ $3\frac{1}{2}$ $5^{11}/_{12}$ $8^{234}/_{567}$	*Fractions*
	new azaleas bloom where	*new azaleas bloom where*	*Contextual alternates*

Quotation marks are also converted to typographer's quotes when text is imported with the Place command. To turn this off, uncheck the Convert Quotes option in the Place dialog box.

White Space Characters

InDesign supports all the white space characters which QuarkXPress does, with the exception of the flex space. In addition it provides a flush space (which we describe in Chapter 48), a hair space, and a thin space. While InDesign doesn't support as many non-breaking white space characters as XPress, any character or characters can be made non-breaking by applying the No Break character attribute.

Break Characters

InDesign's Insert Break Character menu contains five invisible characters that control how text flows into multiple frames. When you insert one of these characters, text is forced to the next column in the current frame, to the next threaded frame, to the next page, or to the next even or odd page.

Auto Page Numbers and Jump Lines

The Insert Special Character submenu includes three characters used to reference pages in a document. The Auto Page Number is the equivalent of XPress's Current Page Number—usually placed on master pages to create page numbers. The other two characters—Previous Page Number and Next Page Number—are used when stories jump from page to page, as they often do in newsletters or magazines. In InDesign, it usually works best to place these characters in a separate frame for a jump line (for example, Continued on Page *x*). Position the jump line so it overlaps the main story frame, and then it can correctly call out the page you're jumping to or from. All three characters work exactly the same way as in XPress.

Typography

Unicode Mapping Problems

While InDesign's support for Unicode encoding and OpenType fonts is generally a good thing, you should be aware of one little glitch which you may run into you. In QuarkXPress, you expect that you can type characters which represent keyboard positions (for example, the letters a, b and c), and when you select those characters and switch the font to a pi font (like Symbol or Zapf Dingbats), the characters in those same keyboard positions will be called out.

In InDesign, it doesn't work this way—at least not by default. As far as InDesign is concerned, the letter "a" is Unicode 0061 (which you can see in the Glyphs palette if you pause the cursor over the glyph), and the Greek "alpha" glyph is Unicode 03B1. So when you select the letter "a," and change the font to Symbol, what you see is a pink blotch—meaning the font is missing!

So what's the solution? You have two options: If you hold down Command-Option/Ctrl-Alt when selecting the new font, InDesign handles the switch the way you expect and overrides the Unicode mapping. Or, you can select the pink splotch, and just retype the characters again.

52

Find and Change

The Find/Change command is one of the workhorses of a page layout program. The feature is rarely mentioned in application feature lists, but learning how to use it well can save you much production time. For both QuarkXPress and InDesign, the Find/Change function is controlled with a dialog box which acts as a palette (so it can be left open as you work; see Figure 52-1). In InDesign, you open it by choosing Find/Change in the Edit menu (or press Command-F/Ctrl-F).

Figure 52-1
The Find/Change
dialog box in
its minimized
configuration, used
for character searches.

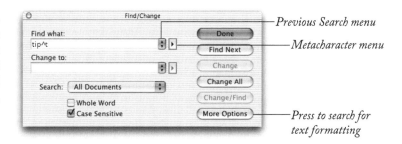

Previous Search menu

Metacharacter menu

Press to search for text formatting

Setting the Search Range

In QuarkXPress you can search the current story or the current document. InDesign can find/change using both these search ranges, and it can also search a text selection, multiple stories, or all open documents. In the Search menu, select the range to be searched: Selection, Story, Stories, To End of Story, Document, or All Documents. (The choices are context sensitive, so Stories is only available if you have more than one story selected with the Selection tool.) Note that InDesign's document searches include the master pages (in XPress, you have to do that as a separate search).

Specifying the Text

After setting the search range, type or paste the characters to be searched for in the Find What field. InDesign remembers the last 15 searches you've performed, and you can select them in the Previous Search popup menu (just to the right of the field). If you want to replace characters, type or paste the characters into the Change To field. This field also has a Previous Search menu with previous replacement characters.

Special Characters

In QuarkXPress, if you want to search for special characters like a Tab or a New Paragraph, you must remember the code to type in the Find What or Change To fields, or a keystroke. In InDesign, to search and replace these kinds of special characters, you can choose them from the Metacharacter popup menu, to the right of the Find What and Change To fields. If you're really into codes, InDesign supports those, too (see Table 52-1).

Wild Card Characters

QuarkXPress has one *wild card* code which can stand for any character in the Find/Change command. InDesign has four of them: Any White Space Character (like a tab or space), Any Character, Any Digit, or Any Letter. These are all in the Metacharacters popup menu. As in XPress, the wild card characters can only be used in the Find What field, not in the Change To field.

Other Options

Both QuarkXPress and InDesign have two other options when performing a Find/Change command. When you check Whole Word, the search is limited to entire words only. Turning on the Case Sensitive option is the same as turning *off* Ignore Case in XPress.

Performing a Text Search

The buttons in the Find/Change dialog box are almost identical to those in XPress: Find Next, Change, Change/Find or Change All. When you are finished searching, click Done or click the close palette button. Note that unlike XPress, InDesign lets you continue searching while the Find/

Table 52-1

Find/Change codes
(if you don't want to
use the Metacharacter
popup menu)

To Enter This Character	Type
Auto Page Numbering	^#
Section Marker	^x
Bullet	^8
Caret	^^
Copyright Symbol	^2
New Paragraph	^p
New Line	^n
Inline Graphic Marker	^g
Paragraph Symbol	^7
Registered Trademark Symbol	^r
Section Symbol	^6
Tab Character	^t
Right Indent Tab	^y
Indent to Here	^i
Em Dash	^_
Em Space	^m
En Dash	^=
En Space	^>
Flush Space	^f
Hair Space	^|
Non-breaking Space	^s
Thin Space	^<
Discretionary Hyphen	^-
Non-breaking Hyphen	^~
Double Left Quotation Mark	^{
Double Right Quotation Mark	^}
Single Left Quotation Mark	^[
Single Right Quotation Mark	^]
Any White Space (space or tab)	^w
Any Character	^?
Any Digit	^9
Any Letter	^$

Change palette is closed: Just select Find Next from the Edit menu, or press Command-Option-F/Ctrl-Alt-F.

Finding/Changing Formatted Text

Many people don't realize you can search for or change text attributes in XPress because you have to first turn off the Ignore Attributes checkbox

Typography

in the Find/Change palette. When you do so, XPress allows you to find/replace style sheets, or the font name, font size, font color, and character-level Type Style formatting.

Similarly, to find or change formatted text in InDesign, click the More Options button in the Find/Change dialog box. InDesign now presents the expanded form of the dialog box showing its Format controls (see Figure 52-2). You can then click the Format buttons to choose the formatting you wish to find or replace.

Figure 52-2

The Find/Change dialog box in its enlarged configuration, used to search and replace text formatting.

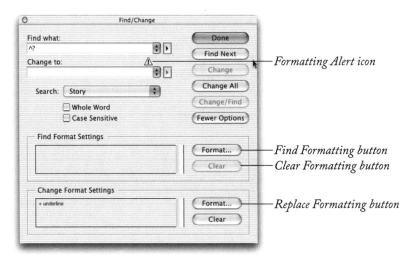

Specifying Formatting

When you click one of the Format buttons, you see the Find Format Settings or Change Format Settings dialog box (see Figure 52-3). On the left side of this dialog box, select a type of formatting, and then specify the attributes which you want to find/change. InDesign's choices are considerably more extensive than in XPress: You can Find/Change style sheets, basic and advanced character attributes, indents, spacing, keep options, drop caps, composer, character color, and OpenType features. (You can't Find/Change paragraph rules, tabs, or H&J settings.)

As in QuarkXPress, formatting attributes in this dialog box can have one of three states—on, off, or ignore—representing whether the search is finding or changing text with or without this attribute, or whether this attribute is to be ignored. In Figure 52-3, text is being changed to include the Underline attribute (it is checked), the Strikethrough attribute is being removed (it is unchecked), and the other attributes are being ignored (they either show a line through the checkbox or they show a field or menu which is empty).

Figure 52-3

The Change Format
Settings dialog box

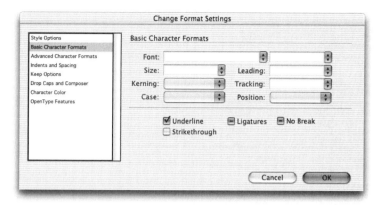

Applying Formatting

After making choices for finding or changing formatting in the dialog box, click OK. When you return to the Find/Change dialog box, the formatting you've specified is listed in the Find Format Settings and Change Format Settings sections. When you are satisfied with your choices, use the Find Next, Change, Change/Find or Change All buttons as described above.

While XPress cannot undo a search and replace, InDesign can: choose Undo from the Edit menu or press Command-Z/Ctrl-Z. One common mistake is to inadvertently leave formatting attributes from a previous search. InDesign helps you recognize that formatting is being searched for or replaced by placing a yellow Formatting Alert icon next to the field where formatting is designated. To clear the formatting, press Clear.

Using Wild Cards to Apply Word Underlining

To show you the power of the Find/Change dialog box, we'll show you how to use it to apply word underlining. This is a character attribute found in QuarkXPress, but not in InDesign. However, with three simple steps, you can apply it in InDesign:

1. Select the text and apply the Underline style (press Command-Shift-U/Ctrl-Shift-U).

2. While the text is still selected, open the Find/Change dialog box (Command-F/Ctrl-F) and choose Selection from the Search popup menu.

3. Choose White Space from the Metacharacter popup menu beside Find What (^w will appear in the field). Click the Format button in the Change Format section. In the Basic Characters Formats section, *turn off* Underline (click it twice, so there's nothing in the box), and click OK. Now click Change All and the underlining is removed from the white space characters.

53

Find Font

InDesign's Find Font dialog box is the equivalent of the Font panel in the QuarkXPress Usage dialog box—it tells you what fonts are used in your document and lets you replace them with other fonts. You can get to Find Font in one of three ways. First, if you open an InDesign file which uses fonts which are not open on your system, the Missing Fonts dialog box appears (see Figure 53-1). You're given the immediate opportunity to substitute a different font by clicking on the Find Font button (which takes you to the Find Font dialog box). Second, you can open the Find Font dialog box by choosing Find Font from the Type menu. Third, when preflighting your document (see Chapter 91) you can press the Find Font button on the Fonts panel of the Preflight dialog box.

Figure 53-1
The Missing Fonts
dialog box

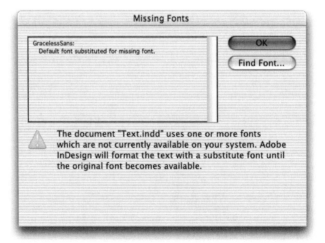

Find Font Dialog Box

The Find Font dialog box allows you to see where in your document missing fonts are located, to replace fonts with other fonts on your system, or to gather information about the fonts in your document (see Figure 53-2). The button labeled Less Info toggles with More Info to open or close the bottom portion of the dialog box.

Figure 53-2
The Find Font dialog box in its expanded (More Info) state.

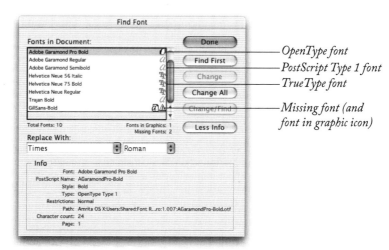

OpenType font
PostScript Type 1 font
TrueType font

Missing font (and font in graphic icon)

XPress's Usage dialog box only displays the fonts which are on document pages or on master pages, but not both at the same time. Similarly, when you replace fonts in XPress, you can only do this on either document or master pages. InDesign makes no such distinction, and it can find or replace on master pages at the same time as document pages. Furthermore, the Find Font dialog box also lists fonts which are located in EPS or PDF files (but it cannot replace them).

Finding Information

When you select a document font in the list, you can click the Find First button to find the first instance of the font in the document. The text that uses the document moves into view. If the font is in a graphic, the Find Font button changes to Find Graphic.

InDesign indicates in the font list whether a font is PostScript Type 1, TrueType or OpenType by its icon. If the lower portion of the dialog box is open, clicking on a font provides more information—the PostScript name, the location of the font, and the number of characters using the font, for instance. (The font type may be Unknown if the file format of the graphic doesn't provide information about the font.)

Replacing a Font

To replace a font, select it and then select a replacement font from the two Replace With popup menus. Click Find First, and then you can do one of the following:

- Click Change to change that instance of the font.
- Click Change/Find to change that instance and find the next instance.
- Click Change All to change all instances of the fonts selected in the list.

When all the instances of a font are removed, the font disappears from the list. InDesign shares QuarkXPress's limitation that font replacements don't change the fonts which are defined in a paragraph or character style. They apply the font change locally to the text, but they don't change the font in the style itself. This is, in our humble opinion, extremely annoying in both programs.

Note that to replace fonts which are in graphics, you have to open the application which originally exported the graphic, then update the graphic in InDesign.

PART 5

Styles

○ ○ ○

Paragraph Styles \ Styles \ atches \

about cyber - head

Address street

ADDRESS1

big head

body

bold description

54

Paragraph Styles

If your workflow depends heavily on the time-saving benefits of style sheets, you'll find that InDesign styles meet or beat the capabilities of the style sheets in QuarkXPress. InDesign splits the lists of styles for paragraphs and characters (described in the next chapter) into separate Paragraph Styles and Character Styles palettes, while QuarkXPress keeps both lists in a single Style Sheets palette. Be careful not to confuse InDesign's Paragraph Styles and Character Styles palettes with its Paragraph and Character palettes; the latter pair only apply local formatting that isn't attached to a style.

To open the Paragraph Styles palette, choose Paragraph Styles from the Type menu or press its keyboard shortcut (F11). Unlike XPress, empty style palettes don't have any default style sheets such as Normal, just the No Style option that removes the style tag. If you find yourself looking for the commands that would be on the context menu for the Style Sheets palette in XPress, you'll find them in InDesign's Paragraph Styles palette's flyout menu.

Creating Paragraph Styles

The fastest way to create a new style is to click the Create New Style button at the bottom of the Paragraph Styles palette (Fig. 54-1). InDesign adds a style cleverly named "New Style," based on the formatting of the currently-selected text. It's usually advisable to hold the Option/Alt key when clicking to customize the style's name and attributes as the style is created. You can also select New Style from the palette's flyout menu.

Figure 54-1

You can create a new paragraph style by clicking (or Option/Alt-clicking) on the Create New Style button at the bottom of the Paragraph Styles palette. Or, as here, we drag another style on top of the button.

The Modify Paragraph Style Options dialog box lets you set up or edit the style (see Figure 54-2). Select any of the panels along the left side of the dialog box to enter attributes for the style.

In general, all the options available in QuarkXPress' Edit Paragraph Style Sheet dialog box are available in InDesign's Modify Paragraph Style Options dialog box, but the layout is very different. InDesign uses 12 panels in the dialog box. However, InDesign has the advantage that you can preview a style while modifying it; turn on the Preview option to do this.

All character attributes can be made part of a paragraph style, but unlike XPress, a character style can't be part of a paragraph style—InDesign paragraph and character styles co-exist independently. However, you can create similar functionality by making a paragraph style where only character attributes are specified, and then base other paragraph styles on that parent style.

Figure 54-2

The Modify Paragraph Style Options dialog box

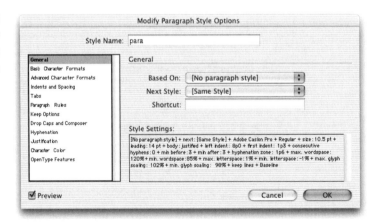

When you're done setting up a style, click OK and the new style name appears in the Paragraph Styles palette. We cover applying styles in Chapter 56.

Duplicating Paragraph Styles

You can use an existing paragraph style as the foundation for a new style by dragging the name of the original style on top of the New Style icon at the bottom of the palette. InDesign duplicates the style and appends "Copy" to the style's name. We discuss editing styles in Chapter 57.

However, in many cases it may be better to simply base a new style on an existing style (its "parent") and change only the attributes that are different. As in XPress, this can simplify production because the attributes in common between the parent and child styles update automatically when they're edited in the parent style. In XPress, you would accomplish this using the Based On option in the Edit Paragraph Styles Sheet dialog box; InDesign uses the same name for the option and you'll find it in the General panel of the New Paragraph Style dialog box.

55

Character Styles

When we upgraded to QuarkXPress version 4 we were excited about the addition of character styles, and now can't imagine working without them. As in XPress, you can use InDesign's character styles to create, save, and apply a group of style attributes to a few selected words or characters (as opposed to an entire paragraph, which occurs when using paragraph styles). Creating, applying, and editing character styles generally works the same way as paragraph styles do, except for the differences outlined in the next section. Display the Character Styles palette using the command of the same name on the Type menu (or press Shift-F11).

Note that unlike QuarkXPress, InDesign only changes attributes that are specifically identified within a character style when it is applied. Leaving an attribute blank in the Character Styles palette will cause InDesign to not change that attribute of the text when the character style is used (see Figure 55-1). For instance, in XPress a character style always includes font, size, color, baseline shift, and so on; in InDesign, a character style can simply be the color "Red." In many cases, this allows you to create fewer character styles than you'd need to in XPress. In this example, you only need one style to apply the red color to characters in paragraphs to which any paragraph style is applied.

Figure 55-1
Leaving style attributes unchanged will cause these features to be unchanged when the style is applied to text.

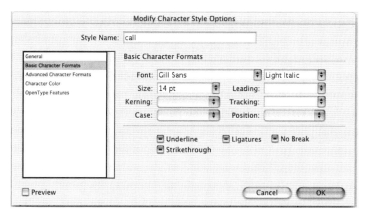

Styles

56

Applying Styles

InDesign and QuarkXPress are almost identical when it comes to applying paragraph and character styles.

Applying Paragraph Styles

To apply a paragraph style, you can place the text cursor in a paragraph and click on the name of the style within the Paragraph Styles palette, or you can press a keyboard shortcut to apply the style (if you've set one up). Unlike XPress, you can't apply a style from the main menu bar, but since that was the slowest of all methods, you're unlikely to miss it.

With InDesign, you define keyboard shortcuts for styles using the Shortcut option in the General panel of the Modify Paragraph Style Options dialog box. The main difference between how InDesign and XPress use style shortcuts is that InDesign only lets you combine a number on the numeric keypad with one or more modifier keys (such as Shift); XPress lets you use function keys as well.

Applying Character Styles

Character styles take a bit more care to apply. As in XPress, you must first select the exact range of characters you want to change, then select the style to be applied from the Character Styles palette. You can also assign and use a keyboard shortcut for character styles.

Overriding Local Attributes

Any text formatting on top of the given paragraph or character style is called *local formatting*. For example, making a single word italic is applying local formatting to it. As in XPress, InDesign adds a plus ("+") symbol to the style name when the text insertion point is within styled text that has local formatting (Figure 56-1).

InDesign, like XPress, does not override local formatting when you apply a character or paragraph style (so your italic words won't get wiped out). If you want to apply a style so that it removes all local formatting (except character styles), hold down the Option/Alt key when you click the style you're applying (this works in XPress, too). If you also hold down the Shift key, both local formatting and character styles are removed.

Figure 56-1
Like XPress, InDesign informs you of local formatting by placing a plus symbol after the style name.

Copying Styles

You may have used the Shift-Option trick in XPress to copy formatting from one paragraph to another. In InDesign, you can copy both paragraph and character formatting using the Eyedropper tool (see Chapter 82).

Styles

57

Editing Styles

It's at least as easy to edit styles in InDesign as it is in XPress. The procedures are quite similar in the two programs, though InDesign offers a much cooler way to edit styles: Redefine Style.

Modifying Character and Paragraph Styles

You can edit an existing style by double-clicking it in the Paragraph Styles or Character Styles palette. Either the Modify Paragraph Style Options dialog box or the Modify Character Style Options dialog box appears (see Figure 57-1). Make the desired changes and click OK to save them.

However, be very careful when editing styles: When you double-click on the style's name, you apply that style to any text you have selected (even if you have only selected a text frame with the Selection tool). This can cause much grief, believe us. Fortunately, you can edit a style without affecting any text by holding down Command-Shift/Ctrl-Shift while double-clicking the style name. Or you can make sure nothing on your page is selected by choosing Deselect All from the Edit menu (or press Command-Shift-A/Ctrl-Shift-A).

Redefining styles

While XPress insists that you change style definitions in a dialog box, InDesign is more flexible. You can actually change a style right on your

Figure 57-1
The Modify Style
Options dialog box

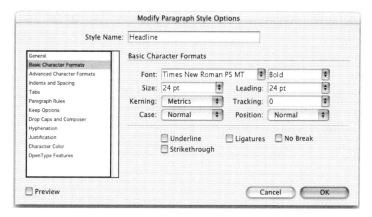

document page. Select some text that is tagged with the paragraph or character style you want to change, then apply local formatting to it. Make sure the text insertion point is in the paragraph with the replacement formatting, then choose Redefine Style from the flyout menu on the Paragraph Styles or Character Styles palette. Or quicker: press Command-Option-Shift-R/Ctrl-Alt-Shift-R to redefine the paragraph style and Command-Option-Shift-C/Ctrl-Alt-Shift-C to redefine the character style.

Deleting Styles

You can delete a paragraph or character style by selecting it and clicking the trash icon in the Paragraph Styles or Character Styles palette, or choosing Delete Style from the palette's flyout menu. But before you delete a paragraph style, stop and think. Unlike XPress, when you delete a style you don't get a chance to apply a replacement style to text that was tagged with the style you're deleting. Therefore, you may want to first use the Find/Change palette to locate and change the paragraph style of any text that uses a style you're about to delete.

Note that you can also delete more than one style at a time: Just Command/Ctrl click on each style in the palette before clicking the Delete button. If you want to delete all the styles that are unused in your document, first choose Select All Unused from the palette's flyout menu.

58

Importing Styles

You can copy paragraph and character styles between InDesign documents. You can also import styles from text that is placed into your InDesign documents from word processing files.

Appending Styles from InDesign Documents

In QuarkXPress, you may have brought in styles from other XPress documents using the Append feature. InDesign has a similar feature, but the InDesign user interface uses the term "load" instead of "append." You can import external styles into an individual InDesign file, or to the default styles available in all documents.

Importing All Styles from a Document

You can append all of the paragraph and character styles from a saved document into your current document by selecting Load All Styles from the flyout menu of either the Paragraph Styles or Character Styles palettes. Regardless of which palette you use to select this command, it imports both character and paragraph styles.

Importing Only Paragraph or Character Styles

If you only want to import only the paragraph or only the character styles from another document, you can select Load Paragraph Styles from the

Paragraph palette's flyout menu or Load Character Styles from the Character palette's flyout menu. Unfortunately, there is no way to specify *which* particular styles are imported (by name), as you can in XPress.

Importing Styles as Defaults

As in XPress, importing styles when no documents are open adds them to the list of default styles available in all new documents.

Importing Styles from Word Files

If you apply styles to your text while using a word processing program such as Microsoft Word, when you Place the text file into InDesign, the styles will come along, too. If the InDesign file doesn't have styles with the same names, then placing the text file imports those styles automatically.

Note that when you import text, you have the choice of turning on the Retain Format option in the Place dialog box (see Figure 58-1). When this is on, InDesign applies the formatting to the imported text (including applying the appropriate paragraph and character styles). When you turn it off, InDesign still imports the styles, but it won't apply them to the text; instead, it applies whatever paragraph style happens to be selected in the Paragraph Styles palette at that moment.

Figure 58-1

The Place dialog box

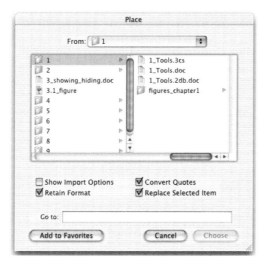

59

Exporting Text

As in QuarkXPress, you can save text from your InDesign document to disk—either selected portions of a story or the entire text of the story. And like XPress, only text is exported; graphics and inline objects aren't included. Use one of these methods to export the text, depending on how much text you need to export:

- To export only a portion of text from a story: Select the text range to be extracted by highlighting the text, and then select Export from the File menu.

- To export an entire story (text flow): Place your cursor in the story to be extracted (without actually selecting any text) and select Export from the File menu.

Either way, you then have to choose a file format from the Formats popup menu (see Figure 59-1).

Text Formats

When exporting text you'll encounter a pop-up menu of export formats which is somewhat different than what you'd see in XPress. Many of the formats export entire pages instead of just text, so choose carefully (see Chapter 11). The formats that only export text are listed below.

Text Only

Choose this option if you need the text to be usable on any computer operating system and any software. The Text Only option extracts the

Figure 59-1
The Export
dialog box

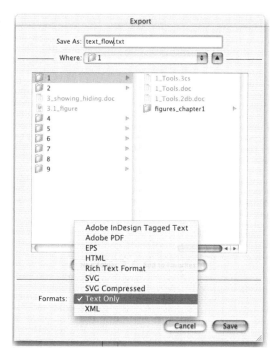

text and places it in a standard file format that virtually any text editing software will be able to read. Text Only removes any and all formatting you've applied to text and only exports the characters.

The Text Only option allows you to apply the characteristics of the computer platform where the files will be used, regardless of which computer operating system on which you are using InDesign (see Figure 59-2). By selecting Macintosh or PC, the text is structured so that characters will display and print properly when opened on the computer type you select. The Encoding option allows you to specify Unicode if necessary to preserve special characters.

Rich Text Format

The Rich Text Format (RTF) saves your text with most of its formatting (including styles, fonts, and so on). You should use RTF if you're going to open the exported text file with Microsoft Word or place the text in an application that recognizes this file format, such as PageMaker or QuarkXPress for Windows. You can use this option to extract your text to a word processing program for further editing and then re-import the text back into InDesign to complete a page layout (but you may lose some InDesign-specific formatting in the process).

Figure 59-2
The Text Only
export option

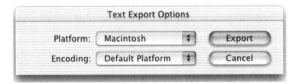

Adobe InDesign Tagged Text

The most robust text-export format is InDesign Tagged Text, which is similar to XPress Tags. Tagged text saves all your text formatting, but other programs can't read it. We cover this option in more detail in the next chapter.

Tagged Text

The InDesign Tagged Text format is similar to Text Only, except that codes are written into the text to identify how the characters and paragraphs will be formatted (see Figure 60-1). This format lets you interchange text among InDesign documents without losing any formatting (useful when copy and paste isn't available, like when having to e-mail a formatted text story to someone). You can also produce formatted text in any text-editing software and then place the formatted version into an InDesign document.

Figure 60-1

You can export formatted text with codes called tags.

The original formatted story

The same story saved in InDesign Tagged Text format

229

InDesign Tagged Text versus XPress Tags

Although many of the InDesign Tagged Text tags resemble the XPress Tags format which allows for a similar capability in QuarkXPress, they are not interchangeable. While Adobe InDesign does not directly support the import of XPress Tags, Late Night Software (*www.latenightsw.com*) has developed a plug-in called Tag-On that you can purchase to help import all XPress Tags into your InDesign documents.

Tagged Text Export Options

You can export text in the InDesign Tagged Text format by selecting a text story (or a portion of the story), choosing Export from the File menu, and selecting Adobe InDesign Tagged Text from the Formats popup menu. InDesign then offers you a choice of how the text of the story and the tags should be saved to disk (see Figure 60-2).

Figure 60-2
InDesign Tagged
Text options

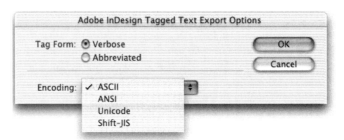

- Verbose writes the tags in a longer form. For example, <StrokeColor: Red> as opposed to the Abbreviated option which would write <sc:Red>. If a human will be reading or editing the tags, you should export using Verbose.

- ASCII is used for most PC systems and is the most common format for representing English characters.

- ANSI includes the ASCII characters and also special punctuation marks and symbols that are not included with the ASCII character set. The Macintosh operating system typically writes text using the ANSI format for plain text.

- Unicode can describe a much larger character set, including thousands of different glyphs, supporting non-European languages.

- Shift-JIS is used for Japanese characters that are to be represented as plain text.

For a detailed description of every code available using the InDesign Tagged Text export option, locate the Tagged Text.pdf file located on your Adobe InDesign CD. This file is also available for download from the Adobe Web site.

Styles

PART 6

Graphics

Links		
EdnasPoemsPart2.pdf	?	47
Big Hair.eps		50
eyeglasses.gray.psd		47
gorillaCMYK72dpi.tif		48

61

Importing Graphics

Importing graphics into your InDesign documents can be very similar to the way you work in QuarkXPress, but InDesign also offers some new ways for you to be more creative and efficient when building your pages. For instance, it supports more flexible ways of creating graphic frames and a wider range of import options.

Placing Graphics

As in QuarkXPress, you can build placeholder frames on your page and import graphics into these frames. Instead of the Get Picture command in QuarkXPress, you use the Place command from the File menu (or press Command-D/Ctrl-D) to select an image to import into the frame. (We discuss the file formats which InDesign supports in the next chapter.)

Flexible Frames

As we discuss in Chapter 10, any frame may contain any content—you do not need to build frames specifically for text or pictures. In fact, you have to be careful here: If you select a text frame with the Selection tool when you place a graphic, InDesign deletes the text and replaces it with the picture! As we discuss in Chapter 69, if you place a graphic when you have an active text insertion point (with the Type tool), the graphic becomes anchored in the text as an inline object.

If you don't want to replace the currently-selected picture or text, or anchor the image in your text, then turn off the Replace Selected Item option in the Place dialog box. This way, InDesign ignores the selected item and simply loads the Place gun. (Or, if you forget and the image replaces a frame's content, you can press Command-Z/Ctrl-Z to reload the Place gun.)

The Place Gun

Unlike QuarkXPress, you can choose the Place command even if you have not preselected a frame. Once you have selected a graphic in the Place dialog box and click OK, the Place command changes your cursor into either a paint brush or an Acrobat cursor (the latter if you choose a PDF file), indicating that it is ready to place a graphic (see Figure 61-1). You can then move this "loaded graphic cursor"—what we've called the "Place gun" since the old PageMaker days—over any empty frame. When you see parentheses around the cursor, click to place the image into the frame.

When you put the Place gun over a frame, it changes slightly

You can also create a frame at the same time you are importing a graphic. Either click and drag with the Place gun to manually define the frame size, or click once and InDesign builds a frame to the size of the image bounding box. This freedom lets you actually build a page at the same time you are importing images, so it is no longer necessary to create a dummy layout with empty boxes prior to importing the images.

Drag & Drop Importing

In Chapter 10, we also describe how you can select one or more files in the Windows or Macintosh Desktop or in Windows Explorer and simply drag the files into InDesign. This is David's favorite method of importing images, especially when he wants to place more than one picture at a time. Remember that if you drag in a single image, you can drag the picture onto any frame on the page (even if it's not selected) to place the graphic inside that frame.

Additional Options

There's one other option in the Place dialog box that affects graphics (the other two are for text files): If you turn on the Show Import Options checkbox, InDesign displays another dialog box (after you click OK), providing specific options for particular graphic file formats. We discuss this in the next chapter. (You can also choose this option by holding down the Shift key when you click OK.)

Graphics

62

Think Outside the Box: InDesign and Graphic File Formats

Because you may be creating documents for different purposes, and because your artwork may be coming from a variety of sources, InDesign allows you to import 14 different graphic file formats. Except for a couple of little-used formats (like PhotoCD), anything QuarkXPress can import, InDesign can, too. However, InDesign lets you import two file formats that XPress does not: native Photoshop (.PSD) and Illustrator (.AI) files.

Importing Native File Formats

The ability to import Photoshop and Illustrator files (native files) without having to first save into flattened .EPS, .JPG, or .TIFF formats can significantly speed the creative process, as you can link in InDesign directly to the original Photoshop or Illustrator files. That way, InDesign can update immediately when you make changes to the graphic. This also means that you can simplify your workflow and only save a single version of each graphic file, rather than two (the original and the flattened version).

Another advantage of placing native Photoshop and Illustrator files is that they can contain transparency which InDesign recognizes. (EPS files don't support transparency.) In some cases, this can eliminate the need for creating clipping paths, as we discuss in Chapter 68.

To Import or Not to Import

The problem is that native Photoshop files—especially those with many layers—can be huge. It probably doesn't make sense to import ten 200 MB .PSD files into InDesign, because when it comes time to send your file to the printer, you have to send those Photoshop files, too. Printing these files isn't a problem (though it takes InDesign a little longer to print because it has to flatten the images before sending them to the printer), but managing them is.

This problem is exacerbated when your native files are higher resolution than you need. For instance, many people manipulate 300-ppi images in Photoshop, but when it comes time to print, they downsample to 225 or 250 (which can save a huge amount of disk space and is plenty of data for 133 or 150 lpi halftones).

If you're dealing with very large Photoshop files, it may make more sense for you to use a more-traditional "downsample, sharpen, flatten, convert-to-CMYK, then export as TIFF" workflow (see David's *Real World Photoshop* for more on Photoshop production issues). On the other hand, there's rarely a problem using native Illustrator files—as they're rarely unwieldy—or smallish Photoshop files.

Native File Format Details

You can place Adobe Illustrator version 5.5 and later files directly into an InDesign document. Version 9 and later support transparency, and this transparency is maintained after importing the graphic into InDesign. In the next chapter, we show how you can even copy editable objects from Illustrator into InDesign.

InDesign can also place Adobe Photoshop version 4.0 and later files into your InDesign documents. All layers and layer masks are flattened when the image is placed in the document (the original image file remains untouched). However, vector objects (like type) are currently rasterized into bitmaps at print time, and InDesign cannot deal with .PSD files that include spot colors.

Alternatives to Native Formats

You might also consider saving your Photoshop files as layered PDF or TIFF files. Most people don't realize that TIFF files can include layers and transparency, and that InDesign can read that information just as easily as if the image were a .PSD file. The reason is that layered TIFF files are a combination of a flattened TIFF and a layered .PSD file. Programs that can read the layered information (like InDesign), do so; programs that cannot (like XPress), read the flattened part. The problem is that layered TIFF files are even bigger than .PSD files. For that reason, many people prefer flattened TIFF files.

In general, Photoshop PDF files are the most flexible format; they can be flattened or layered, include vector and transparency information, and are often surprisingly small on disk. Unfortunately, InDesign can't read spot colors inside Photoshop PDF files. (XPress 4 cannot read Photoshop PDF files at all, though XPress 5 can, with some limitations.)

Recommended Prepress Formats

As we said earlier, InDesign can accept almost any graphic file format you'd want (though it doesn't handle specialized 3-D file formats, Painter files, or CAD files). There's no problem with your using flattened TIFF, EPS, and JPG files rather than native file formats. Here are a few tips that might be useful:

- **TIFF.** This is normally the format we use for saving bitmapped images (if we're not using a native .PSD format). TIFF files can even contain alpha channels or clipping paths created in Photoshop.

- **EPS.** The Encapsulated PostScript (EPS) file format usually contains a low-resolution, low-quality PICT or TIFF preview which, by default, InDesign uses to display the image on screen (like QuarkXPress). However, unlike XPress, InDesign can also interpret the PostScript code in the EPS file and display a high-quality version on screen (see Chapter 66). InDesign can also produce its own proxy preview if one doesn't exist. When printing to a non-PostScript printer, InDesign rasterizes the PostScript so you get a high-quality print, much better than you'd get from XPress.

- **JPEG (.JPG).** The Joint Photographic Experts Group (JPEG) uses a "lossy" compression mechanism which can cause image quality to deteriorate significantly. InDesign can import and print JPEG files, but you should make sure you use a minimum of compression (maximum quality) or else you will likely see image degradation, especially artifacts appearing around sharp high-contrast edges. (Of course, if you're printing to newsprint, no one will notice.)

- **PDF.** As we noted above, PDF is a very flexible and robust file format. We now generally prefer this over the EPS format for vector artwork. However, note that when you make a PDF file, the default in every program we've seen (Distiller, Photoshop, and even InDesign) is to compress bitmapped image data with JPEG compression, degrading them in the process. If you want to save all your image data, turn off compression or use the ZIP setting instead of JPEG (ZIP is a "lossless" form of compression).

- **DCS.** Desktop Color Separations (DCS), developed by Quark, is a version of the standard EPS format. The only good reason to use DCS is when you have a Photoshop image with spot color channels. However, note that DCS files don't support transparency—you can't even put something transparent over them—because InDesign can't get at the high-resolution data (see Chapter 94).

Inappropriate File Formats

Just because InDesign can import and print some file formats doesn't mean you should run out and use them. Here's a list of file formats that InDesign supports, but which we recommend avoiding if you're doing prepress work: GIF, PNG, BMP, PICT, WMF, PCX, Scitex CT. (If you're doing multimedia work, exporting PDFs from InDesign for the Web, then some of these may be appropriate.)

Import Options

The options available when you place a graphic are dependent on the file format of the graphic you are placing. The import options appear in a new dialog box when the Show Import Options checkbox is turned on in the Place dialog box (or if it's off and you hold down the Shift key when clicking OK). Generally, the options you set remain in effect for that file format until you change them.

Here's a list of the primary image import options:

- **Apply Photoshop Clipping Path.** When you place a TIFF or Photoshop file which contains a clipping path, turning on this option applies the clipping path automatically. If you leave this off, you can still apply the clipping path later (see Chapter 68). Note that this option is available with EPS files, too, but it will likely get you in trouble if you turn it on because it makes it appear that you can edit that clipping path in InDesign when you really can't.

- **Color Settings.** There are three color management options which can be selected for individual graphics—Enable Color Management, Profile, and Rendering Intent. We discuss these in Chapter 87.

- **Read Embedded OPI Image Links.** Available only for EPS files. We discuss this in Chapter 95.

- **Proxy Generation.** Available only for EPS files. Select Use TIFF or PICT Preview to use the embedded preview stored in the file or choose Rasterize the PostScript to have InDesign create a preview.

- **Place PDF Options.** When you choose Show Import Options for a PDF file, the Place PDF dialog box appears. You can click the arrows under the preview or type a page number to select the page of a multi-page PDF. The Crop menu lets you choose how much of a PDF page to place. The Preserve Halftone Screens option overrides InDesign's settings when the PDF contains halftone screens. When the Transparent Background option is chosen, the background of a PDF containing transparency is honored; if turned off, the background is opaque.

63

Copying Objects To and From Adobe Illustrator

While InDesign can place native Illustrator (.AI) files, you can also copy Illustrator objects directly into InDesign through dragging and dropping or copying and pasting. When you copy objects from Illustrator they usually remain fully editable in InDesign with some proper setup. In our tests, this also works with Macromedia FreeHand. Even more cool, you can copy InDesign objects and paste them into Adobe Illustrator (not FreeHand). None of this is possible in QuarkXPress.

Setting Up Illustrator

Although you can always copy and paste objects from Illustrator into InDesign, if you are using Illustrator 9 or later you may not be able to edit the objects in InDesign unless you first set up the Illustrator's preferences properly. In Adobe Illustrator, select the Files & Clipboard Preferences (see Figure 63-1). Choose the AICB option in the Clipboard portion of the preferences to keep objects editable when copied from Illustrator into InDesign (AICB is the Adobe Illustrator Clipboard format, similar to EPS).

Copying Objects Into InDesign

When you copy and paste one or more objects from Illustrator into InDesign, they become InDesign objects, and they can usually be edited just as if

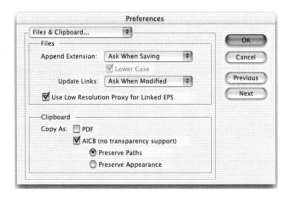

Figure 63-1
To edit Illustrator objects after pasting, set Illustrator's preferences to copy objects using AICB.

they were created using InDesign drawing tools. When objects are copied into InDesign they are not linked to the original file and do not appear in the Links palette. The same thing goes for objects that are dragged from Illustrator onto your InDesign page.

Of course, InDesign does not have all of the drawing tools or features found in Adobe Illustrator. Because of this, certain objects will not be editable when copied from Illustrator to InDesign. For example, an object with a gradient mesh becomes an embedded EPS file when it is copied and pasted into your InDesign document. This can be problematic, and we suggest you avoid it when possible.

Similarly, when text is copied from Illustrator, it has limited editability. It appears in InDesign as an image and can't be selected with the Type tool, but it prints in high resolution.

Copying Objects from InDesign into Illustrator

Our friend Sandee Cohen discovered that you can also copy paths from InDesign and paste them into Illustrator 10. To do this, you must set InDesign's General Preferences to Copy PDF to Clipboard. We recommend that you only use this method for very simple objects, but it's nice to know you can do it!

One tip here: When you paste an InDesign object into Illustrator, you actually get the object plus a clipping mask object. You will probably need to select Release from the Clipping Mask submenu (under the Object menu in Illustrator) and then select Ungroup from the Object menu before you can do anything useful with the shape. Also note that the InDesign object must have a stroke, a fill, or content, or else Illustrator ignores it.

Scaling Graphics Precisely

It's easy to scale a graphic inside a picture box in QuarkXPress. It's just as easy in InDesign, but InDesign also has some ways of handling graphics that may make you a little crazy until you learn how they're different than QuarkXPress.

Big Differences

In XPress, when you make a picture box and use Get Picture to put an image in it, only the box appears as a editable object: you can move a picture within the box with the Content tool, but you can't see the bounding box handles of the picture itself. When you place a picture in InDesign, the program sees it as two objects: the frame and the graphic nested inside of it. If you choose the Selection tool, you can manipulate the frame. If you choose the Direct Selection tool, you can manipulate the content—the graphic itself, including its bounding box. Fortunately, InDesign displays the graphic bounding box in a different color (the inverse of the current layer color).

When you apply numeric scaling to graphics in XPress, there is only one scaling value, which appears in the Measurement palette or the Modify dialog box. However, since InDesign gives you access to both the frame and the graphic bounding box, in some cases each may have a different scaling value!

So, when you manipulate a picture in InDesign, *always pay attention to which tool is selected.* Select an image with the Direct Selection tool to adjust only the image, or select it with the Selection tool to adjust *both* the image and its frame together. If you want to change the frame but not its contents, first Option/Alt-click on the frame with the Direct Selection tool, or turn off the Scale Content option in the Transform palette's flyout menu.

Scaling Images

There are several ways to scale images in InDesign, most of them similar to ways you do it in XPress.

Scaling with Fitting Commands

First, as in QuarkXPress, you can choose menu commands (or a context menu, or keyboard shortcuts) to center or fit the graphic to the frame or the frame to the graphic (see Figure 64-1). Select the graphic frame with the Selection tool and choose among these commands:

Figure 64-1
The context menu
for fitting images

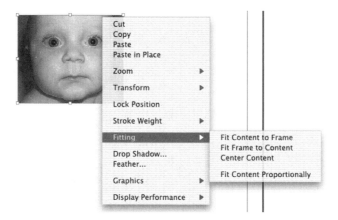

- Choose Fit Content Proportionally from the Fitting submenu (under the Object menu) or press Command-Option-Shift-E/Ctrl-Alt-Shift-E to resize the image to the maximum size that will proportionally fit the frame.

- Choose the Fit Content to Frame option (or press Command-Option-E/Ctrl-Alt-E) to scale the image to the frame size, allowing it to distort.

- Use the Fit Frame to Content option (or press Command-Option-C/Ctrl-Alt-C) to resize the frame so that it is the same size as the imported image.

- Use the Center Content option (or press Command-Shift-E/Ctrl-Shift-E) to center the graphic in the frame.

Scaling With Key Commands

As in QuarkXPress, you can also use keyboard shortcuts to change the size of an imported graphic. Press Command-./Ctrl-. (period) to increase the size of a selected image or press Command-,/Ctrl-, (comma) to reduce the size of an image. In either case you are adjusting the size in one percent increments. You can increase or decrease the size in five percent increments by adding the Option/Alt key.

Scaling with the Transform Palette

After selecting an image, you can use the Transform palette, the Scale tool, or the Free Transform tool to scale an image to a specific value (we discuss these methods in Chapters 17 and 18). If you use the Transform palette, you can enter the percent to scale vertically or horizontally. If you want the horizontal and vertical values to be the same, type one value and then press Command-Enter/Ctrl-Enter to duplicate the value to the other field.

Also, use this palette to determine the scaling previously applied to an imported image, but be certain to click on the image with the Direct Selection tool to obtain an accurate reading of its scaling.

Scaling a Graphic by Dragging

You can also scale graphics interactively (but not precisely) by dragging the bounding box handles with the Selection tool as we describe in Chapter 17. To scale a graphic frame and its contents together, hold down the Command/Ctrl and Shift keys while dragging. Note that when you use this method, the frame doesn't retain the scaling value (the scale fields in the Transform palette return to 100 percent). If you select the image with the Direct Selection tool, however, you can see the true scaling value.

Graphics

65

Linking & Embedding Graphics

InDesign handles imported graphics similarly to QuarkXPress: By default, the program links to the image on disk rather than embedding the high-resolution data. However, InDesign not only makes it easier to manage linked graphics but it also lets you do things with these images that XPress does not.

The Links Palette

You can use InDesign's Links palette just as you would the Pictures panel of the Usage dialog box in QuarkXPress. InDesign uses the Links palette to list the placed graphics within your document, informing you whether any files have been modified or are missing. Like XPress's Usage dialog box, the palette can also show you the image's file path on disk.

To open the Links palette, choose Links from the Window menu or press Command-Shift-D/Ctrl-Shift-D. The Links palette also opens automatically if it detects a missing or modified file when you open a document; it then gives you the option of fixing the links immediately or waiting until later. The Links palette tracks all the linked graphics and text or word processing files in your document (we discuss text linking in Chapter 39). You can sort the list by name, page, or status by choosing these options on the palette's flyout menu.

Updating and Changing Graphic Links

If you have edited an image or changed it in any way, InDesign displays a yellow triangle icon adjacent to the its name in the Links palette (see

Figure 65-1). If you want InDesign to relink to the updated version, select the file's name in the Links palette and click the Update Link button or choose Update Link from the Links palette's flyout menu.

InDesign lacks QuarkXPress' option for Auto Picture Import. However, it's easy to update all your graphics at once. Simply deselect all the linked graphic names by clicking in the blank space at the bottom of the palette.

Figure 65-1

The Links palette

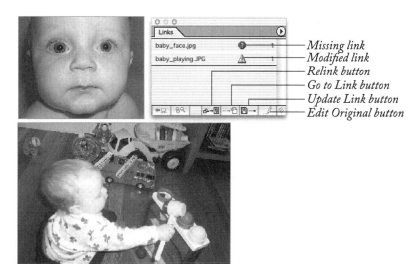

Missing link
Modified link
Relink button
Go to Link button
Update Link button
Edit Original button

Then click the Update Link button, and all the modified graphics will be updated at once.

InDesign alerts you to images that it can no longer find on disk with a red stop sign icon in the Links palette. You can help InDesign locate the missing file by clicking the Relink button or choosing Relink from the palette's flyout menu. This command lets you then navigate to the new location of a file or specify a new file to use in place of the current file. (If you've placed a PDF file, relinking conveniently remembers what page you placed.)

Go to the Graphic

When you have lots of graphics spread across many pages, you can select a graphic on the palette, and tell InDesign to display the image by clicking the Go to Link button or selecting Go to Link from the palette's flyout menu. This is equivalent to XPress's Show button in the Usage dialog box. An even faster way is to Option/Alt-double-click a file name in the Links palette.

Information about Graphics

QuarkXPress displays information about each linked graphic in the Pictures panel of the Usage dialog box. You can get similar information— including file path, modification date, page number, color information, and file type—by either double-clicking on a graphic's name or choosing Link Information from the palette menu. In the Link Information dialog box, you can click the Next and Prev buttons to navigate through all your graphic links, and even relink to other graphics.

Editing the Original Graphic

A nice feature of InDesign is the ability to open an original graphic directly from the Links palette. To do this, select the graphic and click the Edit Original button. You can also select Edit Original from the Links' flyout menu or from the context menu (under the Graphics submenu).

Embedding Graphics

You can avoid the need to update or relink images by embedding the graphics into your InDesign file (XPress can't do this). While this eliminates the need to keep track of separate files, this option limits the flexibility of being able to manipulate the separate files.

To embed a file, select it in the Links palette and choose Embed in the palette's flyout menu. An Embed icon indicates an embedded file in the Links palette. Later, you can select the embedded file name and select Unembed command from the palette menu if you need to relink to the original image file (or if you lost the original and want to get the picture out again).

Because embedding images can create very large InDesign files that are more susceptible to becoming corrupt, we (and our service providers) prefer to keep our image files linked as opposed to embedded. On the other hand, if the image is small (like a 20K EPS file that you're using as a bullet in fifty places throughout your document), embedding isn't so bad.

Display Options

One of the great technologies that Adobe has put under the hood of InDesign is its ability to display graphics based upon their high-resolution information. Since QuarkXPress is always limited to low-resolution proxy previews of graphics (unless you use a third-party XTension) this is a major step forward and provides you with a better representation on screen of what your printed piece will actually look like.

View Menu Settings

InDesign gives you the ability to display each open window with a different display setting. To change the setting, choose from the View menu: Optimized Display, Typical Display, or High Quality Display (see Figure 66-1).

- **Optimized.** Select this setting (or press Command-Option-O/Ctrl-Alt-O) to gray out all images and turn off transparency effects—useful when proofing or entering copy in long documents.

- **Typical.** You can choose this setting (or press Command-Option-Z/Ctrl-Alt-Z) to view images with low-resolution proxy previews similar to the way they are displayed in QuarkXPress.

- **High Quality.** When you choose this setting (or press Command-Option-H/Ctrl-Alt-H) you can see your images at the same resolution

Figure 66-1
Display Quality

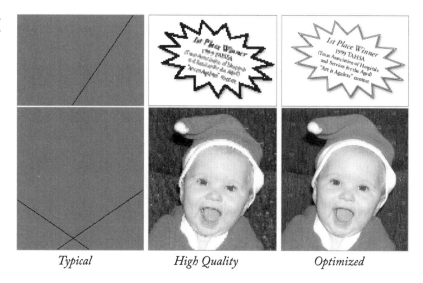

Typical   *High Quality*   *Optimized*

they display in Photoshop and Illustrator. This is more or less "Display PostScript."

You might think that higher quality is always better. However, the High Quality display setting is calculation intensive and will slow down all but the fastest computers. If working in High Quality mode works for you, then go for it. But if you find InDesign displaying your pages very slowly, try using Typical or Optimized, or only applying the High Quality display mode to images that really need it (see below).

Individual Image Display Settings

InDesign lets you apply a display choice to each image via the Display Performance submenu in either the Object menu or the context menu. For instance, we often use Typical display for the document and then apply High Quality display on vector EPS images (which are notoriously difficult to see on screen).

If you have applied local display settings but then want to override them, choose Ignore Local Display Settings from the View menu. You can also remove an image's local display setting by selecting Use View Setting from the Display Performance submenu.

Setting Display Defaults

The three display settings are generally good enough, but InDesign lets you tweak them in the Display Performance panel of the Preferences dialog box (see Figure 66-2). If you really care about what these settings do (we can't imagine that there are many who do), go see David's book *Real World InDesign 2*.

Figure 66-2
Display
Performance
Preferences
dialog box

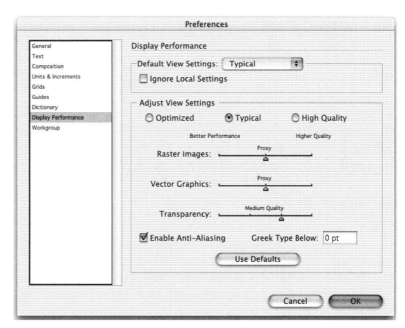

67

Colorizing Images

Both QuarkXPress and InDesign let you apply color to a grayscale or black-and-white (Bitmap) TIFF image. They both also let you apply a color to the background of an image's frame to create a "fake-duotone effect." However, when applying colors, XPress users have to get accustomed to using the right tool to select the right item.

If you want to colorize the image itself (only grayscale or black-and-white TIFF, JPEG, or PSD files), you must select it using the Direct Selection tool. As we explain in Chapter 64, this selects the graphic, rather than the frame. Then you can use either the Swatches or Color palette to apply a color to the image. Using the Tint slider on the Swatches palette has the same effect as choosing a Shade from XPress's Style menu.

InDesign also lets you change the fill color of the graphic frame by clicking on it with the Selection tool. Unfortunately, there's no way to tell InDesign to overprint the image on the background color, so it always knocks out. It's pretty ugly; we don't recommend it.

By the way, QuarkXPress's Contrast and Halftone features originated in early versions of XPress when most users didn't use an application like Adobe Photoshop. These days, most graphics professionals would choose to use Photoshop to manipulate their images with much more control than the crude settings XPress offers. Adobe has chosen not to implement these features in InDesign.

68

Clipping Paths

Clipping paths are PostScript (Bézier) paths that clip out a portion of an image. Clipping paths have long been the primary way to create "transparency" effects in QuarkXPress, but there are two problems with clipping paths. First, they can take a long time to create. Second, they always have very sharp edges (part of the image is either in the path or outside of it). Because InDesign can now read image transparency, you may not have to take the time to draw a clipping path; also, the transparency features support soft edges.

Nevertheless, you may still need to deal with a clipping path from time to time, so we'd better explain how InDesign handles them. In short, InDesign deals with clipping paths almost exactly the way XPress does. (Of course, InDesign also adds a few fun options not available in XPress, too.)

Using Embedded Paths

Paths or clipping paths that you have saved within images in the TIFF, PSD or JPEG formats and imported into InDesign can be used to silhouette images. (Clipping paths in EPS files are *always* used.) You can apply a clipping path by selecting an image with the Selection or Direct Selection tool and choosing Clipping Path from the Object menu (or press Command-Option-Shift-K/Ctrl-Alt-Shift-K). Then, in the Clipping Path dialog box, select Photoshop Path from the Type popup menu. If there's more than one path embedded, choose which one you want to use (see Figure 68-1).

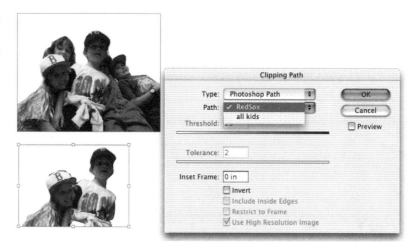

Figure 68-1
The Clipping Path
dialog box

Creating Clipping Paths

If you import an image without an embedded clipping path, you can ask InDesign to create one using the Detect Edges option, which is similar to QuarkXPress's Non-white Areas clipping path feature. You can use this feature to drop out a solid colored (white or near-white) background behind an image. After selecting an image to clip and choosing the Clipping Path command from the Object menu, choose the Detect Edges option from the Type popup menu in the Clipping Path dialog box.

With the Detect Edges option selected, you can determine how close to the color white a pixel must be before it is ignored and removed from the visible area with the Threshold control (see Figure 68-2). Lighter backgrounds require a lower threshold whereas darker images require a higher value. The Tolerance setting determines how different a pixel is from the Threshold value for it to be recognized in creating the clipping path. Finally, the Inset Clipping Path choice lets you shrink the resulting clipping path, often to remove a white fringe around the image.

If the image has an extra channel in it, you can also tell InDesign to base the clipping path on it by choosing Alpha Channel from the Type popup menu in the Clipping Path dialog box. In this case, anything 50-percent black or darker in the channel is outside of the path.

In general, we usually shy away from using either the Detect Edges or the Alpha Channel features except perhaps for a quick comp. They're just too clunky.

Figure 68-2
Clipping path made
with Detect Edges

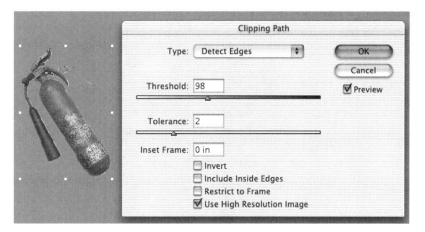

Editing a Clipping Path

Both QuarkXPress and InDesign allow you to edit a clipping path which is imported or created. You might do this occasionally, for example, to perform a "quick fix" on a poorly created clipping path. In InDesign, in the anchor points of the clipping path appear whenever you select the image with the Direct Selection tool. You can then use any of the path-editing tools to edit a clipping path. If you open the Clipping Paths dialog box now, you'll see the Type popup menu has changed to User-Modified Path.

InDesign has an advantage over QuarkXPress when editing clipping paths because you can turn on the High Quality Display choice on the View menu or the context menu to zoom in as you're editing the path; XPress is limited to a low-resolution preview.

Converting Clipping Paths to Frames

Every so often, you need to convert a clipping path into an actual shape on the page. For example, you might want to place text around an image in the same shape as the clipping path. This is simply impossible in QuarkXPress. However, you can do it easily in InDesign: First, choose the graphic with the Direct Selection tool so you see the clipping path. Then Control-click/right-click on the clipping path to open the context menu, from which you can select Convert Clipping Path to Frame. InDesign replaces the image's frame with a new frame in the shape of the clipping path (see Figure 68-3).

Figure 68-3

We used Detect Edges to make a clipping path, and then used Convert Clipping Path to Frame to get a frame on which we could place the text.

PART 7

Where Text Meets Graphics

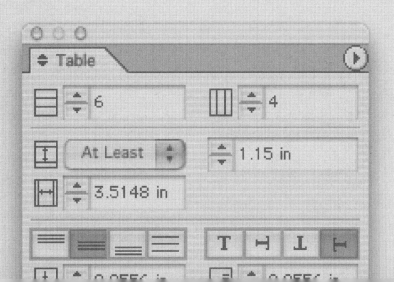

Inline Objects

What QuarkXPress calls anchored boxes, InDesign names *inline objects*. As we describe in Chapter 13, InDesign actually takes the concept further by allowing any frame to be embedded in another other frame—and they can be nested as deeply as you like. This chapter is where we talk about how you can anchor objects in text, so they flow when the text changes.

The current versions of both QuarkXPress and InDesign allow you to include text frames, graphics frames, frames without content, paths, text paths, and groups as inline objects. If you want to anchor multiple objects, you need to group them first. Neither application allows you to link text in an inline object to another text frame.

Creating Inline Objects

There are two ways you can create inline objects in InDesign:

- You can use the XPress method: Select the object with the Selection tool and copy it to the Clipboard. Then use the Type tool to click an insertion point where you want the object to be anchored, and use the Paste command under the Edit menu.

- You can click an insertion point with the Type tool and choose Place from the File menu. Select a graphic file, and click Open. (Choosing a text file just inserts the text into the text flow in the original frame.)

We usually find the first method is more practical because you can size your inline object more easily before pasting.

Manipulating an Inline Object

Once an object is inline, it's treated like a character in the text flow, exactly as in XPress. If you want to move an inline object, you can't drag it because it's embedded in the text: You'll need to select it with the Type tool, and then cut and paste it to another position. (The easiest way to select an inline object "character" is to click an insertion point with the Type tool just before or after it, and then press the Left or Right Arrow key while pressing the Shift key.) To delete the object, select it—either click on it with the Selection tool or drag over it with the Type tool—and press the Delete key.

You can transform an anchored object in a variety of ways. You can use the Selection tool to drag the handles of a frame to change its size. Unlike XPress, you can extend the boundaries of the inline object past the right edge of the text frame, and you can apply transformations on an inline object with the Scale, Rotate, Shear, or Free Transform tools, or the Transform palette. You can change the object's color or transparency. There are almost no limitations on these kinds of manipulations.

Adjusting Leading and Spacing

The object you paste or place must fit within the height of the text frame, though it can be wider. When you paste or place an object, you will probably have to adjust the space around it within the text. Here are some tips for doing that.

- If you want the object to sit between paragraphs of text, place it in a paragraph of its own. Select the object as we describe above, and set the leading to Auto on the Character palette Leading menu so the leading can expand, and it won't overlap the previous line. You can also adjust the paragraph Space Above or Space Below values.

- If you want the object to float within a line of text (for example, an icon graphic to be used in a manual), reduce its size with the Selection tool to fit the leading.

- To adjust the position of the inline object vertically, you can drag it up or down with the Selection or Direct Selection tool. However, we prefer to select the object with the Type tool, and adjust its position with Baseline Shift on the Character palette because it's more accurate.

- To adjust the object's position horizontally, place an insertion point before or after the frame and adjust the Kerning value.

The No Ascent Workaround

When you create an anchored box in XPress, you can select it and set whether the box aligns with the text's ascent or baseline in the Modify dialog box, or on the Measurements palette. If you select Ascent, XPress automatically runs text around the object.

Unfortunately, InDesign doesn't offer an ascent option, and there is also no way to set text wrap for an inline object. However, there is a workaround which, while not as easy as the XPress method, often works. Typically, you need this effect at the beginning of the paragraph (see Figure 69-1). You can create an ascent effect by using InDesign's Drop Cap feature.

Figure 69-1

Using a graphic frame as a drop cap

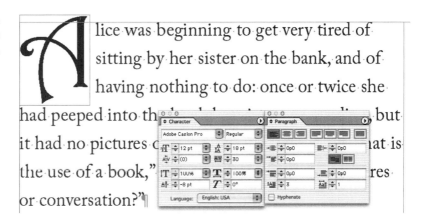

Here's how you can do it:

1. Paste the inline object into the text as described above.

2. In the Paragraph palette, adjust the Drop Cap Number of Lines menu to create the ascent. To fine-tune the vertical position, use Baseline Shift on the Character palette or drag the inline graphic up or down.

3. Place the text insertion point between the inline frame and the first character of the paragraph and pressing Option/Alt-Right Arrow to adjust the space with a positive kern value.

70

Paragraph Rules

Paragraph rules are a paragraph attribute which places lines above, below, and sometimes through the text of a paragraph. The way they are implemented is very similar in QuarkXPress and InDesign, yet there are some subtle differences which can affect the way they are used.

Setting Appearance

In both programs, you can add a paragraph rule using a dialog box or in a paragraph style. In InDesign, select one or more paragraphs with the Type tool, and then choose Paragraph Rule from the Paragraph palette's flyout menu (or press Command-Option-J/Ctrl-Alt-J). The Paragraph Rules dialog box appears (see Figure 70-1). Unfortunately, while InDesign allows you to set both a Rule Above and a Rule Below in the same paragraph, you must select one or the other from the popup menu, and you can only look at the settings for one at a time. Be sure to turn on the Preview option, which works similarly to XPress's Apply button.

QuarkXPress lets you set a rule's Width, Color, Shade and Style. In InDesign, you can set the Weight, Color, and Tint. Sadly, there are no options to include a styled rule (dashed or dotted, for example) in the Paragraph Rules dialog box. To add one, you must create it as an inline object (see Chapter 69). On the other hand, InDesign lets you use any color you've created in the Swatches palette, including gradients. InDesign also lets you apply "[Text Color]", which is defined as the color of the first character in the paragraph for a Rule Above, or the last character for a Rule Below. In InDesign, you may also set the rule to have an overprinting stroke.

Figure 70-1
The Rule Above applied to the heading of this poem is so thick that it makes the heading appear "reversed out."

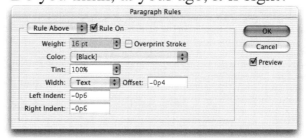

Positioning the Rules

There are two attributes used when positioning a rule or rules in a paragraph: The vertical position (the "Offset") and the horizontal position.

Vertical Position

QuarkXPress allows you to set the Offset using either absolute positioning (a specific value from the baseline) or with a percentage of the space between this paragraph and the one before or after it. InDesign, however, only allows absolute positioning. As in XPress, the offset for Rule Above is measured from the baseline of the top line of the text to bottom of the rule. The offset for Rule Below is measured from the baseline of the last line of text to the top of the rule.

Note that to make the reversed type heading in Figure 70-1, a *negative* Offset value was used to begin the rule four points below the baseline. This is often done when you want to use the rule to create a reversed out effect or a tint background to the paragraph. XPress has strict limits as to how large the negative Offset can be; InDesign does not—you can even place the rule outside of the text frame!

Horizontal Position

As in QuarkXPress, you may set a paragraph rule to be the width of the text or the column—a choice you make in the Width popup menu—and adjust that based on the Left and Right Indent values. However, the indents work a little differently in the two programs. In QuarkXPress, the column width is the width of the text (including any paragraph indents). In InDesign, the column is the column as defined by the text frame and the Text Inset value (from the Text Frame Options dialog box).

Both InDesign and XPress let you use negative values for the indents, but XPress never allows the rule to extend past the edge of the text box. In InDesign, you can push the rule out as far as you want (even bleeding off the page).

Text Wraps

When text meets graphics, or any two objects on your page overlap, your page layout application lets you choose how the two shall meet. In QuarkXPress, this choice is called runaround, and it's controlled in the Runaround panel of the Modify dialog box. In InDesign, it's called *text wrap*, and you make your choices in the Text Wrap palette.

Wrap Options

When you want to set the text wrap around an object, open the Text Wrap palette from the Window menu (or press Command-Option-W/Ctrl-Alt-W) If necessary, choose Show Options from the palette's flyout menu to see the contour options at the bottom of the palette (see Figure 71-1).

Both QuarkXPress and InDesign let you set the text wrap for almost any object—graphic frame, text frame, path, text path, or contentless frame. To set a default runaround in XPress (for new objects you create), you set your choices in Tool Preferences. In InDesign, you set your default options on the Text Wrap palette with no object selected.

QuarkXPress lets you create three types of runarounds: None, Picture Bounds (a rectangular runaround to the edges of a picture), and a contour which can be shaped around an object. InDesign gives you five choices. The first three—No Text Wrap, Wrap Around Bounding Box, and Wrap Around Object Shape—correspond to the XPress options. In addition, you can choose the Jump Object option (which forces text in any column touching the text wrap boundary to skip past the object), or Jump to Next

Figure 71-1
The Text Wrap
palette

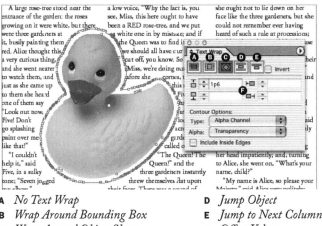

A *No Text Wrap*
B *Wrap Around Bounding Box*
C *Wrap Around Object Shape*
D *Jump Object*
E *Jump to Next Column*
F *Offset Values*

Column (which forces text into the next column or text frame when it encounters a text wrap).

To create a text wrap in InDesign, select the object you want to wrap text around with the Selection or Direct Selection tool, and click one of the buttons in the palette. When you choose a rectangular wrap, you have the opportunity to set offset values on four sides of the object.

Creating Contours

Both QuarkXPress and InDesign provide several ways to create contours that follow the shape of a frame, the graphic inside a frame, a path, and so on. In InDesign, when you choose Wrap Around Object Shape, the contour options at the bottom of the palette become available. Table 71-1 compares the choices for creating contours in the two applications.

Contour Choices

Both QuarkXPress and InDesign can read paths and clipping paths which are stored in TIFF, JPEG or EPS files, and InDesign can read them in Photoshop PSD files, too. To do this in InDesign, select Photoshop Path from the Type popup menu in the Text Wrap palette, and then select the name of the path you want to use for the wrap in the Path menu. Similarly, if the image has an extra channel, you can use it by choosing Alpha, and then selecting the name of the channel to use. Note that InDesign, unlike XPress, treats an image's transparency mask (the boundary of transparent areas) as an additional channel.

Table 71-1

Runaround versus Text Wrap terminology

What QuarkXPress calls…	InDesign calls…
Item	Graphic Frame
Embedded Path	Photoshop Path
Alpha Channel	Alpha Channel
Same as Clipping	Same as Clipping
Non-white Areas	Detect Edges
Auto Image	[No equivalent]

The other contour options are similar to the choices in XPress: Graphic Frame follows the shape of the frame the graphic is in. Same as Clipping follows a clipping path saved with the graphic. Detect Edges uses InDesign's automatic edge detection, which only really works with graphics where there is a distinct edge to detect (when the image is against a white background).

To let text appear on the inside of an object, select Inside Edges on the Text Wrap palette. To run text on the inside of an object rather than the outside, choose the Invert option.

Editing the Contour

In QuarkXPress, you must select a menu command to see a runaround path and edit it. InDesign displays the runaround path in a tint of the layer color whenever you select the graphic with the Direct Selection tool. Then you can use the Direct Selection tool and any of the path editing tools to edit the runaround path (see Chapter 12).

Controlling Text Wrap

In QuarkXPress, runaround can only be applied when the text is below the runaround object (in the stacking order). In InDesign, text wrap operates whether the wrap object is above or below the text. This can really mess up a new user, as text starts disappearing for "no reason." Unfortunately, text wrap also even operates when the wrap object is on a hidden layer.

When you need to prevent text from wrapping around an object with a text wrap, select the text frame, choose Text Frame Options from the Object menu (or press Command-B/Ctrl-B), and turn on the Ignore Text Wrap option.

Two other differences between QuarkXPress and InDesign: In XPress, text normally wraps on only one side of a graphic, and you have to choose

Where Text Meets Graphics

a text box option to run on both sides. In InDesign, text always wraps on both sides of a graphic. Also, you can apply runaround to objects on a master page in XPress. For some silly reason InDesign doesn't let you do this (you can do it, but the wrap is ignored on your document pages).

72

Converting Text to Outlines

Each of the characters in the fonts we use in page layout is composed of resolution-independent outlines which can be scaled to any size. Sometimes you want access to these character outlines to create special effects with type. Both QuarkXPress and InDesign allow you to convert text to outlines, and to manipulate the character shapes once you have converted them to paths.

Creating Outlines

To convert text to outlines in InDesign, either select a text frame with the Selection tool, or select characters with the Type tool. Then choose Create Outlines from the Type menu (or press Command-Shift-O/Ctrl-Shift-O). In QuarkXPress, you're limited to converting only one line of type at a time, but InDesign has no limit on the number of lines you can convert.

QuarkXPress, by default, creates the outlines as a separate item, outside of the text box. By contrast, InDesign's default behavior is to literally convert the text into outlines, anchoring them as a inline object within the text frame. (We discuss inline objects in Chapter 69.) If you want to make the outlines a separate copy, hold down the Option/Alt key when choosing the Create Outlines command (or add it to the keyboard shortcut). Then a copy of the type is created on top of the original; use the Selection tool to move it elsewhere.

If you didn't realize that your outlines were an inline object, and you need to remove them from the frame, click on the outlines with the

Selection tool, then cut the outlined text to the Clipboard and paste it elsewhere.

Conversion Issues

You can convert PostScript Type 1, TrueType or OpenType fonts to outlines. However, you must be using a font whose manufacturer allows the type to be outlined (some fonts are restricted in their use).

When type is converted to outlines, its hinting (the built-in rules that makes a font look good at small sizes or low resolution) is lost, so outlined text may look somewhat different than the editable original. In addition, if you have applied a stroke around type in InDesign, the program is smart enough to put the stroke around the *outside* of the characters. When you convert that text to outlines, the letterforms become paths, and the strokes are *centered* on the paths (which is true of all PostScript paths). The appearance of outlined type can change dramatically (see Figure 72-1).

Figure 72-1
Stroked text converted to outlines alters the appearance because of the way the strokes are applied.

You should also be careful not to convert too much text to outlines at the same time. InDesign allows you to convert many lines at a time, but the resulting paths may not be printable if they are too complex!

Manipulating Outlines

When type is converted to outlines, the resulting outlines are compound objects. (We discuss compound objects and how to edit them in Chapter 16.) You can use the Direct Selection tool to select the subpaths in the outlines, and use any of the path editing tools to edit the shapes. If you need to work with the individual paths which make up the compound path, choose Release from the Compound Paths submenu (under the Object menu).

After text has been converted to outlines, there are many ways you can use them, including the following:

- You can edit the individual character shapes.

- You can place text or graphics in the outline frame.

- You can use the Paste Inside command as we describe in Chapter 13 to nest another object inside the outlines.

Where Text Meets Graphics

73

Text and Graphics on a Path

Both QuarkXPress and InDesign let you set text along a path. In fact, since both programs also support inline objects (which we discuss in Chapter 69), text on a path can be extended to include graphics on a path as well. We discuss both features in this chapter.

Creating Path Type

To create path type in QuarkXPress, you use one of the four tools dedicated to that function or you convert a text box into a text path. InDesign works a bit differently. It doesn't use specialized tools to create the path: Instead, you can use any of the path creation and editing tools which we describe in Chapter 12. You can create path type on any open or closed path (but not compound paths). InDesign can't convert shapes to paths.

When you want to change a regular path into a text path, choose the Path Type tool, normally hidden under the Type tool (or press Shift-T). Then move the cursor over the path until you see a small + cursor. This indicates that if you click, or if you click and drag, you'll turn an ordinary path into a path type text frame (see Figure 73-1).

Clicking or Clicking-and-Dragging

If you click with the Path Type tool on an open path, an insertion point appears at the start of the path by default. (If the current default paragraph settings are not flush left or if they include an indent, the cursor may appear somewhere else on the path.) When you type or paste text, the text can

Figure 73-1

When using the Path Type tool, look for the small + indicator when you're over a path. Then click, or click and drag to change the path into a path type text frame.

extend the full length of the path. If you click on a closed path (like an oval), InDesign places the insertion point exactly where you clicked.

If you click and drag with the Path Type tool along the path instead, you determine where the text begins and ends on the path (you can't do this in XPress). Where you start dragging, a *start handle* appears, and as you're dragging an *end handle* moves along the path, indicating the end of the text (see Figure 73-2). After dragging to indicate where the text will go, type or paste text on the path.

Figure 73-2

Watch the cursor change when you're working with path type text.

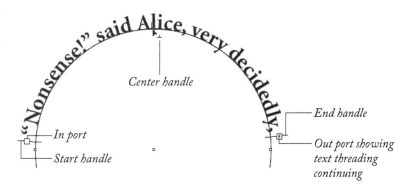

At the center of the path text, a small vertical *center handle* also appears. In addition, because path type works like a single-line text frame, you also see an in port and out port which can be used for threading the text to or from another text path or a regular text frame.

Path Type Controls

QuarkXPress offers several options for styling text on a path in the Modify dialog box. InDesign has similar path type controls in the Path Type Options dialog box, which you may open in one of three ways (see Figure 73-3). The easiest method is to double-click the Path Type tool. You can also select Options from the Type on a Path submenu (under the Type menu), or you can use the context menu when path type is selected.

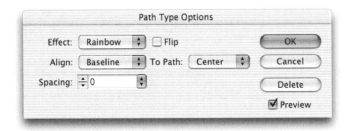

QuarkXPress offers four styles of path type which vary how the text is oriented to the line; XPress's styles don't have names, only icons and buttons in the Modify dialog box. InDesign offers five similar Effects (see Figure 73-4):

- **Rainbow.** This is the default style, and it corresponds to XPress's default style in which characters follow the path, rotating along the curve.
- **Skew.** This effect rotates the characters along the curve, then skews them so they remains upright.
- **3D Ribbon.** This skews the characters, but doesn't rotate them.
- **Stair Step.** Here, the characters are neither rotated nor skewed.

Figure 73-4
Path type effects

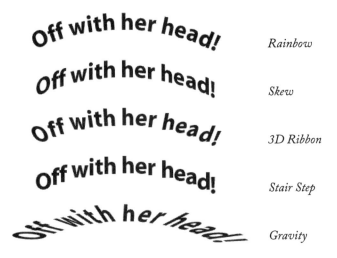

- **Gravity.** Not available in XPress, this strange effect keeps the bottom of the characters' baseline on the path while keeping each vertical edge in line with the path's center point.

As in QuarkXPress, you can align the text to the path based on the text's baseline, center, ascender or descender. You can also adjust to the path's top, center or bottom. There is a Flip checkbox like in XPress which allows you to flip the type you've created across the path. (Unlike XPress, you can also use the Selection or Direct Selection tool to drag the center handle of path type across the path to flip it.)

The Spacing control lets you compensate for the fact that characters spread out when they are over a tight curve (XPress can't do this). By entering a positive value, InDesign removes extra space from characters near a curve, but leaves the spacing of those on straight segments unchanged.

Editing Path Type

You can use the Selection or Direct Selection tools to drag the path type handles, manipulating the position of the type along the path. (Be careful not to click the in port or out port.) You can also drag the center handle to finesse the positioning.

Because path type is a special kind of text "frame," its position is also controlled by the settings on the Paragraph palette. For example, clicking the Center icon (or pressing Command-Shift-C/Ctrl-Shift-C) centers the type along the path between the start and end handles. You can also use tabs and indents to move text along a path, but manipulating the handles is usually easier.

Threading Text

If not all your text fits on the path type frame, it gets overset. However, because path type has in and out ports, you can continue the text flow using InDesign's threading methods to create connections from one path to another, or between paths and regular text frames. Just use the Selection tool to click the in and out ports using the techniques we describe in Chapter 40.

Deleting Path Type

If you want to remove type from a path, select Delete Type from Path from the Type on a Path submenu (under the Type menu). This turns the path type "frame" into a regular path. If the path text is threaded, it will flow to another frame; if it is not, the text is deleted.

Where Text Meets Graphics

Graphics on a Path

For special effects, you can also create graphics on a path. Since both InDesign and XPress support inline objects, you can paste graphics onto a text path. In Figure 73-5, we pasted a pig image onto a path a number of times, and then used the tracking and baseline shift features to control their position along the line.

Figure 73.5

Creating graphics on a path

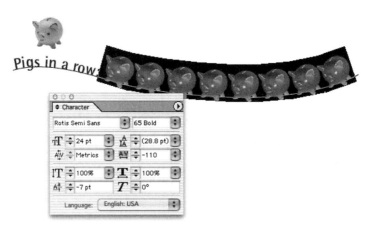

Creating and Importing Tables

Tables have been used as a visual way to communicate structured information for hundreds of years. While commands for creating and editing tables have long been available in word processing software and applications which work with structured documents like Adobe FrameMaker, Quark-XPress and InDesign have added table support only relatively recently. Table creation and editing is now available in QuarkXPress 5 and InDesign 2, but InDesign has far more table features than XPress.

Tables are a relatively deep issue so our discussion will continue in the next several chapters. In this chapter we talk about what tables are and how to create or import them. In the next chapter, we discuss how to format the table itself, in Chapter 76 we focus on formatting the text inside a table, and in Chapter 77, we talk about how to incorporate graphics. Finally, Chapter 78 completes the subject by discussing how to adjust a table's alignment and spacing.

Table Terminology

Before we describe how to create a table, we should discuss what a table is and how it differs from tabular material. A table is a grid of *cells*, arranged in horizontal *rows*, and vertical *columns* (see Figure 74-1). In QuarkXPress the cells can contain text or graphics; InDesign only has text cells, but allows table cells to contain inline graphics. In InDesign, a cell can expand as text is added to it by default, or it can be set to an absolute size; XPress's cells cannot auto expand.

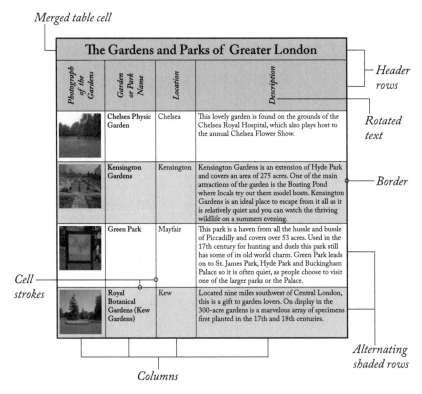

Figure 74-1
Tables are grids
of cells.

Tables have their own specialized terminology, so it's worth taking a moment to be clear what the different parts of a table are called. The line which may surround a table is called the table's *border*. Each cell has a *fill* *(cell color* in XPress), and it is surrounded by *strokes (gridlines* in XPress). While QuarkXPress cannot make cells or gridlines transparent (only solid color or a blend), InDesign lets you set the fill or stroke to None (transparent), a color, or a gradient. InDesign even lets you set the stroke attributes on each side of the cell individually, which XPress does not.

Tables versus Tabs

Desktop publishers have long used tabs to create simple tables (see Chapter 49). However, tables—especially as they're are implemented in InDesign—are much more powerful. Here are some reasons to use tables.

- You can have multiple lines of text in a single cell, which is impossible with tabs.

- Adding background colors and rules is much easier with tables.

- Alignment and spacing can be set very precisely inside and outside of InDesign tables.

- Editing a table is much easier than editing tabular material. You can easily select cells, rows, columns or the entire table to make changes quickly.

Creating a New Table

In QuarkXPress 5, you create a new table by dragging out a rectangle the size of the table area with the Table tool. You can also select text which contains tab and return characters, and choose to convert the text to a table. For XPress, a table is a new kind of page item which works like a grid of text or picture boxes linked together.

For InDesign, a table is always an inline (anchored) object in a text frame. To create a new table, place a text insertion point in a frame and choose Insert Table from the Table menu (or press Command-Option-Shift-T/Ctrl-Alt-Shift-T). In the Insert Table dialog box (see Figure 74-2), you define the initial structure of the table—the number of rows high, and columns wide. When you click OK, InDesign creates a table the width of the enclosing text frame. We describe how to adjust this initial structure of rows and columns in the next chapter.

Figure 74-2
The Insert Table
dialog box

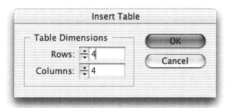

Like XPress, you can also convert text which contains tab and return characters (a tabular structure) into a table. First, turn on Show Hidden Characters in the Type menu and make sure that there are tab characters where you want columns to be formed, and return characters at the end of each line where you want a row to be defined. Then select the text, and choose Convert Text to Table from the Table menu.

Entering Text in a Table

To enter text into your table, use the Type tool to place a text insertion point in a cell and start typing. You can press the Tab key to advance from cell to cell. (If you press Tab in the last cell, a new row will be created.) Press Shift-Tab to move to the previous cell. Press Return to add a paragraph return within a cell. As you add text (unless you have defined the cell to be a fixed size) the cell expands vertically, but not horizontally. You can also use the Left, Right, Up, and Down Arrow keys to move between cells.

You can also copy and paste text into cells, or use the Place feature to import text into a single cell. We'll talk about placing graphics, inline objects and other tables within a table cell in Chapter 77.

Importing Tables

Unlike QuarkXPress, InDesign also allows you to import tables created in Microsoft Word and spreadsheets created in Microsoft Excel—just place the file as you would any other text file. You can also copy and paste from Word and Excel documents.

InDesign retains as much formatting from the Word or Excel table as its import filter will allow. However, you can always reformat it in InDesign using the methods we describe in the following chapters. Also, InDesign retains a link to the Word or Excel file in the Links palette. As we describe in Chapter 39, it's usually wise to choose Unlink from the Links palette menu to remove the link to the external file.

Converting Tables to Text

It's also possible in both QuarkXPress and InDesign to convert a table to tabbed text. When InDesign does this, it adds tab characters between each column, and return characters at the end of each row. The best reason to do this might be to create tab-delimited text which can be imported back into a spreadsheet application.

Formatting Tables

Once you've created or imported a table, it's time to begin formatting it. In this chapter, we begin by discussing how to select tables and parts of tables. We then discuss the three main tools for formatting tables—the Table Options and Cell Options dialog boxes and the Table palette. We cover how to change a table's structure—its size, and the rows and columns that make it up. Finally, we talk about formatting the table's border and the strokes and fills of the individual cells.

Selecting Tables

To format a table, you need to know how to select it and its elements. As we discussed in the previous chapter, tables are always contained within a text frame. To perform any selection, you must start by choosing the Type tool.

Selecting Cells

If you want to select a single cell, click an insertion point or select text with the Type tool, then choose Cell from the Select submenu (under the Table menu or from the context menu). Or, faster, just press the Escape (Esc) key.

You can select multiple cells by clicking in a cell and dragging horizontally, vertically, or diagonally. Another method to select several cells is to select a single cell and then press the Shift key with the Up, Down, Left or Right Arrow keys to extend the selection.

Selecting Rows or Columns

When you want to select rows or columns, you can also use either menu commands or the mouse. The slow way: select text in the row or column you want to select, then choose Row or Column from the Select submenu (under the Table menu). The fast way: If you want to select a row, move your cursor along the left edge of the row until you see the right-pointing arrow cursor (see Figure 75-1). Click to select the row. Dragging upward or downward extends the selection to other rows. Even faster: Press Command-3/Ctrl-3.

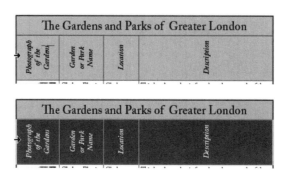

Figure 75-1
Move along the left side of the table. When you see the right-pointing arrow click to select the row. The down-pointing arrow selects columns. The diagonal arrow selects the entire table.

Selecting columns with the mouse is just as easy. To select a column, move your cursor along the top edge of the column until you see a down-pointing arrow cursor, then click (or drag). Or, just press Command-Option-3/Ctrl-Alt-3.

Selecting the Entire Table

There are three ways to select every cell in a table: First, you can place the text cursor in the table and then choose Table from the Select submenu (in the Table menu or context menu). Next, you can also move your cursor to the upper-left corner of the table and when you see the diagonal arrow cursor, click to select the table. Third (and fastest), type Command-Option-A/Ctrl-Alt-A.

Tools for Table Formatting

You can find almost every table-related feature in the Table menu, and most table-formatting features in the Table Options dialog box (press Command-Option-T/Ctrl-Alt-T; see Figure 75-2).

Figure 75-2
The Table Options
dialog box

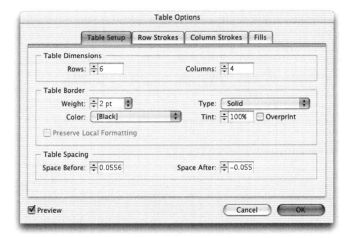

There is also the Cell Options dialog box (press Command-Option-B/
Ctrl-Alt-B; see Figure 75-3), where you can set the attributes of selected
cells. These include text attributes that we talk about in the next chapter;
the stroke and fill attributes; row height, column width, and keep options
(we also discuss the latter in the next chapter); and diagonal lines which
can be applied across a cell.

InDesign also has a Table palette which contains the most common
formatting options (see Figure 75-4). If it's not open, choose Table from
the Window menu.

Figure 75-3
The Cell Options
dialog box

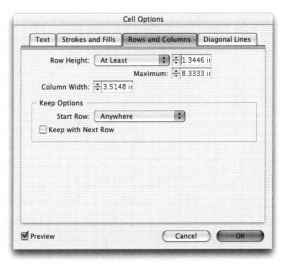

Figure 75-4

The Table palette

A *Number of rows*
B *Number of columns*
C *Row height*
D *Column width*
E *Alignment icons*
F *Text rotation icons*
G *Cell inset values*

Editing a Table's Structure

Tables almost never spring into being perfectly; you'll likely need to change the overall size of the table or of the rows and columns, add or delete rows or columns, merge two or more cells into one, or split a cell into smaller cells. It's all possible, and it's all easy.

Scaling the Entire Table

InDesign allows you to scale an entire table by dragging. First, click anywhere in the table with the Type tool, and move the cursor over the lower-right corner of the table. When you see the diagonal double-headed arrow cursor (see Figure 75-5), drag to scale the table. Holding down the Shift key constrains the scaling proportionally. (You can't scale a table if the table spans more than one text frame.)

Unlike QuarkXPress 5, there is no modifier to scale the content along with the table. Of course, you can always scale the text frame that contains the table (using the Scale or Free Transform tool, or the Transform palette; see Chapters 17 and 18).

Figure 75-5

Cursors for scaling the table and dragging cell or row boundaries.

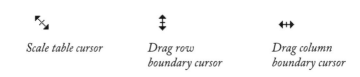

Scale table cursor   *Drag row*   *Drag column*
                           boundary cursor   *boundary cursor*

Adding Rows and Columns

There are several ways to add rows or columns to a table. First, you can use the Insert dialog box: Place the text cursor in a row or column next to where you want the new row or column to appear. Next, choose either Row or Column from the Insert submenu (in the Table menu or from the context menu). Then enter the number of rows or columns and whether you want them above, below, to the left, or the right of the current cell.

You can also add rows by dragging: Position the Type tool over a row or column boundary until you see the double-headed arrow cursor (see Figure 75-5). Hold down the mouse button, and then press the Option/Alt key while dragging downward (for rows) or to the right (for columns).

Finally, you can use the Table Options dialog box or the Table palette to add rows or columns. Increasing the number of rows or columns in the dialog box or the palette adds rows at the bottom of the table, or columns on the right side of the table.

Deleting Rows, and Columns, and Tables

You have similar flexibility when deleting rows and columns. Using the Type tool, you can click in a cell (or select multiple cells) and then choose Row or Column from the Delete submenu (under the Table menu). You can also use the dragging method to delete cells on the right or bottom side of the table: Position the Type tool over the bottom or right side of the table until you see the double-headed arrow cursor. Hold down the mouse, then press the Option/Alt key. If you drag upward or to the left, rows or columns are deleted.

Finally, you can reduce the dimensions of a table by changing the Rows or Columns fields in the Table Options dialog box or the Table palette.

If you want to delete the entire table, when there is an insertion point or a selection, choose Table from the Delete submenu (under the Table menu).

Merging and Splitting Cells

You can merge together cells in the same row or column by selecting them, then choosing Merge Cells from the Table menu (or context menu). If there is content in the cells, InDesign combines into one cell.

To split a cell into two smaller cells, use the Type tool to click inside the cell and then choose Split Cell Horizontally or Split Cell Vertically from the Table menu (or context menu).

Changing Row or Column Size

You can change a table's row or column size by dragging or numerically. If you like working interactively, just click and drag a row or column boundary (you'll see the double-headed arrow cursor if you're in the right place). Note that this changes your table's width or height; in fact, you can extend it beyond the right edge of the text frame. If you want to change a row or column boundary without resizing the whole table, hold down the Shift key while you drag. You can also resize all the rows or columns proportionately by holding down the Shift key while dragging the right edge (for rows) or bottom edge (for columns) of the table.

To change row width or column height numerically, first select the rows or columns to be resized (or just place the text cursor in any cell in the row or column). Then you can choose Rows and Columns from the Cell Options submenu (under the Table menu or context menu). Similarly, you can change the values in the Row Height and Column Width fields of the Table palette.

When you don't know exactly how high a row should be, choose At Least from the popup menu next to the Row Height field. This sets a minimum row height that autoexpands as text or graphics are added to the cells in the row. Alternatively, you can use the Exactly option to set the row height to be a particular value.

One last trick: You can give selected rows or columns the same height or width by selecting the rows or columns you want to change, and choosing Distribute Rows Evenly or Distribute Columns Evenly from the Table menu. Unfortunately, you cannot set this numerically, as you can in XPress.

Setting Strokes and Fills

You can set the fill and stroke attributes for the table as a whole, or for individual cells. The colors available are those which have been created in the Swatches palette. While you can set the fill of a cell to None (which you can't do in XPress), you can't include dashed or dotted lines in a table stroke, as you can in XPress.

Both the Table Options dialog box and the Cell Options dialog box let you apply formatting to table cells—the first globally, and the second to local selections—and the settings in the Table Options dialog box typically override formatting applied to fills and strokes in individual cells. However, if you turn on the Preserve Local Formatting option in Table Options, local formatting won't get overridden.

Specifying the Table Border

The line which surrounds the table is called the *border*. To set the border attributes, choose Table Options from the Table menu. In the Table Border section of the dialog box, you can set the border's line weight, color, line type, and overprinting attribute. Later in this section we show how you can also set the border attributes using the Stroke palette. If you don't want a table border, choose a stroke color of None.

Using the Cell Options Dialog Box

To set the fills and strokes for table cells with the Cell Options dialog box, select the cells you want to affect, choose Cell Options from the Table menu, and click on the Strokes and Fills panel. Here you can set the characteristics for the strokes of the selected table or cells: their weight, color, line type, and overprinting attributes. In the same dialog, you can set the fill color and overprinting characteristics.

When setting stroke attributes, use the proxy image to select which segments you want to apply the change to (see Figure 75-6). Click the segments to select and deselect them—selected segments are blue, deselected segments are gray. For example, to change the outside strokes of the selected cells, click on the inside segments to deselect them. (Here are some shortcuts: Double-clicking any outside segment toggles selects or deselects all the outside segments. Double-clicking works similarly on inside segments. Triple-clicking anywhere in the proxy toggles between selecting and deselecting all the segments.)

You can use the Preview checkbox to preview the results, but because selecting cells inverses their color, you can't really see the resulting colors until you click OK and deselect the cells. (You can, however, watch the stroke and fill icons in the Tool palette to get some color-picking feedback.)

Figure 75-6

The stroke proxy in the Cell Options dialog box

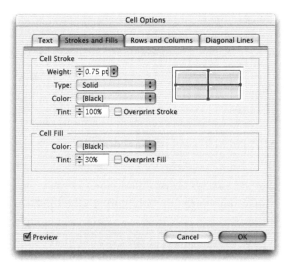

Where Text Meets Graphics

Using the Stroke and Swatches Palettes

An alternative way to set stroke and fill attributes for cells is to use the Stroke and Swatches palettes. First, select cells whose attributes you want to change. Then, to set stroke attributes, make sure the Formatting Affects Frame button is selected on the Swatches or Tools palettes (otherwise, the stroke will be applied to text within the cell; see Chapter 14). On the Stroke palette, click segments on the stroke proxy as described earlier to choose the strokes of the selected cells you want to affect, and then pick the stroke weight and line type in the Stroke palette. You can change the stroke color in the Swatches palette.

To select fill attributes, make sure the Fill button and Formatting Affects Frame buttons are selected on the Swatches or Tools palettes, and then select a color in the Swatches palette.

Adding Diagonal Lines

You can also apply diagonal lines to cells. Select the cells you want to affect, and choose Diagonal Lines from the Cell Options submenu (under the Table menu). In the Diagonal Lines panel, you can select the type of diagonal line you want, and whether it prints in front of or behind the contents of the cell. You can also choose the line's weight, line type, color, and overprinting attributes.

Creating Alternating Patterns

It's often helpful to apply an alternating pattern of strokes or fills to the cells of a table to make it more readable or to improve its appearance. Unlike QuarkXPress, InDesign lets you create these alternating patterns automatically. That means that as you subsequently edit the table, adding or deleting rows and columns, the pattern remains true. As we noted earlier, alternating patterns override local table cell strokes and fills unless you turn on Preserve Local Formatting.

Adding Alternate Strokes

To create alternating strokes in your table, click anywhere in the table and choose Table Options from the Table menu. Then, in the Alternating Row Strokes panel (or the Alternating Column Strokes, depending on what you're trying to do), choose an alternating pattern: every other row, every second or third row, or whatever. You may wish to skip a certain number rows at the top or bottom of the table—for example, the header rows at the top. Specify that in the Skip First and Skip Last fields.

Adding Alternate Fills

You can also specify alternating fills across rows or columns by choosing the Alternating Fills panel in the Table Options dialog box. Similar to the alternating stroke choices above, you can choose the frequency and fill colors of your pattern for either rows or columns (see Figure 75-7).

Figure 75-7
Alternating Fills in
Table Options

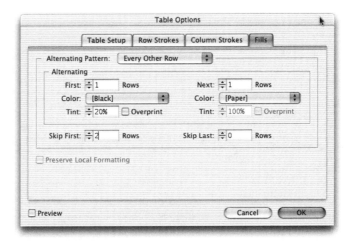

76

Formatting Text in Tables

It's time to talk about formatting text inside table cells. Because InDesign allows tables to break between text frames, we discuss in this chapter how to control the way a table is split. We also talk about how to use copying, pasting and deleting to change a table's content.

Text Formatting

Text inside a table cell acts almost exactly like text inside any text frame, and you can format it to your heart's delight. If you need to format a bunch of cells in the same way, select them all and use the Character and Paragraph palettes (or apply a paragraph or character style). You can even delete all the text from all selected cells by pressing the Delete key. Note that you can format table cells even with no text in them. That way, the text in each cell gets formatted automatically as you type.

Tabs within Tables

Ordinarily you wouldn't type a tab character inside a table cell, but if you need one—to align decimal numbers within a cell, for example—you can add one by either using the Insert Special Character submenu (see Chapter 51) or by typing Option-Tab on the Macintosh. Alt-Tab switches applications in Windows, so set up your own keyboard shortcut. Then you can use the Tab palette to set up tab stops within the cell, just as though the cell were a text frame (see Chapter 49).

Overset Text in a Cell

By default, cells auto expand vertically when you add text or graphics. However, if you've set rows to have a fixed height, when you add text or graphics beyond that size, you may see a small red dot appear in the lower right corner of the cell (see Figure 76-1). This indicates overset text. You can either make the cell bigger or make the cell's contents smaller. We discuss how to handle overset graphics, inline graphics, and tables in the next chapter.

Figure 76-1
The red dot indicates overset text in a cell.

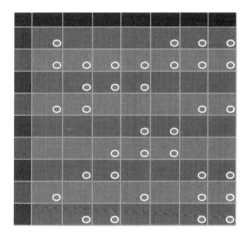

Text Rotation

Sometimes it's useful to rotate the text within a table cell, like for table headers. InDesign allows text to be rotated in multiples of 90 degrees (unlike XPress, which allows an arbitrary rotation). To rotate text, select the cell or cells you want to affect and click on one of the text rotation buttons in the Table palette. You can also use the Text panel of the Cell Options dialog box. Note that you can get text at any angle by pasting in rotated text as an inline graphic.

Table Flow Between Text Frames

One of the reasons tables are implemented within text frames is so you can flow a table from frame to frame—excellent for multi-page tables. We discuss how to thread text between text frames in Chapter 40. When a table is contained within the text flow of a story (or even if it is the only element in the text frame), each row acts like a line of text, so the table always breaks between rows; you can't break the table part way through a row.

Just as in working with paragraph text, you can use Keep Options to control where a row begins and whether it is kept with the next row. However, here, the Keep Options are in the Rows and Columns panel of the Cell Options dialog box. In the Keep Options section of the dialog box, choose whether the row can begin in any location, or in the next column, text frame, page, or even or odd page. You can also choose the Keep with Next Row option.

The problem with breaking tables across pages is that the header and footer rows often need to be repeated. Unfortunately, InDesign provides no automatic facility for doing this. Use the copy and paste method described in the next section to duplicate header and footer rows.

Copying, Pasting, and Deleting Content

You can copy, paste, and delete text and other content from selected cells. Keep in mind that to be successful when you're replacing content, you must paste into a table structure which is at least as many cells wide and tall as the cells you're pasting.

For example, what do you do if a Excel or Word table gets updated and you need to update it in InDesign, too? If the table were still linked to the original file and you updated it, you would lose all your InDesign-applied formatting. Here's what you do.

1. In Word or Excel, select contiguous cells with the updated data, and copy them to the Clipboard.

2. In InDesign, click an insertion point in an empty text frame, and choose Paste from the Edit menu. A small table will appear containing just the cells you copied.

3. Select this new table, and copy the cells to the Clipboard.

4. Select the cells whose content is to be replaced in your formatted table, and choose Paste from the Edit menu. Of course, the pasted cells may need to be formatted again; if you're using character styles, just apply them.

Actually, the best way to retain the formatting in a table is to use Wood-wing Software's SmartStyles plug-in (*www.woodwing.com*), which lets you record and reapply a bunch of formatting quickly and easily.

Using Graphics within a Table

What if you want to put a picture inside a table cell instead of text? It's not impossible, though it's not quite as easy to do as in XPress.

Pasting or Placing Graphics

The only way to get a picture into a table cell is to insert it as an inline (anchored) object. Once pasted or placed, it can be manipulated like any inline object. (We discuss what inline objects are and how to work with them in Chapter 69.) This is also true for placing lines, other tables, or any other object inside a table cell. Note, however, that you can also insert a table inside a table cell by choosing Insert Table from the Table menu.

We've found that you'll get the most control over the process if you place your graphic on the page first and scale it to the approximate size of the cell *before* you paste it into a table cell. You should also consider setting the row height, cell alignment, and clipping options for the cell *before* placing the graphic, as described below.

Fitting Graphics

There are several variables which control how a graphic fits into a table cell. These include the settings for row height, cell alignment, and whether the graphic is set to be clipped. You can also adjust the size and positioning of the graphic, or perform other transformations once it's been pasted or placed.

Row Height

As we describe in the previous chapter, InDesign's default behavior is to auto expand a cell vertically when text or graphics are added to it. We highly recommend leaving this set to At Least if you're going to put a picture inside the cell. If you set an exact row height, and the size of the graphic exceeds the space available within the cell, it may cause the cell to overset (see "Handling Overset Graphics," below).

Cell Alignment Options

Whether a graphic fits into a cell is also determined by two kinds of alignment settings. When you select one or more cells and choose Text from the Cell Options submenu (under the Table menu), or press Command-Option-B/Ctrl-Alt-B, InDesign lets you set options for Text Inset, Vertical Justification, and First Baseline Offset for the cell. (We discuss these in detail in the next chapter.) Also, on the Paragraph palette, the paragraph attributes of alignment (left, center, right, or justified), and indent values also affect where the graphic appears within the cell.

We find one option, in particular, useful for working with graphic content: When you set First Baseline Offset to Fixed, InDesign ignores the height of the graphic, and you can use the Min. setting to specify the distance from the baseline (bottom) of the graphic to the top of the cell.

Clipping the Graphic

A third variable which affects graphic placement is whether the graphic is clipped by the cell boundaries. In the same Text panel described in the previous section, you can clip the contents of the graphic to the cell boundary by turning on the Clip Contents to Cell option. If the graphic is larger than the cell and it's not clipped, it will extend above and to the right of the cell boundary (see Figure 77-1).

Transforming the Graphic

Once a graphic has been placed in a cell, you can still adjust its size and position (or rotation, skew, and so on) by using the Selection tool. For instance, you can hold down Command/Ctrl and Shift and drag the corner of the graphic bounding box to rescale the graphic frame and its contents together (see Figure 77-2). You can also move the graphic frame within the cell with the Selection tool to position it vertically.

Figure 77-1

The graphic is pasted into the table cell with the Clip Contents to Cell turned off (above) and with the clipping turned on (below).

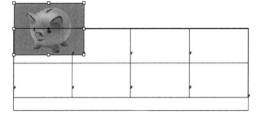

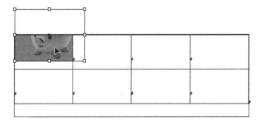

Figure 77-2

The graphic has been resized with the Selection tool to fit the cell.

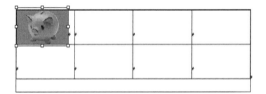

Choosing the Right Tool

It's a little confusing at first when working with graphics in a cell because you have to learn to use the correct tool to do what you want:

- To select the cell or cells so you can set cell options or resize the cell boundaries, choose the Type tool. If necessary, click in the cell to get an insertion point. Then pressing the Escape (Esc) key toggles between selecting the cell and the cell's contents (the graphic).

- To perform transformations of the graphic frame and its content, use the Selection tool to select the graphic's bounding box. Then use any of the transformation tools, or drag to move the graphic frame into position.

- To select only the content of the graphic frame, use the Direct Selection tool.

Where Text Meets Graphics

Handling Overset Graphics

You may sometimes see an overset condition when you paste or place text or graphics. This is because the object being placed exceeds the space available for it. Our experience is that this most often happens with graphics when the Text Inset values are too large, or when you make the cell height smaller than the First Baseline Offset value. InDesign usually tries to let a graphic expand above and to the right of the cell, even if it doesn't fit. In addition to the methods suggested in Chapter 76, you can also select the cell and adjust the Text Inset or First Baseline Offset values to get the graphic to fit.

If you place a table inside a cell, and the table is taller than the cell, InDesign places as many rows as will fit, and oversets the rest (extra width extends to the right of the cell). To fix the overset, either undo after pasting, or cut the pasted inline table to the Clipboard, and paste it on the page. Then adjust it to fit before copying and pasting it into the table again.

78

Table Alignment and Spacing

Just when you thought you had read enough about tables, here we are again—this time discussing how to align objects within table cells using cell alignment options and the Paragraph palette. We also discuss how to a table is spaced and aligned in relationship to the text frame of which it's a part.

Alignment and Spacing Within a Cell

Each cell is like a miniature text frame, and it's not surprising that the options for alignment and spacing are very similar to those of text frames. The Text panel of the Cell Options dialog box is the equivalent of the Text Frame Options dialog box (see Figure 78-1 and Chapter 50), and it mainly affects vertical alignment within the cell. In addition, you can use the controls on the Paragraph palette to control horizontal alignment, indents, and the spacing between paragraphs inside a cell.

You can also set some of these options, such as Cell Inset, in the Table palette.

Alignment and Spacing Around a Table

A table always sits inside of a text frame, so you must also consider its relationship to that frame. Here are how some ways you can do that.

- **Horizontal Alignment.** The table may not fill the width of the text frame. If that is so, then you can click an insertion point to the right or left of the table (the blinking insertion point should appear as tall as

Figure 78.1

The Text panel of the Cell Options dialog box

the table). Then use the Paragraph palette horizontal alignment controls to set how the table aligns to the frame.

- **Space Before and After.** You can set the space above and below a table using the Space Before and Space After fields in the Paragraph palette, but you have to put the cursor in the same paragraph as the table (not inside the table). Or, put the cursor inside the table and choose Table Setup from the Table Options submenu (under the Table menu). In the Table Spacing section of the dialog box, you can set the space before and after values. Space Before doesn't apply when the table is at the top of a frame.

- **Adding Text Above a Table.** If your table is at the top of the frame, you may decide you want to add text above it. Remember that tables are themselves just inline objects, so you can click an insertion point to the right of (or below) the table. Then press the Left Arrow key once to move the cursor to the left side of the table, then begin typing to enter text.

PART 8

Color and Transparency

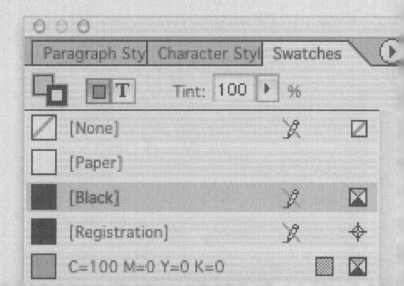

79

Creating Colors

QuarkXPress lets you define and manipulate colors in several places—the Edit Color dialog box, the Styles menu, and the Color palette. InDesign uses two different palettes to create and manipulate colors. One of them, the Swatches palette, follows the XPress model of working with named colors. The other is the Color palette—similar to the Color palette in Adobe Illustrator—which allows you to use sliders to mix colors, and which can create and apply colors without naming them.

As in QuarkXPress, you can mix colors in InDesign in CMYK, RGB, and Lab (but not HSB) color models, and you can define colors as either process or spot. We discuss working with color libraries like Pantone and Trumatch in Chapter 83.

Swatches Palette

We recommend that you use the Swatches palette to create and edit your colors. The advantage of creating named colors here is that, as in QuarkX-Press, it makes it easier for you or your service provider to globally change the colors in your document later on, should that be necessary.

The Swatches palette in InDesign looks somewhat similar to XPress's Color palette. If it's not open, choose the Swatches palette from the Window menu, or press F5 (see Figure 79-1). The palette lists all the colors currently in your document, along with icons indicating the color model and whether the color is spot or process. There are controls for applying color to fills and strokes which we describe in the next chapter. Unlike

Figure 79-1
The Swatches palette

A *Fill/Stroke control*
B *Text/Object control*
C *Tint slider*
D *Color swatch*
E *Gradient swatch*
F *Tint swatch*
G *Spot color*
H *Process color*
I *RGB color*
J *CMYK color*
K *Show All Swatches button*
L *Show Colors button*
M *Show Gradients button*
N *New Swatch button*
O *Delete Swatch button*

XPress' Color palette, you can also save tints and gradients in the Swatches palette (we discuss gradients in Chapter 81).

There are four built-in swatches which always appear in the Swatches palette and which can't be removed: None, Black, Registration, and Paper. The first three are the same as XPress; the last, Paper, simulates the paper color on which you're printing. By default, Paper is the same as XPress's "White" color, but you can double-click on the swatch to edit its composition if you're going to print on non-white stock. (It is for on-screen preview only, and will not print.)

InDesign also includes swatches for cyan, yellow, magenta, red, green, and blue. These are the same as XPress, but with one important difference: Unlike XPress, these red, green, and blue swatches are defined as true process colors, so it's okay to use them. (They're RGB colors in XPress.)

Creating Swatches

To create a new color, choose New Color Swatch from the palette's flyout menu. This opens the New Color Swatch dialog box (see Figure 79-2). A faster way of opening the dialog is to select any color other than None or Paper and then Option/Alt-click the New Swatch button on the palette. Here you can name your swatch, choose its color model, and specify whether the color is process or spot. When editing the color composition, you can either drag the sliders or type values. For process colors the default is to name colors by their color components, but if you turn off the Name with Color Value option, you can give a color any name.

Beware: If an object is selected on your page when you create a swatch, InDesign automatically applies the color to it. This makes David crazy, so he tries to remember to press Command-Shift-A/Ctrl-Shift-A to deselect all objects before creating a color.

Tint Swatches

InDesign lets you create swatches that are tints (shades) of other swatches. For example, if you use 20-percent cyan behind every sidebar in your publication, make this a swatch to apply it quickly. Later, if you decide you want 15-percent magenta instead, you can edit the swatch (by double-clicking on it) and all the tints will change throughout your document. To make a tint swatch, select a color in the palette and choose New Tint Swatch from the flyout menu.

Displaying Swatches

Unlike XPress, you can control how the Swatches palette displays its swatches. From the palette's flyout menu, you can choose to display just swatches by choosing Large Swatch, or you can display each swatch with its name by choosing Name. You can also display more swatches at a time by choosing either Small Swatches or Small Name from the palette menu. At the bottom of the palette, there are buttons to show all swatches, only color swatches, or only gradient swatches.

Default Colors

As with QuarkXPress, you can create colors that will be available for all future documents you create. Like the default preferences we discussed in Chapter 7, default colors are added to your swatches when you have no documents open.

Figure 79-2
The New Color Swatch dialog box

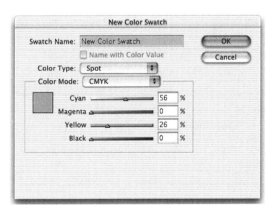

305

Color & Transparency

Color Palette

The second option for creating new colors is the Color palette, which works more like creating colors in Illustrator or Photoshop. When creating new colors with the Color palette they are not automatically saved in the Swatches palette for future use. If it's not open, choose the Color palette from the Window menu, or press F6 (see Figure 79-3), then choose a color mode (Lab, CMYK, or RGB) from the palette's flyout menu. Shortcut: You can toggle through these modes by Shift-clicking in the color bar at the bottom of the palette.

Finally, you can pick a color either by moving the sliders, typing a value, or clicking in the color bar. Remember that if an object is selected on your page, playing with the Color palette will apply the color to that object. If that's what you want to do, then at least be careful to identify whether you want to color the fill or the stroke before creating the color.

Figure 79-3

The Color palette

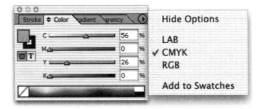

Saving Unnamed Colors

The Color palette is nice if you like working interactively. However, we don't like it for two reasons. First, it's too easy to get fooled into trusting the color you see on screen instead of picking colors from a printed swatch book. You cannot trust what you see on screen unless you have spent time setting up the color management system (see Chapter 87). Second, unnamed colors are a hassle for everyone, especially your output provider.

Fortunately, you can turn unnamed colors into named swatches by dragging the color proxy in the Color palette into the Swatches palette or by choosing Add to Swatches from the Color palette's flyout menu. Even better, if you've created a bunch of unnamed colors in your document you can add them all to the Swatches palette by choosing Add Unnamed Colors from the Swatches palette menu.

80

Applying Colors

In Chapter 14, we discuss how InDesign uses different terminology than QuarkXPress for describing page objects: What QuarkXPress calls a box's color, InDesign calls a frame's *fill*; and what XPress calls a frame, InDesign calls a *stroke*. In this chapter we describe the different ways InDesign can apply color to fills and strokes using the Swatches and Color palette. Another way to apply color is with the Eyedropper tool which we discuss in Chapter 82.

Applying Colors to Frames and Text

Before using QuarkXPress's Color palette, you need to tell XPress whether you want to color the selected box's background, content, or frame, right? InDesign works the same way: Select one or more boxes, and then select whether you want to change the fill or the stroke attributes. These choices are found in three places: on the bottom of the Tools palette, and on the upper left corner of the Swatches and Color palettes (see Figure 80-1). You can also toggle between these two options by typing the letter X. If you pick the wrong attribute—fill instead of stroke, or *vice versa*—Shift-X swaps the fill and stroke colors.

Applying Colors to Frames

Once you select Fill or Stroke, you can then apply a color by clicking a swatch in the Swatches palette or choosing a color from the Color palette (see Chapter 79 for more information about the differences between these methods). You can also apply colors by dragging a color swatch from the

Figure 80-1

Determining what
gets colored: stroke,
fill, text or frame

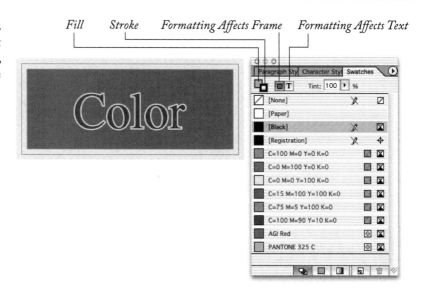

Swatches or Color palettes onto the fill or stroke of a frame, even if the
frame is not the selected object.

Changing the Color of Type

When selecting a text frame, you also need to tell InDesign whether
you want to color the frame or the type inside the frame. There are two
additional buttons found on the Tools, Swatches, and Color palettes:
Formatting Affects Frame and Formatting Affects Text. It's crucial to
pay attention to these because unlike QuarkXPress, InDesign can apply a
stroke color to text without converting the text to outlines. You can even
apply a fill color of None to make the text transparent (though of course
you'll probably want to give the text a stroke or drop shadow to make it
visible in some other way).

Applying Color to Lines

Coloring lines (paths) works the same as applying color to frames. Just
select the path's stroke or fill attribute, and then use the Swatches or Color
palette to pick a color. Note that InDesign is more flexible than XPress
because you can also apply color to the fill of an unclosed path. (Filled lines
act just like closed paths; it's as though there were an invisible line from
the end point to the beginning point of the line.)

81

Gradients

In QuarkXPress you can create *blends* which can be applied to the background of boxes. InDesign allows you to create *gradients* which are considerably more flexible in several ways: Gradients can be applied to the strokes of frames, paths, groups of objects, and even to text. You can create and save gradients in the Swatches palette (so you can later globally change them throughout your document), and you can define gradients that have more than two colors.

Gradient Swatches

Creating gradients is similar to creating color swatches: Select New Gradient Swatch from the Swatches palette's flyout menu. In the New Gradient Swatch dialog box you can set the color and tint of each end separately by clicking on the little box (called a "stop") under the Gradient Ramp at the bottom of the dialog box (see Figure 81-1). Then you can either choose from colors listed in your Swatches palette (by selecting Named Color from the Stop Color popup menu), or mix a new color by choosing a color model such as CMYK. You can also choose between a Linear or Radial gradient from the Type popup menu.

Unlike XPress, you can add additional colors to your gradient by clicking just below the Gradient Ramp and selecting the color for the new stop. You can, of course, drag the stops around (even reversing the order of the blend by switching the two end stops) or move them by typing a percentage value in the Location field. To remove a stop, just drag it from

Figure 81-1
The New Gradient
Swatch dialog box

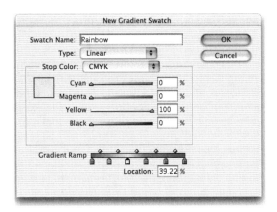

the ramp. You can even move the midpoint between two stops by dragging the diamonds on top of the Gradient Ramp.

Gradients are applied to objects and text just like any solid color, which we discuss in detail in Chapter 80. Select the object you want to change and either select a gradient color on the Swatches palette, or drag the gradient to the object.

Controlling Gradients

InDesign also gives you two other tools for working with gradients: the Gradient palette and the Gradient tool.

Gradient Palette

You can also create and edit gradients with the Gradient palette, which you can open from the Window menu (choose Show Options from the palette's flyout menu to make it look like Figure 81-2).

Figure 81-2
The Gradient palette

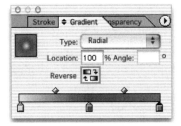

This palette is the equivalent of the Color palette—that is, it lets you create local, unnamed gradients on objects. Because we'd rather have named gradient swatches, we rarely use this palette to create blends. However, if you like working interactively like this, you can use this palette in a similar way to the New Gradient Swatch dialog box—clicking on color stops, editing colors using the Color palette, and so on.

We do use two features in the palette frequently because there are two features here not found in the dialog box: You can reverse the colors in the gradient by clicking the reverse button, and you can change the angle of the gradient.

Gradient Tool

 The Gradient tool lets you apply or edit a blend, controlling the direction and length of the gradient. First, select the object you wish to modify, then drag the Gradient tool across the object in the direction you wish the gradient to go. The distance you click and drag also controls the start and stop points of the gradient: Drag a short distance to create a gradient with an abrupt transition between colors or drag a greater distance to create a longer gradient. This, too, creates unnamed gradients that are hard to control later. It's a great tool, but we prefer to control gradients using swatches.

Applying Gradients to Multiple Objects

While QuarkXPress allows you to apply the same blend to multiple objects or a group, InDesign lets you apply a gradient which spans the bounding box of more than one selected objects or of a group. To do this, select the objects and drag the Gradient tool across them.

Applying Gradients to Text

Also unlike XPress, you can apply a gradient to text. When you do this, the gradient applies to the bounding box of the text frame. Individual characters are colored by the gradient depending on where they fall in the bounding box. Be careful using the feature because applying a color transition to small text characters may be hard to print accurately on a printing press.

Color & Transparency

82

Eyedropper Tool

Simply put, the Eyedropper tool—found in InDesign's Tools palette but nowhere in XPress—is a cool tool to have in a page layout program. With it you can quickly copy all color attributes from an object, and apply them to one or more objects, either selected or not. In addition, you can copy transparency or text attributes in a similar way.

Copying and Applying Colors

 The Eyedropper tool lets you copy colors used in any open document, including those in placed images. For example, if you wish to match the color of the type in a headline to the color of a car which appears in a placed picture, select the text with the Type tool and then click on the car with the Eyedropper tool.

The Eyedropper immediately applies the color to any selected object, so you might consider pressing Command-Shift-A/Ctrl-Shift-A to deselect all objects before using it.

Eyedropper Tool Status

The Eyedropper tool is ready to pick up formatting when it is filled with white and facing down towards the left. Once you have clicked on something, the cursor changes—filled with black and facing down to the right—meaning its ready to apply formatting. If you've picked up text formatting with the Eyedropper tool, the cursor will also have an I-beam attached to it. If you choose an incorrect color or formatting, hold down the Option/Alt key and resample a different color with the Eyedropper tool.

As long as the cursor is filled with black, you can continue to apply formatting to other objects—selected or not—by clicking on them with the "filled" cursor.

Sampled Colors

The color you select with the Eyedropper tool appears in the Color palette. We highly recommend saving this color into the Swatches palette as a named color (drag the swatch from the Color palette into the Swatches palette, choose Add to Swatches from the Color palette's flyout menu, or choose Add Unnamed Colors from the Swatches palette's flyout menu).

By the way, be aware that if you're sampling color from an RGB image, the color you're picking is in the RGB model, which is often inappropriate for prepress work (depending on how you're managing colors in your document). Also, if you select a color from a vector image, such as a PDF file or Illustrator or FreeHand artwork, InDesign bases the color on the screen representation, *not* the true color as defined in the image!

Copying Text and Other Formatting

The Eyedropper tool can do much more than copy colors. It can also copy and apply transparency and text attributes. Similar to the method we describe above, you can select text that needs to be formatted and then use the Eyedropper tool to click on text with formatting you wish to copy, even if the text is in a different text frame. The formatting is applied immediately. Or, with no text selected, use the Eyedropper tool to click on text with formatting you wish to copy, then drag the tool over text to which you wish to apply formatting. Neither text frame has to be selected for this to work.

Eyedropper Options

You can choose which attributes you want to copy with the Eyedropper tool by double-clicking on the tool in the Tools palette. The Eyedropper Options dialog box has five different sets of settings for copying fill, stroke, transparency, character, and paragraph attributes. By default, all are turned on. Then, within each category you can select the exact choices you want to include by clicking in the checkboxes. For instance, you can tell InDesign to pick up the font, size, and color of text, but ignore its leading and tint.

Color & Transparency

83

Colors & Color Libraries

Color libraries are groups of colors that have been saved together, added to the Swatches palette, and used in your document. Popular color libraries that ship with InDesign include Pantone, Trumatch, and Web-safe colors. Because libraries can contain thousands of colors each, InDesign does not automatically add them all to your Swatches palette; you must add colors one at a time.

You can access colors stored in libraries by choosing New Color Swatch from the Swatches palette's flyout menu and then selecting a library by name (see Figure 83-1). InDesign's 15 color libraries are listed under the Color Mode popup menu following the RGB, CMYK and LAB color models. Unfortunately, InDesign lacks QuarkXPress's ability to create multi-ink colors.

To find a particular color in a library, either scroll through the list or type the color's number code. To add that color to your Swatches palette, click OK. Unfortunately, you can only add one color at a time.

Converting Spot Colors to Process

Some of the libraries contains spot colors, while others are CMYK process colors. You can convert spot colors from a library, such as Pantone colors, to CMYK by selecting the spot color, changing the Color Mode popup menu to CMYK, and changing the Color Type drop down menu from Spot to Process. Be aware that some Pantone colors don't have close CMYK equivalents.

Figure 83-1
Color libraries

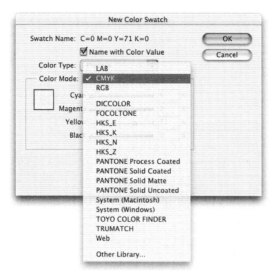

Importing Colors

There are a number of other ways to add colors to your document besides adding them from a library. While InDesign does not have an Append feature like XPress, it does let you grab colors from other documents: In the New Color Swatch dialog box, you can choose Other Library from the Color Mode popup menu and select another InDesign document or an EPS file from Illustrator 8 or earlier (later versions of Illustrator won't work because they use a different format). Then, in the dialog box that next appears, select the colors to add as described above.

Of course, when you open a PageMaker or QuarkXPress document the colors are imported automatically. And as in XPress, when you import an EPS file, InDesign adds the graphic's spot colors (if there are any) to the Swatches palette; InDesign does the same when you place an Illustrator file, even including the named tints and gradients. Copying objects from one InDesign document to another copies the named swatches, too.

Even cooler, you can copy one or more swatches from one document to another by dragging: Open the two documents side by side and make the Swatches palette in the source document visible. Select the swatches in the source document (Shift-click for contiguous swatches or Command/Ctrl-click for discontiguous swatches), and then drag the selected swatches onto the target document window.

Figures 83-2

Converting colors

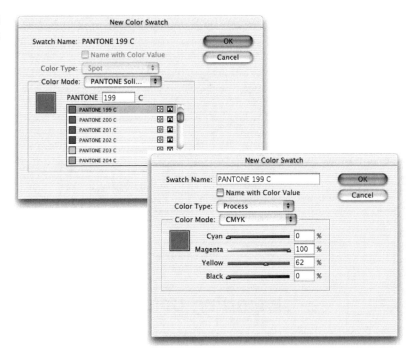

Editing, Merging, and Deleting Colors

You can edit a color by selecting a color in the Swatches palette and choose Swatch Options from the palette menu. Even faster: simply double-click the swatch. Watch out: this applies the color to any selected objects on your page!

You can duplicate a swatch color (perhaps in order to edit it to make a similar color) by selecting a swatch and choosing Duplicate Swatch from the palette menu. But it's even faster just to click on the color and then click the New Color Swatch button at the bottom of the Swatches palette (or Option/Alt-click to duplicate and immediately edit it).

Deleting and Merging Colors

You can delete individual swatches by selecting one or more and either choosing Delete Swatch from the palette menu or dragging the swatches to the Delete Swatch button. Like in XPress, InDesign asks you if you want to replace the color with another swatch; InDesign also gives you the option to leave the color alone (it becomes an unnamed color). If you want to delete all the unused colors in your document, first choose Select All Unused from the Swatches palette's flyout menu and then press the Delete Swatch button.

Deleting spot colors which come from EPS files can sometimes be tricky. If you delete the EPS file, the added spot colors appear to be locked. To remove them, Select All Unused from the menu, deselect any colors which should be retained, and then use the Delete Swatch command.

You can also eliminate colors from your Swatches palette by selecting them and choosing Merge Swatches from the flyout menu (see Figure 83-3). Select the color you want to keep first, then select one or more you want to delete.

Figure 83-3

Merging swatches

Color & Transparency

84

Transparency

QuarkXPress exemplifies page layout as it has been done for decades: opaque objects laid out next to each other or overlapping one another. If you want a non-rectangular edge around an image, you can create a clipping path in Photoshop. If you need soft edges, drop shadows, feathering, or any other sort of raster effect in XPress, you have to either buy an XTension or create it in Photoshop. The result: Many designers spend more time doing "layout" in Photoshop than in XPress.

Adobe decided that this was silly, and added all kinds of cool transparency effects to InDesign. That's what we're going to talk about in this chapter. However, when it comes to printing transparency effects, we'll hold off until Chapter 94. (Suffice it to say for now that this stuff really does print. This is Adobe we're talking about here.)

Importing Transparent Objects

With InDesign you can import transparent graphics saved as native Photoshop (.PSD), Illustrator (.AI), or Acrobat 5 PDF documents (PDF 1.4 or later). For example, you can create a cloud with wispy, feathered edges in Photoshop (fading out to Photoshop's checkerboard transparency) and when you bring it into InDesign the soft edge is retained, revealing any InDesign objects under it (see Figure 84-1).

The most reliable file formats to use for transparent imported graphics are the newest ones: Photoshop 6 or later, Illustrator 10 or later, and PDF 1.4 or later. Photoshop 6 and later can also save TIFF files with transpar-

Figure 84-1
Transparent objects
from Photoshop
or Illustrator retain
their transparency in
InDesign.

In Photoshop   *In InDesign*

ency (see Chapter 62). However, if you flatten an image in Photoshop, you lose all transparency (we discuss flattening in Chapter 94).

Applying Transparency

InDesign also lets you can make any page object—frames, lines, or imported graphics—transparent with the Transparency palette (under the Window menu or press Shift-F10). The two settings you can make here are Opacity and Blending Mode. To change a selected object's Opacity, choose an level of transparency by either entering a percentage or using the slider. The lower the value the more transparent the object becomes. Note that you can't change the opacity of individual characters—it's all the text in a frame or nothing—so select text frames with the Selection tool to apply transparency.

Blending Modes

You can control how transparent objects blend with colors beneath them by choosing one of the blending modes within the Transparency palette. If you're familiar with Photoshop, you may already know these.

- **Normal.** At 100-percent opacity, the top color completely replaces the bottom color—that is, transparency is turned off.

- **Multiply.** Darkens the base color by multiplying its values with those of the blend color. Multiplying dark colors results in the biggest changes; multiplying with white or Paper color causes no change. This mode is generally the best choice for drop shadows.

Color & Transparency

- **Screen.** Lightens the color by multiplying the inverse of the blend and base colors, an effect similar to projecting two slides on the same screen. Screening light colors results in the biggest changes; screening black results in no change.

- **Overlay.** Multiplies or screens the colors, depending on the base color, but tries to limit the effect so that highlights and shadows are preserved. Overlaying contrasting colors results in the biggest changes; overlaying 50-percent gray results in no change.

- **Soft Light.** Soft Light is like Overlay, but doesn't try to preserve highlight and shadow values. Applying black or white results in no change.

- **Hard Light.** Hard Light is like Soft Light but with more contrast.

- **Color Dodge.** Colorizes the base pixel using the blend pixel hue; light pixels are colorized more than dark pixels.

- **Color Burn.** Colorizes the base pixel using the blend pixel hue; dark pixels are colorized more than light pixels.

- **Darken.** Applies the darker of the base and blend colors, but only where the base color is lighter than the blend color. Where the base color is darker, pixels aren't changed.

- **Lighten.** Applies the lighter of the base and blend colors, but only where the base color is darker than the blend color. Where the base color is lighter, pixels aren't changed.

- **Difference.** Applies the color value that results from subtracting one color from another. Bigger differences between base and blend pixel colors increases the effect, but identical pixels result in black.

- **Exclusion.** A lower-contrast version of the Difference mode.

- **Hue.** Applies the base color's lightness and saturation and the blend color's hue.

- **Saturation.** Applies the base color's lightness and color and the blend color's saturation.

- **Color.** Applies the base color's lightness and the blend color's hue and saturation.

- **Luminosity.** Applies the base color's hue and saturation and the blend color's luminance. This mode creates the opposite effect of the Color mode.

If you're using spot colors, you can't use the Difference, Exclusion, Hue, Saturation, Color, and Luminosity modes. The color math that defines these modes won't create a printable result using spot colors.

Blend Options

If you select Show Options from the Transparency palette's flyout menu, you get two more checkboxes to play with.

- **Isolate Blending.** This limits the effect of grouped objects' individual blending modes to other objects within the group, without affecting objects behind the group. Outside the group, it's as if the Normal blending mode was assigned to the group. Isolate Blending has no effect to a blend mode applied to the group itself, or to objects where the Normal blend mode is applied. By default, this option is off and a blending mode applied to an object affects all objects behind it.

- **Knockout Group.** This limits the effect of grouped objects' individual blending modes to objects outside the group. Inside the group, the objects knock each other out as if the Normal blending mode was applied. It's the opposite of Isolate Blending.

Blend Space

When you blend objects using the Transparency command they are converted either to CMYK or RGB for display purposes—you can determine which color mode by selecting one from the Transparency Blend Space submenu (under the Edit menu). If you create documents for print, select the CMYK option. If you create InDesign documents for viewing online, select the RGB option.

85

Drop Shadows & Feathering

If you have been spending too much time using Photoshop or Illustrator to add drop shadows and soft edges to your objects, you'll be happy to discover that you can achieve them directly within InDesign. These features create transparency, which adds some complexity to the printing process, so be certain to read Chapter 94 to learn about printing transparent objects.

Applying Drop Shadows

You can apply a drop shadow to anything on your InDesign page: imported graphics, text frames, lines, and even tables (see Figure 85-1). Drop shadows are an effect attached to an object, so they can be edited or removed at any time. Apply a drop shadow by choosing a frame with the Selection tool and selecting Drop Shadow from either the Object menu or the context menu (or press Command-Option-M/Ctrl-Alt-M)—then turn on the Drop Shadow checkbox. If you select a text frame with a fill color of None, InDesign applies the drop shadow to the text; if the fill is any other color, the drop shadow applies to the frame itself.

The Drop Shadow dialog box lets you set the shadow's color, opacity, and blending mode (see Chapter 84). You can also determine the location of the shadow—by entering an X and Y offset—and the size of the shadow (how diffuse it is) using the Blur value.

Figure 85-1

Drop shadows

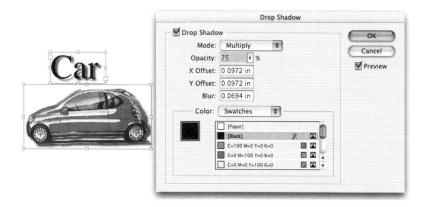

Applying Feathering

The Feather feature (in the Object menu or the context menu) lets you create a soft edge to any object—even text or imported graphics (see Figure 85-2). In the Feather dialog box you can specify the Feather Width and corner appearance (sharp, rounded or diffused). If the command has no effect or makes the original object disappear, the Feather Width value is probably too low or too high.

Figure 85-2

Feathering an imported graphic

Color & Transparency

86

Overprinting Color

As in QuarkXPress, you can specify that an object should overprint objects behind it, instead of knocking them out (completely replacing underlying inks) when you print color separations. By default, both XPress and InDesign overprint anything colored solid black. If, for some really weird reason, you prefer black not overprint, you have the option of turning this feature off in the General panel of Preferences.

Setting Overprints

In QuarkXPress, overprint controls are in the Trapping panel of the Preferences dialog box and in the Trap Information palette. InDesign's overprinting controls are in the Attributes palette (see Figure 86-1), which is available from the Window menu. Here you can set whether to overprint the fill or the stroke of a selected object.

While people commonly use overprinting as a way to manually set the trap on an object, it is better used for intentional ink-mixing effects on press. Building manual traps with overprinting is a recipe for a headache; use InDesign's built-in trapping instead (see Chapter 97). Remember that

Figure 86-1
The Attributes palette

overprinting only occurs when printing color separations. If you're just trying to create a cool effect, you may find using the Multiply blend mode much more flexible and effective than ink overprinting.

Previewing and Printing Overprints

While you can specify overprinting in XPress, there is no way to preview its effect (either on screen or on a color printer) before making color separations. In InDesign, you can: Select Overprint Preview from the View menu to see how overprinted inks will appear. You can work while this is turned on, but it does slow InDesign down a little bit. In addition, when printing composite color prints or making PDF files, you can turn on the Simulate Overprint option. The result is not suitable for final prepress work, but it excellent for inkjet printers and proofing.

Color & Transparency

87

Color Management

Very few people use QuarkXPress's color management system (the Quark-CMS XTension), instead managing the color of bitmapped images in Photoshop and then just assuming that what they see on screen in XPress may or may not be anything similar to what they're going to get on press. In our experience, managing color is easier and more practical in InDesign, partly because the controls are almost identical to those in Photoshop and Illustrator.

If you're not familiar with color management, you should understand that color management is not the same as color correction. Color management helps keep colors more consistent among each device you use—including scanners, monitors and various printers. Like XPress, InDesign relies on industry-standard International Color Consortium (ICC) profiles to convert colors. Both XPress and InDesign allow control over color management at the document level and for individual objects.

If you're looking for an in-depth analysis of InDesign's color management, including how it works with other software, we provide additional resources at the end of this chapter.

Setting Up Color Management

Just about everything in QuarkXPress's Color Management Preferences dialog box can be found in InDesign by selecting Color Settings from the Edit menu and then turning on the Enable Color Management option (it's turned off by default). If you've used Photoshop much, you'll find the settings here pretty familiar (see Figure 87-1). We've outlined the differences between these features and XPress's in Table 87-1.

You can, of course, select a Settings preset that matches your workflow—like U.S. Prepress Defaults or Europe Prepress Defaults, each of which fills in the rest of the dialog box for you. If you've already got this set up properly in Photoshop or Illustrator, it's probably best to choose the same setting you used there. In fact, you can save the color settings from those programs to disk and then click the Load button to import those settings into InDesign.

If you decide to customize the options, they're divided into three groups:

- **Working Spaces.** Defines the RGB and CMYK profiles which are used for non-color-managed and newly created documents that are color managed.

- **Color Management Policies.** Defines what happens when object colors need to be converted from one colorspace to another. We generally recommend that you leave these at their default settings.

- **Conversion Options.** Provides finer control over color conversions by letting you specify the color engine, rendering intent, and black

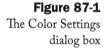
Figure 87-1
The Color Settings
dialog box

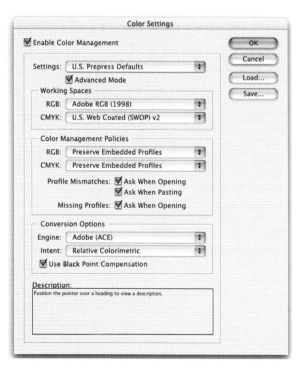

Color & Transparency

point compensation. These choices show up only if Advanced Mode is turned on. These are advanced options that should be left at their default settings, especially for print work. They can be overridden for individual objects using the Image Color Settings command in the Object menu.

The biggest mistake people make in attempting a color-managed workflow is to avoid making a custom ICC profile for their monitor (screen). If you want to even begin to trust what you see on screen, you *must* make a profile for it. You don't necessarily have to calibrate the monitor; but you do want to use something to characterize it (make a profile of it), such the Spyder (from OptiCal)—or at least eyeball it with ColorSync (on the Mac) or Adobe Gamma (on Windows).

Table 87-1

XPress's color management features versus InDesign's

QuarkXPress	Adobe InDesign
Monitor Profile	This is handled automatically; InDesign uses the monitor profile specified in the operating system.
Composite Output	Select a Print Space Profile in the Color Management pane of the Print dialog box (when printing to a composite printer).
Separation Output	Select a Print Space Profile in the Color Management pane of the Print dialog box (when printing separations).
Default Source Profiles	Use Assign Profiles (under the Edit menu). InDesign doesn't support Hexachrome colors.
Color Manage RGB Sources to Destinations	InDesign always color-manages objects when Enable Color Management is on, unless you suppress it for individual objects using the Image Color Settings command.
Display Simulation	InDesign always color-manages the document to the screen when Enable Color Management is on. In addition, you can simulate output conditions using the Proof commands on the View menu.

Color Managing Imported Graphics

You can enable or disable color management for imported images individually, either as you place them or after they're in the layout. The process is very similar to what you would do in XPress. To control color management as you place an image, choose the Place command from the File menu and turn on Show Import Options in the Place dialog box. After you click Choose, select Color Settings from the Image Import Options dialog box. Now you'll be able to specify the profile and rendering intent used by InDesign for this image in the document.

To control color management for an image already on the page, select it and choose Image Color Settings from the Object menu (see Figure 87-2). Again, the profile and rendering intent for the image can be changed here. The Enable Color Management option is different than XPress's Color Manage to RGB Destinations; InDesign's option completely includes or excludes the image from all color management, such as for CMYK images already with the correct color values for the destination press.

Figure 87-2
The Image Color
Settings dialog box

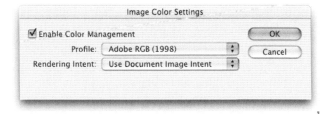

Soft-Proofing Colors

In QuarkXPress, you may have used the Display Simulation popup menu in the Color Management Settings dialog box to simulate different output conditions using your monitor. InDesign has the same capability, called *soft-proofing.* (Alternatively, hard-proofing is proofing on hard copy output.) InDesign makes soft-proofing a feature of the View menu, which is unlike XPress but once again like its Adobe brethren Photoshop and Illustrator. Under the InDesign View menu you'll find the Proof Colors and Proof Setup commands. Here's how they correspond to XPress's soft-proofing features.

First of all, there isn't a direct InDesign equivalent to the XPress's Monitor Color Space option. Whenever Enable Color Management in

Color & Transparency

InDesign's Color Settings dialog box is turned on, colors are adjusted to the monitor color space.

The Proof Colors command is similar to turning on XPress's Display Simulation option and selecting Composite Output or Separation Output in the Display Simulation popup menu. Selecting InDesign's Proof Colors command adds a check mark to indicate that soft-proofing is on. So what exactly is it proofing? The answer is whatever's checked in the Proof Setup submenu. You'll see three options there:

- **Custom.** Opens a dialog box where you can select any profile to proof. In XPress, you can soft-proof only the profiles selected in the Composite Output and Separation Output popup menus. If you wanted to see what the output might look like on other media, you would have to change those menu selections, and then remember to change them back before the job goes out. InDesign's Custom submenu lets you simulate how the document's current color settings might look on any medium for which you have a profile, without having to alter your workflow's actual composite or separation profile settings. This is also the place to simulate output to RGB devices like inkjets and other composite printers. We generally recommend that you leave the Paper White and Ink Black options on to properly simulate the selected profile's dynamic range. As in XPress, color contrast may appear to drop when simulating print media on a monitor, because the simulation must represent the limitations of the output medium.

- **Document CMYK.** This proofs using the document profile, which is set using the Assign Profiles command in the Edit menu. There's no reason why you can't choose the document's CMYK profile in the Custom command, but this command and the next one are convenient shortcuts. If you haven't changed the document profile to be different from the working space, you don't need to worry about this command.

- **Working CMYK.** This proofs using the Working Space you set in the Color Settings command.

For best results when soft-proofing, select High Quality Display from the View menu or from the context menu. This mode, along with soft-proofing itself, takes longer and uses more RAM, so for fast production work you may want to leave proofing off and the display set to a lower quality level.

Color Managing Print Output

When it comes time to print your document, you can tell InDesign how to color manage your output in the Color Management panel of the Print dialog box. Note that the available profiles listed in the Profile popup menu here depend on the Color option set in the Output panel. For example, the Profile menu uses the document's CMYK profile if you set the Color option to Separations, and it sets the composite profile in the Profile menu if you set the Color option to Composite. Also, changing the target printer can change the profile list depending on whether you've targeted a CMYK driver (like an imagesetter) or an RGB driver (like an inkjet printer).

For more detail on the various color management options, see the books *Real World InDesign 2* (by David Blatner and Olav Martin Kvern) and *Real World Color Management* (by Bruce Fraser, Chris Murphy, and Fred Bunting).

Color & Transparency

PART 9

Long Documents

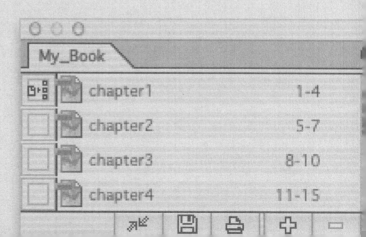

88

Managing Book Files

Like the Book feature that Quark added to XPress 4, InDesign's Book feature lets you effectively manage a number of related files, maintain consistent styles and color definitions across them, or simply print them all at once. With InDesign's Book palette, you can go even farther, preflighting, packaging, and exporting multiple documents to PDF in one easy step.

Building a Book

Just like XPress, you create books by choosing Book from the New submenu (under the File menu). This opens a Book palette, into which you can then add individual InDesign files by using the Add Document command from the flyout menu or clicking the plus icon at the bottom of the palette. You can also drag InDesign files from the Finder (Macintosh) or Explorer (Windows) into the palette.

The Book palette (and the accompanying book file on disk) just stores references to the InDesign files that you add; the documents aren't embedded into the book file. Because of this you will always need to keep both the book file and the original InDesign documents. While they do not need to be stored in the same folder, they need to be accessible to each other—such as on the same network or on the same computer.

Standardizing Attributes

One reason to use the Books feature is to standardize paragraph styles, character styles, swatches, table of contents styles, and trap styles across

Long Documents

335

multiple documents. You can do this by identifying one document as the source document that will be used as the standard for all other documents in the book. By default the source document is the first file you added to the book, but you can change this by clicking to the left of the name of any document in the palette.

Then, just like XPress, you can synchronize the entire book by choosing the Synchronize Book command from the flyout menu (see Figure 88-1) or by clicking the Synchronize icon at the bottom of the Book palette. If you first select two or more documents in the palette, InDesign will only synchronize those files.

Figure 88-1
Although you create and open a book from the File menu, it opens as a separate palette.

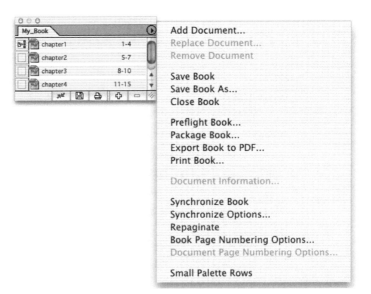

If a style or swatch exists in the source document but not in another book document, it will be added to the book document. If the styles or swatches conflict, those used in the source document will be used to replace the conflicting styles. You can also select which attributes InDesign will synchronize (and which it won't) by selecting Synchronize Options from the flyout menu prior to synchronizing the pages (see Figure 88-2).

Setting Page Order

Another good reason to use the Book feature is to standardize automatic page numbering across multiple documents. InDesign can use the order of the files in the Book palette to correctly set the starting page number

Figure 88-2
Using the
Synchronize
Options dialog
box you can select
which attributes are
standardized across
book chapters.

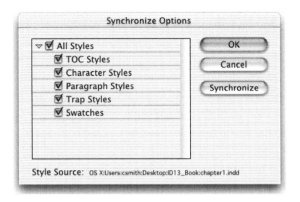

for each document in the book. You can set the page order of your documents by dragging them up or down within the Book palette. After you drag a document, InDesign renumbers all the other files (which can take a little while).

InDesign (unlike XPress) lets you specify how InDesign should number the pages in your book by selecting Book Page Numbering Options from the Book palette's flyout menu (see Figure 88-3). For example, you can force each chapter to start on either odd or even pages, and you can even tell InDesign to insert blank filler pages when needed. You can also indicate if page numbering should be continued from one chapter to the next. Of course, this only works when you've used automatic page numbering to display your page numbers (see Chapter 51).

Figure 88-3
With the Book Page
Numbering Options
dialog box you can set
how each document
in a book will be
numbered.

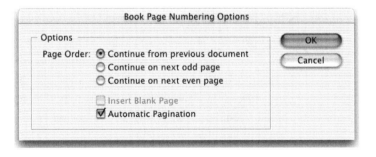

Preparing, Printing & Exporting Books

A great time saving feature of books is the ability to preflight, package, print, or export multiple documents without manually opening each one.

Long Documents

Preparing Books for Printing

Before you print or export, you can check the preparedness of all files in a book by choosing Preflight Book from the Book palette's flyout menu (XPress doesn't have this feature). InDesign checks all the documents listed in the book (or all the selected files, if you have chosen one or more in the palette) for missing or modified images along with possible color space problems and missing fonts. We discuss preflighting in detail in Chapter 91.

You can also use the Package Book feature (in the flyout menu) to collect all supporting elements (fonts, graphics, and so on) used within the book's documents to send them to a coworker or output provider. This is similar to XPress's Collect for Output feature, but XPress can't "package" up all of the files in a book. We discuss InDesign's Package feature in detail in Chapter 92.

Printing Books

You can print an entire book—even if it includes many files—without the need to open a single document by clicking the printer icon at the bottom of the Book palette or selecting Print Book from the book palette's flyout menu. As with synchronizing, preflighting, and packaging you can select a portion of the book to print as opposed to the entire book (Command/Ctrl click to select non-contiguous files in the palette). Note that while XPress cannot currently write book files to disk as PostScript, InDesign has no trouble with this. We talk about printing in Chapters 93 to 95.

Exporting Books to PDF

Like printing, you can export an entire book to PDF without having to open any of the documents contained in the book (XPress does not allow exporting books to PDF). To do this, select the Export Book to PDF command from the flyout menu (make sure no files are selected when you do this, or you'll only export those documents), and choose the PDF export options. We discuss the PDF export options available in Chapter 99.

89

Making a Table of Contents

If you have used paragraph styles religiously, InDesign can create a table of contents (TOC) from your document—or group of documents, if you are using the Book feature. The TOC feature works almost exactly like the Lists feature in QuarkXPress, though the interface is a bit different.

Building a TOC

XPress's Lists feature forces you to define a List, then build the table of contents from the Lists palette. InDesign makes a table of contents in one step, using the Table of Contents feature (which you can select from the Layout menu; see Figures 89-1 and 89-2). In the Table of Contents dialog box you can enter a title (like "Contents") if you wish for one to be automatically added to the beginning of the TOC, and you can apply a paragraph style to the title text using the Style pop-up menu.

Next, you must identify which of your document's paragraph styles InDesign should use to build the table of contents. To do this, double-click the styles you want to include from the Other Styles section of the Table of Contents dialog box (or click once and press the Add button). This adds the styles to the Include Paragraph Styles list. You can tell InDesign what paragraph styles to apply to the text within the table of contents you are building by selecting each style from the Include Paragraph Styles list and then selecting another paragraph style from the Entry Style pop-up menu to format it.

Figure 89-1
The Table of Contents dialog box lets you identify which paragraph styles InDesign should include in your TOC and how they are formatted.

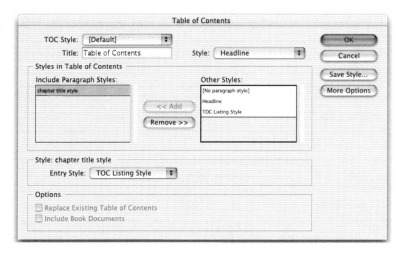

If you are updating an existing table of contents, select the Replace Existing Table of Contents option, and if you are building a table of contents from several Book files, select the Include Book Document option. You can also change the way InDesign creates the table of contents—such as making it alphabetical rather than in chronological order—by clicking the More Options button.

Figure 89-2
A table of contents built using the settings shown in Figure 89-1.

Table of Contents

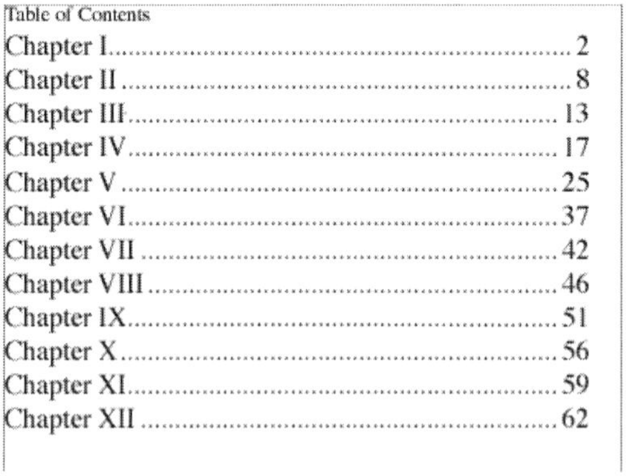

When you're ready, click OK. InDesign builds the table of contents and changes the cursor to the Place icon. You can fill an already-made text frame, or just click to have InDesign create a frame and fill it with the table of contents.

TOC Styles

Just because the feature is called Table of Contents doesn't mean you have to only use it to create tables of contents. Just like XPress's Lists feature, you can make a list of advertisers, a list of illustrators, and a table of contributing authors, all in the same document. The trick is having InDesign keep track of various groups of paragraph styles. These groups of styles are saved as *table of contents styles*, each of which specify a different set of paragraph styles that InDesign is watching, and the paragraph styles that are used to format the text of the list or TOC. You can save all of the settings from the Table of Contents dialog box to easily access them again by clicking the Save Style button. Or, you can select Table of Contents Style from the Layout menu (though this is more cumbersome; see Figure 89-3). Later, to call up the settings for each style, choose the style name from the TOC Style pop-up menu in the Table of Contents dialog box.

Figure 89-3
The Table of Contents Styles dialog box

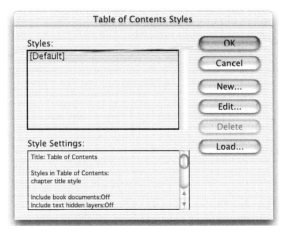

90

Building an Index

Both QuarkXPress and InDesign have more or less the same functionality when it comes to building an index, but neither of them lets you make one automatically. Indexing manually is tough and often tedious, though these tools can speed the process for you a little. Because few people need indexing, we only offer the basics here. For an in-depth look, see *Real World InDesign 2.*

Indexing Topics

Some folks start indexing with a list of topics (or entries) they want to use in an index. For example, if you are writing about animals, you might want to predefine topics (categories) for Felines and Canines, even before starting the indexing process. To create a list of topics, open the Index palette from the Window menu and click the Topic button located along the top of the palette (see Figure 90-1). Then select the New Topic command from the flyout menu or click the New icon at the bottom of the palette. Later, you can attach specific entries, called references, in your document to the topics you have added. Note that creating a list of topics is optional.

Making References

Whether or not you have pre-defined index topics, you can start indexing by clicking the Reference button at the top of the Index palette, selecting a word or phrase in your document that you would like to be indexed, and

Figure 90-1

The Topic option in the Index palette lets you predefine index topics prior to adding references.

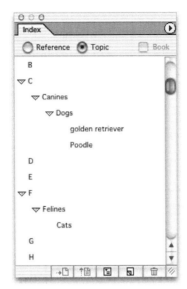

choosing the New Page Reference command from the flyout menu or clicking the New icon at the bottom of the palette. This opens the Page Reference Options dialog box, which lets you specify a scope (index this page, index to the end of the document, or whatever) and create nested entries so that the selected reference appears beneath topics (see Figure 90-2). Items in the first topic appear before second level entries.

Figure 90-2

Making a new page reference.

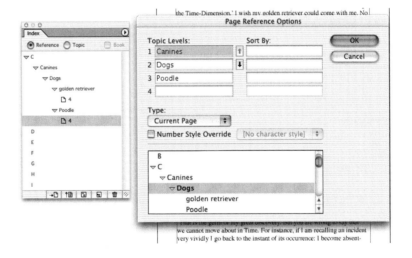

If you have already created topics or subtopics and wish to use these (instead of typing them each time), you can double-click on the topic at the bottom of the Page Reference Options dialog box.

As in QuarkXPress, you can indicate that the index should reference the specific location where your cursor was located when you added the reference, that the topic is located on a range of pages, or even that it should be a cross-reference (such as "*See also* Cuddly beasts"). You can determine this from the Type pop-up menu when in the Page Reference Options dialog box.

Note that if you later want to change an index entry or page reference (such as the type of reference or the level in which it appears), you can double-click on it in the Index palette.

Building the Index

Once you have added all the page references, you can tell InDesign to go and get the page numbers and build the index by selecting Generate Index from the Index palette's flyout menu. InDesign changes the cursor to the Place icon, and you can click on any text frame to place the index. You can also click where no frame exists to have InDesign build a frame for you.

PART 10

Printing

Print

Printer Style: Custom

Printer: PostScript® File

PPD: AGFA SelectSet 5000-X

General
Setup
Marks &Bleeds
Output
Graphics
Color Management
Advanced

Marks & Bleeds

Marks

⊟ All Printer's Marks
☑ Crop Marks
☐ Bleed Marks

91

Preflighting

Preflighting is one of the first stages in preparing your InDesign document for a print workflow. The term, originally coined by industry pundit Chuck Weger, derives its name from the checklist that pilots use when preparing to fly. Preflighting is an automated inspection of your document and its components, including fonts and graphics, so you can see if anything is missing or incorrectly prepared.

QuarkXPress provides only the most rudimentary preflight feature: the report created by Collect for Output includes a list of fonts and graphics. Preflighting in InDesign is integrated into the application, and it provides a great deal more useful information than the XPress feature.

You can preflight an InDesign document at any time. While most people think of doing it as they're preparing to send their file to a service provider, we think it's a good idea to use it at other times as well—for example, when you receive a new file from someone else. In fact, InDesign provides a quick preflight when you open a document, checking for missing or modified graphics and warning you if fonts are missing (we discuss this in Chapters 53 and 65).

The Preflight Dialog Box

Whenever you want to use this feature, choose Preflight from the File menu (or press Command-Option-Shift-F/Ctrl-Alt-Shift-F). In all but the smallest and simplest documents, you'll see a progress bar as InDesign analyzes the document and prepares its report. After a moment, you'll see the Preflight dialog box, set to the Summary panel (see Figure 91-1). Problems are highlighted in the summary with a triangle warning icon.

Figure 91-1

The Summary panel of the Preflight dialog box

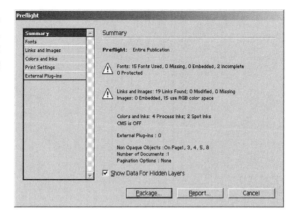

To get more information, click on the name of the panel you want to look at in the left column. (You can also use the shortcut Command/Ctrl-Down Arrow to switch to the next panel down in the list, and Command/Ctrl-Up Arrow to switch to the next panel up.)

Fonts Panel

The Fonts panel tells you about all the fonts in your document and in any linked EPS and PDF files (see Figure 91-2). If any fonts are missing, the panel can tell you the first page in the document where the font is used. If you use a lot of fonts, you may want to turn on the Show Problems Only option. Clicking the Find Font button takes you to the Find Font dialog box where you can find out more information or replace a missing font (see Chapter 53).

Figure 91-2

The Font panel of the Preflight dialog box

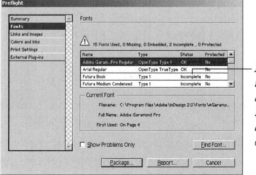

No fonts are missing from this document, but two are incomplete—they are PostScript Type 1 fonts which are missing either their screen or printer font.

Links and Images Panel

The Links and Images panel lists the document's embedded and linked files (see Figure 91-3). Linked images are listed by their name on disk, and embedded images are just listed as "(Embedded)". Note that InDesign also shows linked text files; as we discuss in Chapter 39, linked text files aren't a problem, but we prefer to embed these files. For each image, InDesign lists the file format and color space (unfortunately, the program can't detect RGB color information embedded in EPS or PDF files). In Figure 91-3, fifteen of the images are in RGB—you'd better convert them to CMYK or make sure your printer knows about them.

Figure 91-3

The Links and Images panel of the Preflight dialog box

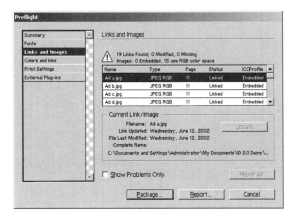

The Update/Relink choice allows you to select an individual linked graphic that is missing or modified, and to update or relocate it without leaving the dialog box (the feature toggles its name depending on the status of the image selected). The Repair All option lets you fix all missing and modified links. (We discuss more about linked graphics in Chapter 65.) Turn on the Show Problems option to only see modified or missing links.

Other Panels and Options

There are three other panels in the Preflight dialog box: The Colors and Inks panel shows you the inks used in your document, including inks specified in EPS or PDF files. This can be useful to identify a document where you have more spot colors than you expect; we discuss how to fix this using the Ink Manager in Chapter 95. The Print Settings panel summarizes the current settings in the Print dialog box. The External Plug-ins panel identifies any plug-ins which are required to reproduce the document (for example, if your document requires the InCopy plug-in).

Printing

There are three buttons at the bottom of the Preflight dialog box. Of course, the Cancel button cancels you out of the dialog box—however, if you have resolved font or link problems within the Preflight dialog box, those changes are not undone. Click the Report button if you want to save a text file of what the dialog box displays. Click Package to package the document and its associated files, which we talk about in the next chapter.

92

Packaging a Document for Print

Packaging is usually the next stage of preparing a document for print after preflighting. It is the equivalent of QuarkXPress's Collect for Output function. Packaging gathers together a copy of the publication, its associated graphics and fonts, and a report about the document for sending to a service provider or anyone else to whom you may be handing off your document.

You can package a document in one of two ways. If you have already performed a preflight (see Chapter 91), just click the Package button in the Preflight dialog box. Or, you can choose Package from the File menu (or press Command-Option-Shift-P/Ctrl-Alt-Shift-P), which automatically preflights the document before packaging. Either way, InDesign always requires you to save the document before proceeding with the packaging.

Printing Instructions

Before InDesign packages the files, it displays the Printing Instructions dialog box, in which you can enter contact information and any special printing instructions. This information gets added to the automatically-generated report, which also includes information about your document (graphics and fonts used, and so on). Since the report (called "Instructions") is stored in the same folder as the packaged document, it can provide valuable information for your output provider if you (and they) choose to use it. After entering the printing instructions, click Continue.

Printing

Packaging Options

Next, InDesign lets you choose how your document is packaged. In Windows, this is called the Package Publication dialog box, while on the Macintosh, it's the Create Package Folder dialog box (see Figure 92-1). Here you specify a name and location for the folder which will contain the files.

Figure 92-1

Package Publication dialog box (called Create Package Folder on the Macintosh)

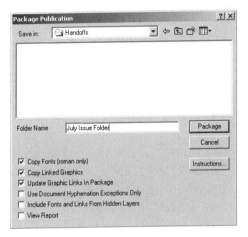

The document and the Printing Instructions report are always copied into the folder. However, you can choose which other items to include. You'll almost always want to use the default choices: copying the fonts, copying linked graphics, and updating the graphic links in the package. Choosing to update graphic links ensures that when your recipient opens the file, all the graphics will be linked and up-to-date. If your file has layers that are turned off (made invisible), turning on the Include Fonts and Links from Hidden Layers option ensures that required components from those layers are also copied. Turning on the Use Document Hyphenation Exceptions checkbox tells InDesign to embed your customized user dictionary in the document, ensuring that there will be no last minute text reflow problems.

When you're finished choosing options, click Package. If you are copying fonts, an alert from the Adobe Legal Department appears warning of the dangers of sending fonts to people who don't own them (as much as we respect the message, we sure wish we could disable this). Click OK to complete the packaging process.

93

Printing

If your first introduction to InDesign was a version before 2.0, you probably remember hating the Print dialog box. It's time to revisit this control center for printing, to see how it's changed. In earlier versions, the printing controls were poorly organized and were tied to particular Adobe-produced printer drivers. Beginning with 2.0, InDesign has totally changed the print dialog box so it matches, and in many ways, exceeds that of QuarkXPress for ease-of-use and capabilities. It supports all common printer drivers so you can choose the one which best fits your printing workflow.

This is such a big topic that we can only cover the most essential features of printing in this chapter. We cover color separation and more advanced printing features in Chapter 95. And we discuss saving and using printer styles in Chapter 96.

Printing Overview

Our discussion about the Print dialog box is made more difficult by differences in how printing is handled in each operating system. Adobe has made an admirable effort to make InDesign's Print dialog box look as similar as possible in both Macintosh and Windows, and between Mac OS 9 and Mac OS X (see Figure 93-1). Aside from some minor rearrangements of features within panels, only the buttons at the bottom of the dialog box vary between operating systems: The Macintosh sports Page Setup and Printer buttons; Windows only has a Setup button.

Figure 93-1

The Print
dialog box
(in Windows)

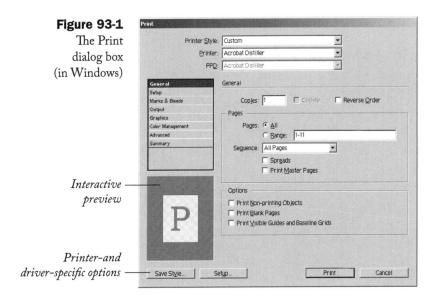

*Interactive
preview*

*Printer-and
driver-specific options*

As you make choices for printing by selecting panels from the panel list, most of the dialog box stays the same, including an interactive preview of the printed page. Note that you can jump from one panel to the next by pressing Command-1/Ctrl-1, Command-2/Ctrl-2, and so on.

Choosing a Printer

How you choose which printer to use depends on which operating system you're using. In Windows, the Printer popup menu in InDesign's Print dialog box displays the printers which you've set up using the Add Printer utility in Windows. In Macintosh OS 9, the menu only displays the current selection in the Chooser, which you access from the Apple menu. (You can also click on the Printer button, and select from printers which have already been set up in the Chooser.) Macintosh OS X is more similar to Windows: The Printer popup menu lists printers that you have defined using Print Center (located in the Utilities folder in the Applications folder).

The Printer pop-up menu includes one other option, no matter what operating system you're using: PostScript File (which we'll discuss below).

PostScript Printers and PPDs

Both QuarkXPress and InDesign were designed for PostScript printers. While InDesign 2 also supports non-Postscript printers (like most desktop inkjet printers), many of the Print dialog box choices won't be available.

For best results, you may find that exporting a PDF (see Chapter 99) and printing from Acrobat or Acrobat Reader is preferable when printing to a non-PostScript printer.

When you pick a PostScript printer, InDesign asks the printer driver for the appropriate PostScript Printer Description (PPD). The PPD is a text file which lists the specific characteristics—for example, paper sizes—available for this printer. You normally select the PPD when you set up your printer using either Add Printer, the Chooser, or the Print Center. InDesign displays the PPD in the PPD popup menu, but the name is dimmed out.

Creating a PostScript File

Writing PostScript to disk is a hassle from QuarkXPress, requiring that you use the printer driver dialog box. InDesign 2 lets you export PostScript easily: Just pick PostScript File from the Printer popup menu. You then have the choice to include or exclude printer-specific PostScript code along with the PostScript code created by InDesign. If you know exactly what printer you're printing this file on, you have its PPD on your machine, and you know what you're doing, then choose the PPD from the PPD popup menu. Otherwise, choose Device Independent.

Previewing Your Printing

While XPress only displays a preview of the printed page in one panel of the Print dialog box, InDesign always gives you an interactive preview in the lower-left corner of the Print dialog box. For example, if you change the page size or orientation, or add printer's marks, that will be reflected in the preview. If you click once on the Preview pane, InDesign displays data about your document; if you click again, InDesign shows you how your page will appear on the paper (most relevant when printing to a roll-fed imagesetter).

Printer-Specific Options

The Print dialog box panels that we describe in this chapter and in Chapter 95 include the features required by almost all printers. However, some printers have special controls which aren't set here (for example, hardware collating features or printer tray selection). You can get access to these options by clicking the Setup button in Windows or the Page Setup and Printer buttons on the Macintosh.

However, if you see choices in the printer driver (for example, page range) which are also in the InDesign Print dialog box, you should ignore the printer driver setting and make that choice in InDesign.

The General Panel

The Print dialog box's General panel is usually the first one you see, and it covers the most common printing choices you make. It includes some items which you find on the Document tab of QuarkXPress's Print dialog box, but also includes a few options which you won't find in XPress.

Here you may set any number of copies up to 999. If you want the Collate feature like in XPress, choose it here, but expect that it will greatly slow printing because your document is being collated "in software." Reverse order is the same as XPress's Back to Front feature.

Choosing Pages

To choose which pages of your document to print, either click All or type a page range with hyphens (or use commas for discontinuous ranges). By default, you have to type the page numbers exactly as they appear on the page. For instance, if you have used the Numbering and Section Options dialog box (see Chapter 37) to start the document on page 13 and you want to print the second page of the document, you need to type 14 into the Range field. If you specified a prefix for page numbering, such as "A-" then you'd have to type A-14.

Unfortunately, InDesign has no symbol for specifying absolute page numbering like in XPress. You can, however, change the Page Numbering option in the General panel of the Preferences dialog box (see Chapter 7) to Absolute Numbering. This way, you could specify the second page of the document by simply typing 2.

The Sequence feature is the same as QuarkXPress' Page Sequence—you can choose All Pages, Even Pages or Odd Pages.

Old and New Options

The General panel also gives you control over printing spreads and blank pages, which are equivalent to the same features in XPress. However, unlike XPress, you can choose to print Master Pages (which prints the all the master pages and could be helpful when designing a document), and the Nonprinting Objects (which overrides the Nonprinting object attribute we describe in Chapter 23). You can also choose to print Visible Guides and Baseline Grids. These print in the color specified in the document, a great feature for page designers.

The Setup Panel

InDesign's Setup panel (see Figure 93-2) is likely the second panel you'll go to when printing a document. It includes similar choices to those on QuarkXPress's Document and Setup tabs—letting you change paper size and orientation, page scaling and positioning, and thumbnails and tiling.

Figure 93-2
The Print dialog box
Setup panel

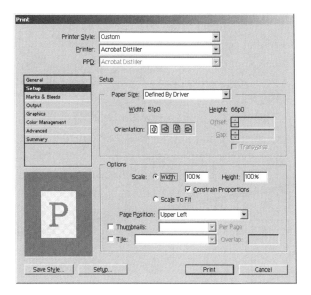

Paper Size and Orientation

The choices of paper size you have in InDesign depend on which choice you have made in the Printer menu:

- If you select a printer, the Paper Size popup menu reads Defined by Driver, which means that InDesign uses the current printer driver's default size. You can override this by choosing a different paper size, based on those specified in that printer's PPD file. Some printers also allow the Custom option, which we discuss below.

- If you choose to create device independent PostScript, no paper size is available because this PostScript file will be handled by post-processing software later in the workflow (like software for imposition, for example).

Printing

- If you choose PostScript targeted for a particular printer, you can also choose the paper sizes listed in that printer's PPD file, or Custom if that is available.

The Orientation feature defines how the page is oriented on the paper (or other media) it's printed on. For high-resolution PostScript imagesetters or platesetters, which image onto roll-fed material, the PPD may also allow the page to be rotated on the media by choosing the Transverse option.

Custom Paper Sizes

High-resolution imagesetters and platesetters can output pages of any size that can fit onto their roll-fed media. Therefore, their PPDs allow the creation of custom paper sizes. When you choose Custom from the Paper Size menu, you may enter any Width or Height value which you wish which fits on the paper. However, there's a much easier and smarter way! InDesign's default for both Width and Height is Auto, which automatically calculates the minimum paper size needed to output the current page with all marks and bleeds, reducing media waste to a minimum.

There are two other options which only appear when selecting roll-fed printers, similar to choices in QuarkXPress: Offset sets the distance between the left edge of the media and the left edge of the page. Gap sets the distance between pages. It's rare that you need to mess with these.

Scaling and Positioning Options

InDesign's Scale Width and Height option allows you to set page scaling. This is the same as QuarkXPress' Reduce or Enlarge option (though InDesign lets you scale from 1 to 1000 percent, much larger and smaller than XPress). Usually, you'll leave the Constrain Proportions option turned on, forcing InDesign to apply the same scaling to the Height and Width. However, non-proportional scaling is also possible, and can be useful for a specialized printing process like flexography. The Scale to Fit feature works exactly like the Fit in Print Area option in XPress.

Similarly, Page Position is equivalent to the same-named feature in QuarkXPress: It's useful when you are printing a small page on large paper; the default is printing on the upper left corner, but centering choices are also available. This is disabled when Scale to Fit, Thumbnails or Tiling is turned on (see below).

Thumbnails and Tiling

You can print several scaled-down pages called thumbnails on a single sheet of paper by turning on the Thumbnails option. Where QuarkXPress only gives you one size of thumbnail, InDesign allows you to select between 2 and 49 thumbnails per page. Use the Preview pane to see how they will fit on your paper.

You may also tile documents like you can in XPress—printing a large page in sections on a smaller paper size—by checking the Tile option. There are three tiling choices: Auto works just like Auto does in QuarkXPress, automatically calculating the number of sheets to print on based on the Overlap value. (Overlap describes how much an edge is repeated between tiles.) Auto Justified calculates using the Overlap value as a minimum; larger overlap may be possible depending on paper size. Manual prints a single tile, just as in XPress: You set the upper left corner by positioning the ruler zero point.

The Marks & Bleeds Panel

The last panel we'll discuss in this chapter, Marks & Bleeds, lets you specify which printer's marks should appear around the printed page, as well as how big the bleed area should be (see Figure 93-3). QuarkXPress offers these choices on the Document and Bleed tabs respectively.

Figure 93-3
The Print dialog box Marks & Bleeds panel

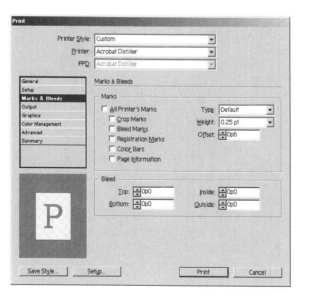

Printing

Printer's Marks

If you want page marks around your printed page in XPress (trim marks, registration marks, page information, and so on), you turn on the Registration checkbox; InDesign offers much finer control, letting you turn on or off five different types of page marks:

- **Crop Marks:** Thin rules which tell your commercial printer where to trim the page.
- **Bleed Marks:** Thin rules which mark the bleed area (described below). We rarely turn this on.
- **Registration Marks:** Printer's targets which are used for aligning color plates (so they're only relevant for color separations).
- **Color Bars:** Gray and colored squares used for measuring ink density.
- **Page Information:** This includes the file name, page number, date and time, and plate color name (when printing color separations).

You can turn on all the marks by checking All Printer's Marks, or you may turn on only those which you wish. The Type popup menu could theoretically let you choose a different sort of registration mark, but we've never seen anything but the Default option available. The Weight of crop and bleed marks can be set in points. The Offset specifies the distance between the edge of the page and the page marks; the default is 6 points (we usually set this higher, to 9 or 12 points).

Bleed Area

When you create artwork that extends all the way to a page edge, you have to actually extend it beyond the edge; this is called a bleed. However, like XPress, InDesign only prints objects beyond the page edge if you increase the bleed settings in the Print dialog box. And, like XPress, you can choose different amounts of bleed for each side of your document.

94

Think Outside the Box: Transparency & Printing

Transparency, as we discuss in Chapters 84 and 85, is the visual interaction of objects which have differing degrees of opacity. InDesign lets you make objects transparent, and you can import transparent graphics from Illustrator, Photoshop and Acrobat. This gives you some design and production capabilities far beyond what you can create in QuarkXPress. However, you must consider some important consequences of using transparency when printing.

Transparency Must Be Flattened

When it comes time to print, the beautiful transparent effects that you've created must be sent to a machine which doesn't know what transparency is. PostScript—the language spoken by most laser printers, imagesetters, and platesetters—only understands objects which are completely opaque. So InDesign (or any application which works natively with transparency) must take the transparent objects and break them into lots of different non-transparent pieces; this process is called *flattening*. The result is a single opaque page that comes out of the printer.

You can control the way flattening occurs by choosing a *transparency flattener style*, which we discuss below.

When Flattening Happens

When you have transparent objects or graphics containing transparency on a page, flattening happens on three different occasions in InDesign:

- When you print, InDesign uses the flattening settings in the Advanced panel of the Print dialog box (see Chapter 95).

- When you export an EPS file, InDesign uses the flattening settings in the Advanced panel of the Export EPS dialog box (see Chapter 98).

- When you export a PDF file in the Acrobat 4 format, InDesign uses the flattening settings on the Advanced panel of the Export PDF dialog box (see Chapter 99). Acrobat 5 PDF format can include transparency so it doesn't have to be flattened.

Figure 94-1 shows four simple objects created in InDesign. Two of the shapes and the type have had their opacity reduced with the Transparency palette. To show the effect of flattening, which normally only appears when printed, we exported the file to an Acrobat 4 PDF file. Then we opened the PDF in Adobe Illustrator, where the flattened objects can be observed. To make the effect more apparent, we offset some of the objects so you can see that they were broken into pieces. Note that InDesign doesn't break up the type, but it does convert some of it into a clipping path.

Figure 94-1
Simple objects with transparency—before and after flattening. Some of the flattened objects were offset to make the results more obvious.

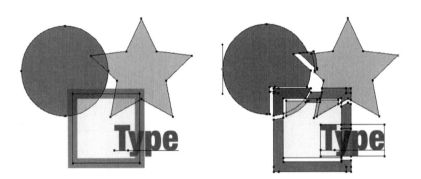

Note that InDesign has to have your high-resolution linked graphics on hand at print time in order to flatten properly. That means printing transparency probably won't work properly if you're printing through an OPI server or if you use DCS images.

How Can You Tell There Is Transparency?

Don't get caught by surprise when objects get flattened. Anytime you have transparent objects or graphics containing transparency there are two signs you can look for to indicate there is transparency on a page or spread:

- A page which has transparency shows a checkerboard background on the Pages palette (see Figure 94-2). This is the same indicator for transparency in a Photoshop layer!

- When you preflight a document with transparency, the Summary panel lists the pages where there are "non opaque objects."

Figure 94-2
A checkboard background on a page indicates transparency.

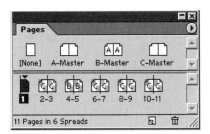

Controlling How Flattening Occurs

Flattening takes time, and usually adds to the time it takes to print a document—how much depends on the complexity of the page. There's just no reason to use the highest quality flattening when printing a proof to a desktop laser printer, but you probably don't mind taking the time to get the best quality on an imagesetter or platesetter. To make the process easier, InDesign ships with three built-in transparency flattener styles: High Resolution, Medium Resolution or Low Resolution. Most of the time, one of these settings will work for whatever you're doing.

You can select one of these flattener styles from the Print dialog box, the Export PDF dialog box, or the Export EPS dialog box. Generally, you can match the style to the resolution of your printer (low for proofing on low-resolution printers and high for imagesetters and platesetters). You can also override the flattener style for an individual spread, found in the Pages palette flyout menu. It's rare that you'd need to do that.

Customizing the Controls

If you're a output service provider, and you really need to fine-tune your transparency output, you can create custom flattener styles by choosing Transparency Flattener Styles from the Edit menu. You'll see the Trans-

Printing

parency Flattener Styles dialog box (see Figure 94-3). To create a new style, choose the built-in style you want to use as a starting point, then click the New button. A second dialog box appears, offering you a number of controls. The Raster/Vector balance slider alters how the flattening occurs: When you select toward Vectors, InDesign tries to maintain as many objects as vector as the complexity of the artwork will allow. This is usually what you want for high-resolution printing.

Figure 94-3

The Transparency Flattener Styles dialog boxes

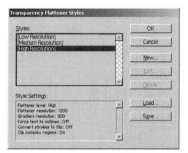

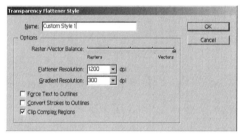

However, if the transparency on the page is very complex, some of the objects may have to be rasterized when flattening occurs. The setting for Flattener Resolution determines the flattening resolution when rasterization is necessary. Gradient Resolution is the resolution for drop shadows, gradients, or Illustrator mesh objects. There are also some controls for special situations—for changing text to outlines to prevent type being only partially rasterized, which can fatten part of the type; for converting strokes to outlines; and for clipping complex regions to prevent an ugly effect called color stitching.

If you're a output service provider, you'll need to know a bit more to optimize your transparency output. We suggest that you look at David's other tome, *Real World InDesign 2*, or refer to the resources we list in Chapter 95, which give more information than we can provide here.

95

Advanced Print Settings

In Chapter 93 we introduced you to the basics of printing and InDesign's Print dialog box. In this chapter, we'll cover some of the deeper print stuff and answer questions like How do I make color separations in InDesign? Can I get two Pantone spot colors with different names to print on the same color plate? How do I print a proof with just low resolution images? What happens if I use an OPI workflow?

The Output Panel

Most of the choices you see in the Print dialog box's Output panel are only available when a PostScript printer is chosen (see Figure 95-1). (This is also true for the other panels described in this chapter.) For instance, on a non-PostScript printer—like those ubiquitous Epson inkjets—only the Color menu and Text as Black option are available. The choices on this panel are similar to QuarkXPress's Output tab.

Kinds of Output

As you prepare to print, you need to consider what kind of output you're expecting from your printer. Are you producing a composite color proof, a grayscale print, or do you want each color in the document to be printed on a separate printing plate? The Color popup menu is where you make that choice:

Printing

Figure 95-1
The Print dialog box
Output panel

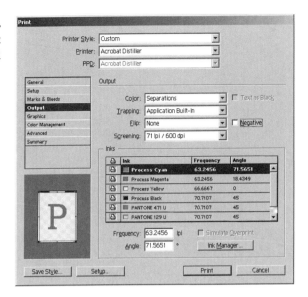

- **Composite Gray.** InDesign sends grayscale information to the printer. Any colors in the InDesign file are converted to grays, though the program can't change colors inside EPS or PDF graphics.

- **Composite RGB.** InDesign sends full-color RGB to the printer. This is best for RGB printers like inkjet printers or film recorders.

- **Composite CMYK.** InDesign sends full-color CMYK to the printer. This is best for CMYK PostScript printers or composite color work-flows (for example, the Scitex workflow).

- **Separations.** InDesign sends the data as CMYK separations with each color (including spot colors) on a separate plate. This is best for pre-separated CMYK workflows.

- **In-RIP Separations.** InDesign sends the data as composite CMYK optimized for separation within the printer's raster image processor (RIP). This choice is only available if you have chosen the PPD of an imagesetter or platesetter which has this capability.

The Text as Black option turns text to black if it isn't colored None, Paper or a zero-percent tint. This is great when printing a proof you're going to fax to someone, but output service providers will probably want to turn this off.

Color Separations

If you choose color separations—either InDesign's or In-RIP—you then have several other choices available, such as trapping and flip. We'll cover the Trapping option in Chapter 97. The Flip choice allows you to print the page so it images right-reading or wrong-reading and on the correct emulsion side when producing film output. The Negative choice turns black to white, and *vice versa*, to produce film negatives. Watch out; while it's nice that InDesign can do these things, output providers often control this stuff better from their RIP software or hardware.

The Screening options provide combinations of screen frequency (in lines per inch) and output resolution (in dots per inch) for printing. This choice may also be available for composite printing:

- For Composite CMYK or RGB printing, a Default setting is available (and is dimmed). This uses the printer's default settings.

- For Composite Gray printing, Default and Custom are available, and, if you choose Custom, you can set a screen frequency and angle.

- For Separations, the settings are those available in the current printer's PPD file, and Default isn't available. You can also set custom halftone values in the Inks section of the dialog box. Note that just because you ask for particular halftone settings doesn't mean you'll get them; an imagesetter or platesetter RIP often overrides your angle and frequencies with ones it knows work well.

Choosing and Changing Inks

You may have applied many colors in your InDesign document (and imported more colors in placed graphics). If the colors are (perhaps accidentally) spot colors, you may find yourself with many more plates output than you expect. The Inks section is where you determine what color plates are produced when color separations are printed.

The Inks list displays all the colors applied in the document, and their output status. For example, in Figure 95-1, six colors are showing, including two Pantone spot colors. The Print icon to the left of the ink name indicates that currently all are set to print. Each ink listed has a screen frequency and screen angle which is determined by the chosen PPD and the chosen screening/output resolution, as described above.

Clicking the Ink Manager button opens the Ink Manager dialog box (see Figure 95-2). While XPress only lets you convert all spot colors to process colors, InDesign's Ink Manager lets you choose whether each individual spot color prints on its own plate, is converted to a process color. (The All Spots to Process checkbox converts them all.)

You can even use the Ink Manager to *alias* one spot color to another. An all-too-familiar scenario for an output provider is that the client has

Figure 95-2
The Ink Manager
dialog box

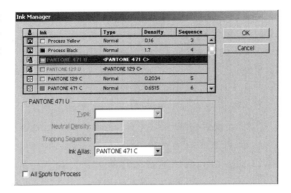

applied two or more different names for the same spot color. If not corrected, these will output on separate plates. In QuarkXPress, this might require you to change the artwork to make the file separate correctly.

In Figure 95-2, you can see that there are two versions of Pantone 471—one ending with "C," and one ending with "U." (These stand for the Pantone Coated and Uncoated libraries, respectively.) To alias one to the other, select a color in the Ink Manager and then select the other color from the Ink Alias popup menu.

The other ink characteristics shown here—Type, Neutral Density and Sequence—are related to trapping, which is discussed in Chapter 97. Note that the Ink Manager is also available in the Export EPS and Export PDF dialog boxes and in the Swatches palette.

The Graphics Panel

The Graphics panel in the Print dialog box has choices similar to those found on the Options tab in QuarkXPress (see Figure 95-3). This panel controls how graphics are output (except for OPI workflows; see below), how fonts are sent to the printer, and the kind of data which is sent to the printer.

The Images option determines how the data in linked graphics is sent to the printer:

- **All.** InDesign sends all the high-resolution data from the placed graphic. This is the default, and this should generally be chosen by service providers when sending to a high-resolution printer.

- **Optimized Subsampling.** InDesign samples down the data in bitmap images based on the halftone screen and printer resolution (set in the Output panel). This prints much faster to printers when you're print-

Figure 95-3

The Print dialog box
Graphics panel

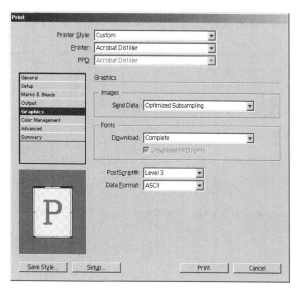

ing low- or medium-resolution proofs. This is the default setting in XPress.

- **Proxy.** InDesign uses only the low-resolution screen preview data when printing graphics. This is even faster than Optimized Subsampling.

- **None.** InDesign replaces all placed graphics with a large X. This prints the fastest of all, of course.

The Font section controls something not available in QuarkXPress: how fonts get downloaded to the printer. In the Download popup menu, Complete (the default) downloads all the document's fonts at the beginning of the print job. Subset downloads only the glyphs (characters) used in the document, but once per page (this is the same option available in Acrobat Distiller). None downloads only references to the fonts and should only be used if you know all the fonts reside on the printer. The Download PPD Fonts checkbox forces all the document's fonts to download, even if the printer's PPD says they are resident in the printer.

Finally, you may select the PostScript level—Level 2 or 3—which is compatible with your printer, though this is usually selected for you, depending on which printer you've chosen in the General panel. (Note that old PostScript Level 1 printers are not supported.) For Data Format, you may choose between Binary (more compact and faster) or ASCII (slower, but required by some older networks and printers).

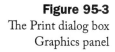

Color Management Panel

We talk about InDesign's options for color management in Chapter 87, so we won't bother discussing them here.

Advanced Panel

The Advanced Panel is sort of a "catch all." It gives you controls for OPI workflows, for printing gradients to certain kinds of printers, and for choosing flattening settings (see Figure 95-4).

Figure 95-4

The Print dialog box
Advanced panel

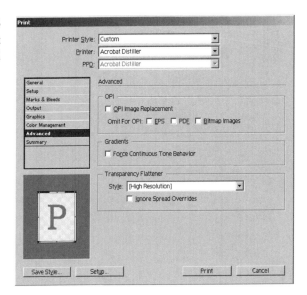

OPI Workflows

You only need to be concerned with the OPI section if you're using an Open Prepress Interface (OPI) workflow. In an OPI workflow, you place low-resolution "proxy" images in InDesign which reference the high-resolution files (which may not even be on your system). At output time, an OPI server automatically replaces the proxies with the high-resolution files.

Turning on OPI Image Replacement allows InDesign to act as an OPI server. For this to work, when placing an EPS file, the Read Embedded OPI Image Links option in the EPS Import Options dialog box must be selected. InDesign must also have access to the high-resolution files. (This workflow can be useful when you're using transparency, and the high-resolution version needs to be used in the flattening process.)

Turning off OPI Image Replacement and turning on one or more of the Omit for OPI options allows InDesign to strip out selected images—based on their graphic formats—EPS (Encapsulated PostScript), PDF (Acrobat files), or Bitmap Images. OPI comments are added to the PostScript instead, to be replaced later in the workflow by an OPI server.

Gradients

The Force Continuous Tone Behavior in the Gradients section is pretty specialized. For color printers which are continuous tone—dye sublimation and continuous-tone laser printers—this choice can help to prevent banding in gradients.

Transparency Flattening

Transparency needs to be flattened when it's time to print. We discuss these options in Chapter 94.

Summary Panel

The Summary panel displays a report of the settings you've made in all the Print dialog panels. It's pretty useless, but there is an option to save this summary, which may be useful for troubleshooting or communicating with others who are handling your files.

Resources for Print Service Providers

We expect that some of you reading this book work for output service providers—printers, service bureaus, and the like. We know you'll need more information about printing than we can cover in this book. Fortunately, Adobe provides a number of resources about InDesign for print service providers regarding printing, handling transparency, trapping, and so on:

- The *Adobe InDesign 2.0 Printing Guide for Service Providers* (in the Adobe Technical Info folder on your InDesign 2.0 installation CD).

- You can find free documentation, including known issues, workarounds and tips, free Adobe classes, and more, at the InDesign Print Service Provider Resources Web site (*http://partners.adobe.com/asn/service/indesign/main.html*.

- Become a member of the Adobe Authorized Service Provider (AASP) program. *http://partners.adobe.com/asn/service/registration/*

Printing

96

Creating Printer Styles

Just as you can create and apply paragraph and character styles to automate the process of applying text attributes, so you can create and apply *printer styles* to automate the process of printing. A printer style is a collection of settings, including almost all the choices you can make in InDesign's Print dialog box. InDesign's Printer Styles commands work almost identically to QuarkXPress's Print Styles feature.

Creating a Printer Style

To create a print style in QuarkXPress, you must select Print Styles from the Edit menu. InDesign is a little more flexible: It lets you create printer styles in two ways—using the Printer Styles command (like in XPress) or from within the Print dialog box. In both programs, the printer styles you create are available application-wide, not just to the current document or to open documents.

In the Print Dialog Box
We find it easiest to create printer styles in the Print dialog box. Open the Print dialog for a typical job in your workflow. Make all the choices necessary in each of the panels, and then click the Save Style button at the bottom of the dialog box. You'll see the Save Style dialog box. To create a new style, type a style name and click OK. To redefine an existing style, choose an existing style name in the popup list and click OK. The style name will now appear in the Printer Style popup menu at the top of the

dialog box. That's all there is to it! You can even press Cancel to leave the Print dialog box without actually printing.

Using the Printer Styles Command

If you have a lot of different devices that you print to, you may prefer to choose Define from the Printer Styles submenu (under the File menu). This displays the Define Printer Styles dialog box (see Figure 96-1), which list the Default style (the settings that appear by default in the Print dialog box) as well as any other printer styles you've created.

Figure 96-1

The Define Printer Styles dialog box

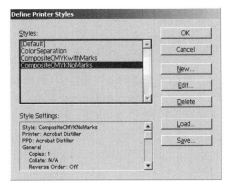

To create a new printer style, click the New button. The Print dialog box appears (see Figure 96-2). It's almost the same as the normal Print dialog box, but there is no preview. Type a name for the style at the top of the dialog box. Then make all the choices in any of the panels. When you're finished, click OK to save changes to the printer style.

Figure 96-2

The Print dialog box when using the Printer Style command

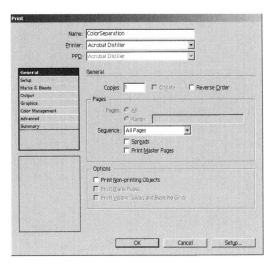

Printing

To edit an existing style, click the Edit button in the Define Printer Styles dialog box. Obviously, you can delete a style by clicking the Delete button. Less obvious is the ability to load and save your styles, which is useful when you want to share your settings among different workstations. To save styles, select the styles you want to include by Shift-clicking or Command/Ctrl-clicking, then click the Save button. Later, you can click the Load button to load the styles.

By the way, there are a couple of items in the Print dialog box which cannot be saved in a style and which must be set individually for a specific job. For instance, specific inks and ink aliasing cannot be saved in a style.

Selecting Printer Styles

When printing, selecting a printer style is as simple as choosing it from the Printer Style popup menu at the top of the Print dialog box or from the Printer Style submenu (under the File menu). If you want to print your entire document with one of your printer styles, hold down the Shift key while selecting the style from the Printer Style submenu—this bypasses the Print dialog box entirely!

97

Trapping

Trapping is the process of compensating for the fact that printing presses sometimes misregister, creating unsightly gaps between areas of adjacent colored inks. When a trap is created, objects on the page overlap a tiny amount to prevent the white gaps. While newer presses and processes like direct-to-plate may somewhat reduce the need for trapping, creating traps will be part of the printing process for the foreseeable future.

In QuarkXPress, there are two ways to trap—you can create color-by-color automatic trapping in the Trapping preferences, and you can create object-level trapping which can be applied to XPress-created items using the Trap Information palette. However, QuarkXPress cannot handle trapping objects like blends, cannot choke type, and cannot handle the trapping of items which touch multiple colors. It also can't trap colors in placed graphics. Many printing professionals turn off XPress trapping, and use professional trapping software instead.

Built-in or In-RIP Trapping

In InDesign, the choice of trapping is made in the Output panel of the Print dialog box (see Chapter 95), but is only available when you are printing color separations. InDesign offers two kinds of trapping from the Trapping popup menu: built-in trapping and In-RIP trapping. InDesign's built-in trapping is surprisingly good, and can handle most trapping needs. However, if your output provider has a PostScript 3 RIP which has In-RIP trapping, InDesign can support that (make sure you have the proper PPD chosen for the RIP).

Printing

InDesign's trapping engine can correctly handle trapping when objects contain multiple colors, like a gradient, when objects cross multiple colors, and even when objects overlap bitmapped images (TIFF, JPEG and PSD formats). The In-RIP trapping also adds the ability to trap colors within placed EPS, PDF, DCS, and Illustrator graphics. (However, we don't actually know anyone who uses PostScript's In-RIP trapping; most output providers rely on other trapping software instead.)

Trapping Controls

InDesign also lets you assign particular trapping to specific pages in your document by allowing you create trapping styles in the Trap Styles palette. For instance, you might want to apply a "no trap" style to a particular spread so that nothing on that page traps. To open the palette, choose Trap Styles from the Window menu (see Figure 97-1).

Figure 97-1
The Trap Styles palette

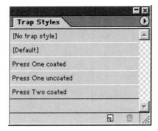

To create a trap style, choose New Style from the palette menu to open the New Trap Style dialog box (see Figure 97-2). You can also import trap styles from other documents by choosing Load Trap Styles from the palette menu. If you're modifying a trap style, select its name in the palette and choose Style Options from the palette menu.

Figure 97-2
The New Trap Style dialog box

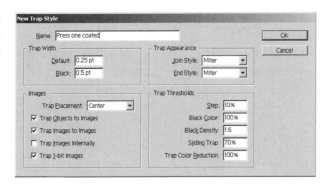

Creating Trap Styles

Trap style settings should only be created or modified by someone who is familiar with press conditions for the job. Here we can only offer a quick overview of the trap style controls. Service providers can find out more information from *Real World InDesign 2* or the resources listed in Chapter 95.

After giving a name to the trap style, you can specify a default Trap Width for the amount of overlap for inks; there is a separate control for trapping black. You can create traps up to 8 points thick with in-RIP trapping; built-in traps are limited to 4 points (which is already a pretty huge trap). For Trap Appearance, you can specify a join style and an end style.

For images, you can specify how placed bitmap images are trapped: There is an option to specify where the trap falls when vector objects (including InDesign objects) trap to bitmap images. There are options for trapping objects to images, images to images, trapping colors within an image, and trapping 1-bit images.

The Trap Threshold section of the dialog box specifies the conditions when trapping occurs: Step controls the degree colors vary before trapping takes place. Black Color indicates the minimum amount of black before black width trapping occurs. Black Density controls the neutral density value which InDesign uses to recognize black ink (neutral density is described below). Sliding Trap tells InDesign the percentage difference between neutral densities of adjoining colors when a more elegant sliding trap is created. Trap Color Reduction reduces trap color to prevent unsightly dark traps when trapping pastel colors.

Assigning Trap Styles

While you probably only need one trap style for a document, you may choose to apply different styles to different ranges of pages. To assign trap styles to pages, choose Assign Trap Style from the Trap Styles palette menu. In the Assign Trap Styles dialog box (see Figure 97-3), select a trap style you want to assign. Either click All or enter the range of pages (continuous or non-continuous) to which you want to apply that trap style, then click Assign. If you have pages where no trapping is necessary, select [No Trap Style], type the page range, and click Assign. Making this choice disables trapping, and these pages will print faster.

Note that trapping doesn't occur when you assign trap styles, only when you actually print color separations from the document. There is no preview

Printing

Figure 97-3

Assign Trap Styles
dialog box

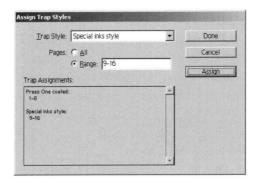

of trapping as there is in some high-end trapping software. The resulting traps only appear on the separation plates.

Ink Controls

We discuss the ink aliasing capabilities of the Ink Manager in Chapter 95, but InDesign hid some trapping controls there, too. Remember that the Ink Manager lives in the Advanced panels of the Print, Export EPS, and Export PDF dialog boxes and in the Swatches palette menu. Since InDesign's trapping happens at the ink level, there are three controls in the Ink Manager that influence trapping. First, each ink can be assigned a Type: Normal for process and most spot color inks, Transparent for clear inks like varnishes, Opaque for heavy, non-transparent inks like metallics, and OpaqueIgnore for heavy, non-transparent inks to prevent trapping along an ink's edges.

Each ink can also be assigned a neutral density (basically, how dark the ink is if you were to see it in grayscale). This value, which may be adjusted to match industry standards in different parts of the world, is used by the trapping engine to calculate trapping requirements. Finally, Sequence indicates the trapping order of inks, which is a press-specific control.

PART 11

Exporting

Export PDF

Style: Custom

General
Compression
Marks & Bleeds
Advanced
Security
Summary

Compression

Color Bitmap Images

Bicubic Downsample to

Compression: Automa

Quality: Medium

Grayscale Bitman Images

98

Exporting EPS

Sometimes you need to use one or more InDesign pages in another application. To do this in QuarkXPress, you would save the page as an Encapsulated PostScript file (EPS) by choosing Save Page as EPS. InDesign lets you save pages as EPS or PDF files (we cover PDF in the next chapter) by choosing Export from the File menu. In the Export dialog box, select EPS from the Formats popup menu, give the file a name, and, for Windows, make sure the file has a .EPS extension. (We discuss graphic formats in more detail in Chapter 62.)

General Options

There are two panels of options to control how InDesign saves your EPS file. The General panel provides many of the same selections as on XPress's Save Page as EPS tab (see Figure 98-1).

An EPS file can only contain one page. However, while QuarkXPress will only let you export one page at a time, InDesign lets you specify a range of pages. For example, if you choose to name your EPS file, "Lightness of Beans.EPS," and there are ten pages in your document, InDesign creates ten EPS documents, appending the page number to each name. If you have created multipage spread, you can check Spreads, and a single EPS file will be created for each spread.

There is no Scaling option as there is in QuarkXPress. Of course, any EPS file can be scaled when you place it, or when being rasterized in Photoshop.

Figure 98-1

The Export EPS dialog box General panel

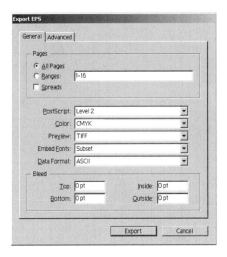

Format Settings

An EPS file contains both the high-resolution data for the printer and a screen preview. The high-resolution information can be written either for a PostScript Level 2 or Level 3 printer. For Color, there are four choices: CMYK is usually the best choice for print. You can also select RGB (though it's rare you'd need it), Gray to turn color to gray values, or Device Independent if you have enabled color management.

The ability to embed fonts in an EPS file is something many XPress users have requested for years. You can set InDesign's Embed Fonts popup menu to Complete (entirely embedded), Subset (to get only the font characters you actually used), or not included. For Data Format, you can write the EPS as Binary (more compact and faster) or ASCII (slower, but required by some older networks and printers).

The preview of an EPS file can be TIFF (best for cross-platform use), PICT (only available on a Macintosh), or None. The latter choice might be useful if you're rasterizing the EPS in Photoshop or re-importing the EPS file back into an InDesign document.

Note that InDesign does not let you export in the DCS or DCS 2.0 formats, but these formats don't support composite workflows or transparency. All EPS files open in Photoshop with a transparent background so there is no need for QuarkXPress's Transparent Page option.

Bleed

The Bleed section of the General panel specifies whether the EPS is cut off at the page boundaries or includes objects within a bleed area. You can enter a Bleed amount for each side of the page of up to 6 inches.

Figure 98-2

The Export EPS
dialog box Advanced
panel

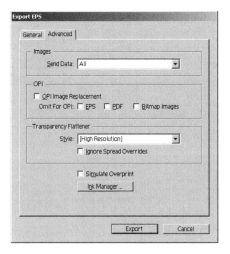

Advanced Options

The Advanced panel is used to specify the handling of images, OPI work-flows, transparency flattening, and ink manager choices (see Figure 98-2). For images in your EPS page, you can either send all the data, or use a low-resolution proxy. The OPI workflow choices are the same as are found on the Advanced panel of the Print dialog box (see Chapter 95). Tranparency needs to be flattened when saving EPS files, so you also have an option for choosing a transparency flattener style (we discuss this in Chapter 94). Finally, the Advanced panel also gives you access to the same Ink Manager capabilities which are described in Chapters 95 and 97.

Exporting

99

Creating PDF Files

One of the most frustrating aspects of QuarkXPress has long been the need to own and use Adobe Acrobat in order to create PDF files. While all graphics professionals should have a copy of Adobe Acrobat in their tool chest, it is nevertheless cumbersome and time-consuming to create PDF files from QuarkXPress. Not so with InDesign, which lets you export your pages directly to the PDF file format. This has some advantages, such as speed, and a few limitations, which we discuss in this chapter.

Exporting PDF

You can export one or more pages to an Adobe PDF file by selecting Export from the File menu and choosing Adobe PDF from the Formats popup menu. After you name the file and tell InDesign where to save it, InDesign displays the Export PDF dialog box. The program ships with four built-in settings for PDF files, which you can choose from the Style popup menu (see Figure 99-1).

- **eBook.** Use this setting for PDF files that will be displayed on screen but may also need to be printed. It is a hybrid between the Screen and Print settings.

- **Screen.** Use this to create the smallest PDF files where a small file size is more important than image quality.

- **Print.** Use this for general office use, when files will be printed on inkjet or laser printers around your office.

Figure 99-1

Preset styles in
the Export PDF
dialog box

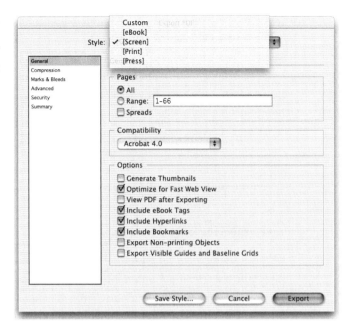

- **Press.** Use this to create high quality PDF files that will be sent to your commercial printer for output using various printing methods, including color separations.

These four default settings will likely meet most of your needs. However, you can always override these settings by changing the options in each of the panels of the Export PDF dialog box—for instance, if you work extensively with spot colors or want password permissions for your PDF files. We discuss the various PDF options below.

An Alternative to Exporting

Note that you can still use Acrobat Distiller to create PDF files from InDesign. The two-step approach of printing a PostScript file to disk and then having the print-to-disk file processed by Distiller is time consuming, but sometimes worthwhile. When creating very small PDF files is our highest priority we use Acrobat Distiller—just as we would from QuarkXPress—because InDesign's Export feature almost always makes larger PDF files than Distiller (though this depends partly on the Export PDF options or Distiller Job settings you choose).

Sometimes InDesign's directly exported PDF files won't print on some printers (primarily non-Adobe PostScript emulators, or "clones"). In these cases, we also use the Distiller to create the PDF files. Of course, as we

Exporting

write this Adobe does not yet have an OS X-native version of Distiller, so we have to endure working with InDesign in Mac OS X, then switching to the Classic mode to process our files. On a side note, this nuisance has Christopher using Dell Pentium 4 laptop more than his G4 Power-Book—but he can happily report that InDesign shares files seamlessly between Mac and PC!

Also, David recently discovered that PDF files exported directly from InDesign would not print on his office printer (a Lexmark PostScript "clone"). Fortunately, the solution was simple: turn off the Optimize For Speed option in Acrobat's Print dialog box.

Customizing PDF Export

XPress has an Export as PDF dialog box (if you use the PDF Filter XTen-sion) which lets you add comments to the PDF file, such as name, keywords, and author information. Similarly, if you type document name and author information into the File Info dialog box (under the File menu), InDesign saves this information in the exported PDF file. InDesign does offer a number of other PDF-specific options that XPress does not. You can select from among the first five of the six panels listed along the left side of the PDF Export dialog box to customize how the PDF is created. Note that you can choose these panels by clicking on them; by holding down the Command/Ctrl key while pressing a number, 1 through 6; or by pressing Command/Ctrl-Page Up or Page Down.

While we cover some of the many PDF options here, Christopher's *Teach Yourself Adobe Acrobat* book has several chapters devoted to settings used when creating PDF files, and David's *Real World InDesign 2* goes into more depth, especially for the more picayune choices.

General

Using the options in the General panel (see Figure 99-1), you can specify which pages will be exported, and if adjoining pages should be exported as spreads. Among the many options listed, the Include Hyperlinks option does exactly the same thing as the feature of the same name in the QuarkXPress Export as PDF dialog box: it lets you export document lists (tables of contents) and index entries as hyperlinks. InDesign also lets you specify if PDF bookmarks will be included (you must have already have used the Table of Contents feature for this to work; see Chapter 89), and if grids and guides should appear in the final PDF file.

Compression

You can use the Compression panel settings to define the quality of placed bitmapped images in the PDF file (see Figure 99-2). The lower the resolution and the higher the compression the smaller the file size–but the tradeoff is reduced quality. This panel is similar to a panel in the Export as PDF dialog box in XPress, and to the Compression panel in the Job Options dialog box in Distiller.

Figure 99-2

The Compression settings in the PDF Export dialog box

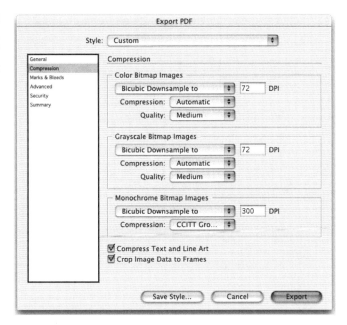

Note that turning on the Crop Image Data to Frames option helps reduce the size of the file by eliminating data that is not visible. This limits the ability for someone else to later to reposition an image within a frame, but this type of editing is rarely performed in PDF files. The Compress Text and Line Art compresses page objects created in InDesign; we can't think of any reason to ever turn this off.

Marks & Bleeds

If you have bled objects off the side of your page, or if you need crop marks around the corners, you'll need to set these up in the Marks & Bleeds panel (see Figure 99-3); the preset Press style doesn't do either of these for you. You can also set the offset (distance from the page) and weight of trim marks you add.

Exporting

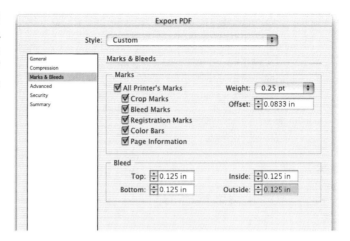

Figure 99-3
The Marks & Bleeds panel of the Export PDF dialog box

Advanced

You can use the Advanced panel settings to define how color is converted when exporting to PDF (see Figure 99-4). You can choose to have all colors converted to RGB or CMYK , or you can leave them unchanged. If you are setting up all of your colors in Photoshop, Illustrator and InDesign prior to exporting this should probably be set to Leave Unchanged. If you are converting the file for posting to a web site, choose the RGB option. We discuss the Ink Manager feature in Chapters 95 and 97 and the color management options in Chapter 87.

Figure 99-4
The Advanced panel of the Export PDF dialog box

Figure 99-5

The Security panel of the Export PDF dialog box

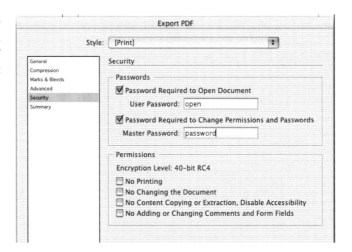

InDesign also lets you determine whether fonts are embedded completely or subsetted. By setting the Subset Fonts Below setting at a high value (like 100%), InDesign only embeds the characters you use in the PDF file and not the entire font family. If you set this at a lower value (like 0%), the entire font will get embedded and not just the characters used in the document. David likes to set this to zero percent for documents destined for a printer or output provider because he likes the whole font to be embedded, but Christopher and Steve tend to set it to 100 percent. To each their own.

Security

If you want to make your printer very unhappy, you can apply security to a PDF file to limit access to the file or restrict printing or editing. Use a Master password to restrict someone from changing or removing your security settings; apply an User password if you want users to input a password before viewing the file. Beware that it is very difficult to remove these restrictions if you forget the password. These security settings only apply to the PDF you are creating, not to the original InDesign file.

After you have finished with the Security settings you can then review all of the settings applied to the PDF you're creating by clicking the Summary panel.

PDF Styles

You can save the settings you've so carefully chosen in the PDF Export dialog box as a PDF style and later call them back up by choosing your style

Exporting

Figure 99-6
Creating a PDF Style for your frequently used PDF settings saves times and reduces the possibility of errors.

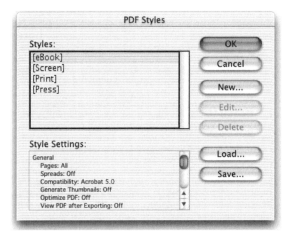

from the Style pop-up menu at the top of the dialog box. You can create a PDF style by choosing PDF Styles from the File menu and navigating your way through the PDF Styles dialog box (see Figure 99-6). However, it is much faster to simply set up the PDF Export dialog box the way you like and then click the Save Style button at the bottom of the dialog box.

100

Exporting to HTML and SVG

Your InDesign documents are probably designed for printing, but you can also export them for viewing on the Web as HTML or SVG documents.

Exporting to HTML

There is no doubt that QuarkXPress (version 5 and later) currently offers more robust tools for exporting HTML files than InDesign. However, most people don't realize that InDesign actually has some reasonably good HTML export tools, too. To export an HTML file from InDesign, select Export from the File menu and choose HTML as the export format. That said, while this option provides a quick method for getting content (text, graphics, and shapes you've drawn on your page) ready for the web, it is not our first choice. Exporting as a PDF file guarantees much better fidelity for sharing documents. Also, when converting documents to HTML, InDesign often converts type to a bitmapped GIF image to maintain its appearance, with incredibly ugly results.

Nevertheless, if you use the HTML export feature you can control a number of settings in the five panels of the Export HTML dialog box (see Figure 100-1):

- **Documents.** In this panel you can control whether each InDesign page of your document is converted to a separate HTML page or a single (long, scrolling) HTML document. You can also control the HTML title and the name of the file.

Figure 100-1

The five panels of the
Export as HTML
dialog box

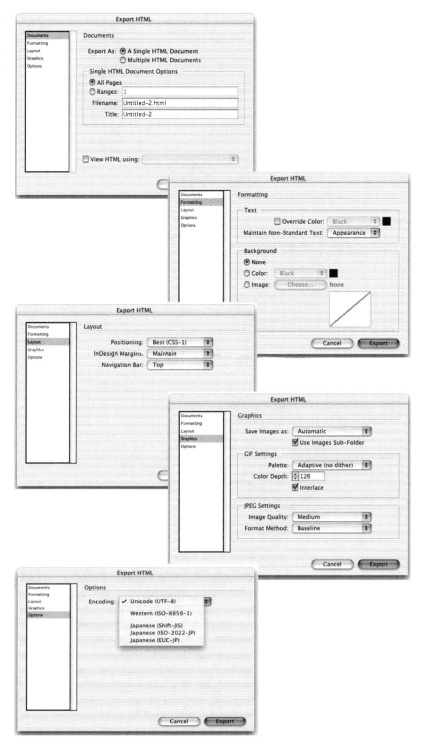

- **Formatting.** Using the Format panel controls, you can override all text colors and force them to become black and you can also apply a background image or color to all pages.

- **Layout.** With the Layout panel controls you can have InDesign add a navigation bar to multiple page documents and you can determine if the HTML will use Cascading Style Sheets to maintain the positioning of objects on your page. (If you're just trying to get content out to import into some other program, then turn off Positioning.)

- **Graphics.** You can use the Graphics panel controls to determine how your imported images are converted for use on the Web. InDesign can automatically determine whether individual images should become GIF or JPEG or you can set them all to one format. The Use Image Sub-Folder checkbox tells InDesign to create a folder for all placed graphics after converting them use on the web. You can also control the quality and size of both JPEG and GIF images in this section. The higher the quality and color depth the larger the size of the images and the longer they take to download. We strongly recommend you use Photoshop to convert images to GIF or JPEG rather than InDesign.

- **Options.** This panel only lets you choose between different text encoding choices.

InDesign does not provide any methods for maintaining, checking, or fixing hyperlinks nor does it provide methods for uploading the file to a web server. For all of these features you can use a web site design and management software program such as Adobe GoLive.

Exporting to SVG

The Scalable Vector Graphics (SVG) file format is a way to describe vector page objects (text, graphics, shapes, and so on) using XML. Some folks are beginning to post SVG files on the Web as an alternative to the Flash format. However, few users have the SVG plug-in required to view SVG graphics, so until Microsoft decides to ship the SVG plug-in with Internet Explorer (or some other major change occurs), there is little practical value to exporting to this format for the Web yet. On the other hand, if you are sure that your audience has the SVG plug-in or a standalone viewer that can display SVG files (perhaps your company's sales force, for instance), then SVG files might be just the ticket.

Exporting

Figure 100-2

Export as
SVG options

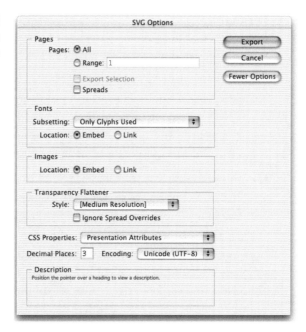

QuarkXPress cannot export SVG files at all at this time (though Quark has said they are committed to the format). Figure 100-2 shows the various options you can set in the Export SVG dialog box. Many of these are similar to those in the HTML and PDF export dialog boxes (see Chapter 99). For more information, see *Real World InDesign 2*.

Converting QuarkXPress files

Converting QuarkXPress Files

Perhaps the greatest concern to XPress users who want to use InDesign is the large store of QuarkXPress files on our hard drives. Fortunately, you can convert most of your QuarkXPress files and templates into InDesign documents. In this appendix, we'll tell you what you need to know to make this feature work for you.

Note that InDesign 2 can open QuarkXPress 3.3 and 4.x documents and templates. It can open QuarkXPress Passport files of the same versions if they have been saved as single-language files. QuarkXPress 5 files must be saved backward to QuarkXPress 4 format. (InDesign can also open Adobe PageMaker 6.5 and 7.0 files as well, but that's less relevant for this book.)

Although we don't know what Adobe has planned for later versions of InDesign, it would surprise us if they ever update this feature so that it can open files from XPress 5 or later; we think of it as a "limited time opportunity."

Conversion Isn't Perfect

When InDesign opens a QuarkXPress file, it must do a file translation into the InDesign format. This is extremely difficult, partly because Quark hasn't made public their secret and proprietary file format information (Adobe had to decode it themselves). Plus, InDesign performs a great many page layout functions differently than XPress does, and there are some XPress features which don't exist at all in InDesign—like custom stripes and multi-ink colors. As with translations between spoken languages, conversions from QuarkXPress aren't flawless. It's our experience that InDesign's conversion can get you about 95 percent of the way there in an "average" document. (These same considerations also apply to Adobe PageMaker files, as well.)

All but the most simple XPress documents will likely require some reworking in InDesign. The more design-intensive your pages, the more likely you'll have to do significant cleanup. That said, we also know of cases in which very complex pages converted without any changes whatsoever. On the other hand, we have heard of at least one case of a commercial printer opening a customer's XPress files in InDesign without consulting with the client first (because he wanted to print from InDesign instead)—this is clearly a *really bad* idea.

What Translates Well

InDesign can read all the paragraph and character styles, master pages, and RGB or CMYK colors in the XPress document (colors other than CMYK and RGB may be an issue, which we'll discuss below). The page geometry (where things are on the page) and XPress-created and linked items will almost always be converted correctly, but proof the files closely for small "glitches," like objects that have moved slightly. Text formatting will usually be converted well, but many line endings may break slightly differently because InDesign uses a different composition engine.

Think "Templates"

In our opinion, your best strategy is to think about opening templates rather than files. That is, open template files, or open old XPress documents that you're going to significantly update anyway. Use the conversion process to create new InDesign templates which can be used to produce new projects. Or, if you have files that have elements which are frequently used in many documents, convert those files only as needed. Converting all your legacy QuarkXPress or PageMaker documents into InDesign documents is probably a waste of time.

Even if you only work in InDesign from now on, you'll probably still want to keep a copy of XPress around to open old legacy documents. This is just a harsh reality of publishing—David still keeps PageMaker around to deal with the documents he created in the late 1980s!

Converting QuarkXPress Files

Converting a QuarkXPress or PageMaker file is usually as simple as choosing Open from the File menu, and selecting the file. However, there are a few preliminaries that we recommend you follow which usually make the process go smoother.

First Steps

First, it's a good idea to open your QuarkXPress document in XPress and make sure that all the fonts and graphics are up-to-date. Then, resave and rename the file using Save As. These steps generally eliminate InDesign errors which occasionally pop up, such as, "There was an error reading the file," "The document includes one or more broken links to external image files," and even "Cannot convert the document."

The conversion also generally works the best if linked graphics reside on your local hard drive, rather than on a network server or removable disk. Also, objects created by some third-party XPress XTensions may not convert properly (or at all). If you have trouble converting the file, you may have to disable the problem XTension and resave the file from XPress.

The Conversion Process

When converting a file, InDesign displays a series of messages describing what it's doing. When it finishes, it may display a Conversion Warnings dialog box (see Figure A-1), which lists objects it had trouble converting and missing resources. However, this isn't necessarily a complete list of everything which didn't convert!

Note that opening an XPress file in InDesign takes much longer than simply opening a normal file. The length of time depends entirely on the

Figure A-1
The Conversion
Warnings dialog box

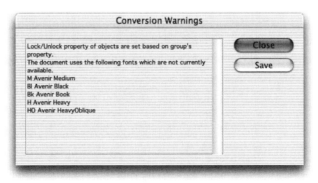

Appendix A

document's contents, but it's not uncommon for the conversion process to take several minutes *per page*. This may be a good time to take a break and go get a latté.

Problem Areas to Look For

Always proof your newly converted document carefully. The following list describes some of the areas which are likely to be the most problematic when converting QuarkXPress files, but it's by no means complete.

- **Runaround.** Text wrapping is handled completely differently by each application. It's likely that you'll have to re-apply text wrap to many graphics (see Chapter 71).

- **Line Styles.** While InDesign can match most of XPress's line styles, custom styles won't be converted correctly, and line weights may occasionally change.

- **Colors.** RGB and CMYK values should remain the same. However, if you've defined objects with the HSB or Multi-Ink modes, or using the Pantone, Trumatch, or Focoltone color libraries, these inks will be converted to RGB definitions. (Spot colors will separate correctly, however.)

- **Keyboard Shortcuts for Styles.** InDesign uses a smaller number of keyboard shortcuts for character and paragraph styles than QuarkXPress. Those shortcuts which don't fit InDesign's restricted range are dropped (the styles are still there, however).

- **Colorized Images.** InDesign supports colorizing only black-and-white and grayscale TIFFs. XPress supports colorizing a few other file formats; these lose their coloring.

- **Special Characters and Type Styles.** QuarkXPress has a few special characters which don't exist in InDesign. These include the flex space (which is converted to an en space) and the superior style (usually converted to superscript). Bold and italic formatting is only maintained if the true font exists (faux bold or italic will appear on the InDesign page highlighted in pink). Shadow and outline styles aren't supported in InDesign.

Getting Help

Adobe has two Support Knowledgebase documents which are helpful for dealing with conversion issues beyond what we can cover in this book.

Support Knowledgebase Document 324146 lists features which are supported in InDesign and which are not. Document 323158 gives some troubleshooting procedures you can follow if conversion fails. Both are available on the Adobe website at: *www.adobe.com/support*.

Other Conversion Options

Opening an XPress document in InDesign isn't the only way to transfer your assets to your new page-layout program. You may find that it is easier, faster, or more convenient to transfer just parts of the document and rebuild the file in InDesign from scratch. Here are a few things to keep in mind.

You can export your text stories as Microsoft Word files (or Rich Text Format files in XPress for Windows) and import them into InDesign. However, you might get more reliable results by exporting in the XPress Tags format and then importing them into InDesign using the TagOn plug-in (which can read XPress Tags) from Late Night Software (*www.latenightsw.com*).

We also find it helpful to use XPress's Collect for Output feature to pull together all the graphics in one place, making them easier to import into InDesign.

One of the best ways to repurpose content from XPress or InDesign or any other program is XML. In our opinion, the Avenue.Quark XML tools that ship with QuarkXPress 5 aren't currently particularly useful. However, there are several other Quark XTensions on the market that help you get XML out of XPress, like RoustaboutXT from Apropos Toy & Tool Development (*www.attd.com*), WebXPress from Gluon (*www.gluon.com*), EasyPress from Atomik (*www.atomik-xt.com*), and Xtract from Noonetime (*www.noonetime.com*). Once you have XML files in hand, you can import them into InDesign. (For more on dealing with XML files in InDesign, see *Real World InDesign 2*.)

index

resizing, 287–288
selecting, 284
table overview, 279, 280
columns (text columns)
creating with guide rules, 132–133
default settings, 30
text frame settings, 197, 198
commands, keyboard shortcuts, 25–28
commas, hanging punctuation, 186
commercial printers
printing instructions file, 351
technical resources for, 371
Complete setting, font downloads, 369
composers, 147, 182–184, 208
Composite CMYK setting, 366, 367
Composite Gray setting, 366, 367
Composite Output setting, 328, 330
Composite RGB setting, 366, 367
composition
highlighting composition problems, 33
H&J settings, 188–191
hyphenation settings, 189–190
justification settings, 190–191
keep options, 180–181
paragraph composers, 183–184
preferences, 33, 184
single-line composers, 147, 182
Composition panel, Preferences dialog box, 33, 184
compound paths, 70–72, 271–273
Compress Text and Line Art option, 387
compression, 240, 241, 387
Compression panel, Export PDF dialog box, 387
Concave corners, 69
Constrain Proportions option, 358
Content tool, 4
context menus, 21–24
continuous-tone laser printers, 371
contours, 268–269
Contrast feature, 254
control handles, 54, 55. *See also* anchor points
Conversion Options settings, 327
Conversion Warnings dialog box, 399
Convert Clipping Path to Frame option, 257

Convert Direction Point tool, 57–58
Convert Quotes option, 149, 203
Convert Text to Table command, 281
converting
anchor points to corner points, 57–58
clipping paths to frames, 257–258
master pages to document pages, 121
QuarkXPress files. *See* converting QuarkXPress files
spot colors to process colors, 314
text to outlines, 271–273
converting QuarkXPress files
alternatives to conversion, 401
conversion process, 399–400
limitations, 397–398
problem areas, 400
technical support, 400
templates, 398
CoolType font technology, 162
Copy PDF to Clipboard option, 31, 32
copyfitting. *See* composition
copying
Alt/Option dragging, 94
copying and pasting, 92–93
copying while transforming, 94
Duplicate command, 93
Eyedropper tool, 7–8, 313
importing graphics, 243–244
Paste in Place command, 93
Step and Repeat command, 93–94
Corner Effects dialog box, 68–69
corner points. *See also* anchor points
converting to smooth points, 57–58
creating while drawing, 55–56
join styles, 66
overview, 54–55
rounded corners, 68–69
Corner Radius attribute, 68
Create Guides dialog box, 132–133
Create Outlines command, 271
Create Package Folder dialog box, 352
Crop Image Data to Frames, 387

crop marks, 360, 387
cross-references in indexes, 344
Current Page Number character, 203
cursors
autoflow cursor, 150
Eyedropper tool, 312
loaded graphics cursor, 236
loaded text cursor, 150, 154, 155
paint brush cursor, 236
Pen cursors, 56
semi-autoflow cursor, 150
text flow cursors, 150
threading cursor, 155
unthreading cursor, 154, 155

D

3D Ribbon path type style, 276
Darken blending mode, 320
dashes, 66–67, 186
Data Format setting, 369
DCS files, importing graphics, 241
Default Source Profiles, 328
default *vs.* document settings, 30. *See also* preferences
Define Printer Styles dialog box, 373–374
Delete Anchor Point tool, 57
Delete icon, Pages palette, 117
Delete Unused Layer command, 104
deselecting objects, 49
Desired field, Justification dialog box, 190
Detach Selection From Master option, 128
Detect Edges option, 256, 269
Device Independent setting, 355
diagonal lines in table cells, 290
dictionaries
adding words to, 157, 160
exception lists, 160, 161
foreign languages, 158
hyphenation points, 161
installing, 159
languages, applying to text, 159
packaging documents for printing, 352
removing words from, 161
user dictionary options, 34–35
Dictionary dialog box, 157, 160–161
Dictionary panel, Preferences dialog box, 34–35
Difference blending mode, 320